New Religious Movements
and Religious Liberty in America

This volume is the forty-fourth published by the Markham Press Fund of Baylor University Press, established in memeory of Dr. L. N. and Princess Finch Markham of Longview, Texas, by their daughters, Mrs. R. Matt Dawson of Waco, Texas, and Mrs. B. Reid Clanton of Longview, Texas.

Library of Congress Cataloging-in-Publication Data

New religious movements and religious liberty in America / edited by Derek H. Davis and Barry Hankins.— 2nd ed.
    p. cm.
Includes bibliographical references and index.
  ISBN 0-918954-92-4 (pbk. : alk. paper)
  1. Cults—United States—Congresses. 2. United
States—Religion—Congresses. 3. Freedom of religion—United
States—Congresses. I. Davis, Derek, 1949- II. Hankins, Barry, 1956-

  BL2525.N487 2003
  323.44'2'0973—dc22

                                    2003018212

Printed in the United States of America on acid-free paper

New Religious Movements and Religious Liberty in America

edited by

Derek H. Davis and Barry Hankins

Second Edition

B

Baylor University Press
Waco, Texas USA

Contents

108489

Preface

All the essays in this book were presented at a symposium at Baylor University entitled "New Religious Movements and Religious Liberty in America," 12-13 February 2001. The J. M. Dawson Institute of Church-State Studies would like to thank Baylor University for its generous funding over the years that has made symposia, lectureships, and books like this one possible. We would like to thank specifically President Robert Sloan and his administration for their gracious support of our work. Chancellor Herbert Reynolds, Provost Donald Schmeltekopf, Vice-Provost Dianna Vitanza, and Arts and Sciences Dean Wallace Daniel, as always, were also supportive of this project.

Several people at the Institute had a hand in bringing both the symposium and this volume to successful completion. Administrative assistant Wanda Gilbert has never left even one stone unturned in the planning of an event, while Janice Losak takes on all tasks with great aplomb. Editorial assistant Pat Cornett seems at times capable of working miracles with computerized text. She has been at the center of this project every step of the way. It would be impossible to plan and execute symposia, conferences, and lectureship without the assistance of these three individuals. Doctoral Fellow Marshall Johnston was a great help in organizing and planning for the conference that spawned this book. Graduate students Hui Fui and Kathy Maxwell performed the tedious yet important task of compiling the index. Also, a special word of thanks is due to those Baylor faculty who serve on our Church-State Studies Faculty Committee and *Journal of Church and State* Editorial Board. They regularly give of their time and expertise in order to keep the work of the Institute and *Journal* moving forward.

Finally, thanks to all of the contributors. In both symposium planning and the editing of this book, you have been most accommodating. Your dedication and commitment to religious liberty for people everywhere and of every religious persuasion has been humbling, and has reassured us that publishing books like this one is a worthwhile endeavor.

Derek H. Davis
Barry Hankins

Baylor University
March 2002

Introduction

Barry Hankins

It has been said that the measure of healthy and civilized society is how well it treats its elderly and indigent. Perhaps it should be said also that the measure of the health of religious liberty in a society is the degree to which minority, nontraditional faiths are protected. This book is a collection of essays on the subject of religious liberty and new religious movements (NRMs). Most of the chapters were first delivered as papers at a conference sponsored by the J.M. Dawson Institute of Church-State Studies at Baylor University in March 2001. NRMs are often called "cults" by popular media commentators and the public at large, but scholars eschew that term because it is so pejorative that it skews the argument from the very beginning. By contrast, the term "new religious movements" attempts to place NRMs squarely in the mix with older, more traditional forms of religion. This is due in part to the fact that in America there should be no correlation between the level of social approval a group has achieved and the degree of religious liberty it enjoys. As the Supreme Court itself averred famously in the 1872 case *Watson* v. *Jones*, "The Law knows no heresy and is committed to the support of no dogma, the establishment of no sect." While often falling short of this ideal, the United States Constitution, specifically the First Amendment, is interpreted by the courts to mean that all groups should enjoy religious liberty, not just those who adhere to long-standing and traditional variations of the Christian faith. Make no mistake from the outset; each author represented in this volume believes that NRMs should enjoy the same liberties as more mainstream religions. If the book has a bias, it is a bias in favor of religious liberty. The authors believe that if the First Amendment is applied to protect the newest, nontraditional, seemingly unusual religions (by the standards of the majority of the population), then nearly everyone is safe as far as religious liberty is concerned.

The book begins with Timothy Miller setting the historical context by showing that in a sense NRMs have been a longstanding part of western history. In centuries past, the majority viewed Christian sectarian groups much as the public views NRMs today. They were not only unusual but also threatening to the social order. Sectarian groups from the Middle Ages and Early Modern Period were at least as radical and controversial as many of today's NRMs, but we tend to be much more tolerant of groups that are safely in the past. Only the NRMs of our own time threaten us.

These supposed threats are sometimes so alarming that anti-cult groups resort to rather extreme measures to combat the influence of NRMs. This is the subject of chapter two. Anson Shupe et al.'s meticulously researched findings concerning the Cult Awareness Network (CAN) raise the age-old question as to whether the proposed solution to a perceived social problem can be worse than the problem itself. This is not to say that NRMs never engage in spurious behavior. No one would make that claim for either NRMs or other, more traditional, religious groups. Clearly, religious groups of all kinds must obey the law. The flip-side of this dictum, however, is that as long as they are, religious liberty requires that they be free to make their cases to the wider public, which includes the right to discredit and refute competing religious groups and win converts for themselves. In addition to its financial irregularities, the problem with CAN, as Shupe and his team show, was that the organization engaged in kidnapping, which violated the liberty of those who adhere to the teachings of various NRMs. This was possible because of an assumption that somehow NRMs operate outside the normal procedures of "acceptable" religious groups, which is a notion that is highly questionable in light of Miller's historical overview.

Following Miller's line of thinking, Gordon Melton shows how the highly developed Sea Org community of the Church of Scientology is much like older religious orders from the Christian faith and from eastern religions. The Sea Org, like the others, is an "ordered religious community." While to outsiders the rigor appears oppressive, for participants the community life is experienced as both voluntary and liberating. Even some ex-members of the Sea Org, whose views are rather negative, still reject the more extreme charges made by ex-Scientology members who were not in the Sea Org.

On the other hand, however, Melton also shows that the worst abuses in Scientology, those often cited by disillusioned ex-members, were indeed committed by Guardian Office (GO) officials of the Sea Org in the 1970s. Since that time, the GO was first reformed, with offending members expelled, then the office was disbanded after leaders determined that it was unsalvageable. Melton, like Miller, makes comparisons with the history of Christianity, specifically with the sixteenth-century Catholic Reformation. Much like the Roman Catholic Church of that time, the Church of Scientology has had to come to grips with its own internal problems and abuses and reform itself.

The point of Melton's essay is not to make an apologia for Scientology. He takes no position on the truth or falsity of the group's claims. Rather, he seeks to show that its practices are not all that different from other ordered religious communities. The upshot, though not argued explicitly, is that Scientology should be treated in the legal domain just as more mainstream groups are. Unfortunately, this is not the case, especially in some European countries where Scientology is considered a dangerous cult that must be highly regulated or shut down.

It is often difficult to pinpoint what facet of NRMs appears as most dangerous to the wider community. Susan Palmer, however, may have identified such a feature in her chapter on gender and sex roles. Again, as Miller's essay shows, there is nothing new about the phenomenon whereby NRMs present a frontal challenge to traditional sex, gender, marital, and familial norms. Shaker founder Mother Ann Lee taught absolute celibacy, even within marriage, and came to be seen by her followers as the female manifestation of Christ. John Humphrey Noyes, by contrast, led his Oneida community into "complex marriage" whereby nearly all the community's males were simultaneously married to all the females. Working from a sociological perspective, Palmer steps back from contemporary NRMs to find patterns in gender roles and sexual relationships. She also finds that the longer an NRM exists, the more it tends to move toward the mainstream. As has been shown so many times in American religious history, American culture has a seemingly inexhaustible capacity to co-opt radical groups and pull them into the mainstream of American life, which is instructive for those who are concerned that NRMs will distort and possibly help destroy American culture. It is more likely that the reverse will happen.

Along with groups practicing nontraditional sex and gender roles, those practicing Satanism and witchcraft have contended for status as most controversial of the NRMs. James Richardson, like Palmer, utilizes the tools of modern sociology to analyze Wicca and Satanism, both of which consist of, as Richardson writes, "small numbers of people doing things that are usually quite harmless to themselves and others," but nevertheless "are defined as major social problems by many in the U.S. and elsewhere." Fostered by "claims makers," such social problems, which by definition must be dealt with and overcome, can lead to a "moral panic" and "perceived danger" that is out of proportion to the actual threat. Richardson traces the recent moral panic that has arisen as a result of Satanism and Wicca and concludes that the anti-cult movement combined with the penchant for melding the identities of Satanism and Wicca will likely continue to foster difficulties for both movements into the foreseeable future.

Perhaps the most disturbing chapter of the book is Stuart Wright's brief exposition of the trial of the Branch Davidians who survived the 1993 siege outside of Waco, just ten miles from the campus where these chapters were first delivered as scholarly papers and from where I write this introduction. Most disturbing is that Wright shows what can happen, in an extreme case to be sure, when a non-traditional NRM is considered as a matter of law to be fundamentally different from more traditional groups. No one excuses the illegal activities David Koresh was involved in—firearms and other weapons violations, alleged child sex abuse, etc.—but the disaster at Waco was a horrific and unacceptable response that resulted in part from recklessness stemming from the Bureau of Alcohol, Tobacco, and Firearms's (ATF) views of NRMs. The ATF used measures that directly violated its own hostage-barricade protocols. Was this the result of an assumption that Koresh and his followers, because they were non-traditional, would not respond rationally or normally to the protocols? Do government officials assume that unusual religious groups are fundamentally different in their rational capabilities and responses? Both Miller and Melton argue that throughout history there are vast similarities in the ways that religious groups of all kinds tend to organize themselves and respond to outside hostility and internal abuses; Wright shows what can happen when authorities ignore the similarities and assume that NRMs are radically different and irrational.

Closely associated with Wright's analysis, Catherine Wessinger offers a way forward that may help American law enforcement agencies avoid such tragedies in the future. Based on her long-standing concern and in-depth research, Wessinger presents a compelling argument that often law enforcement agencies, because of their lack of understanding of NRMs, actually develop a self-fulfilling prophecy. In conflicts between NRMs and law enforcement, both sides often participate in rituals of violence that can escalate into horrific consequences. Sometimes, as was the case with Jim Jones and the People's Temple, the NRM itself engages in such rituals, but in other instances, as with the Weaver family at Ruby Ridge and the Branch Davidians outside of Waco, the NRM and the law enforcement agents enter into a symbiotically destructive pattern of ritualized violence that ends in disaster. From this part of Wessinger's wider research, she hones in specifically on the role that millennialism plays in contests between NRMs and law enforcement. As with the other sociological analyses presented in this volume, she seeks to discover patterns, specifically types of millennialism, and then demonstrates how violence can escalate when law enforcement agents disregard the worldview of an NRM. In a haunting section of her chapter, Wessinger shows how close the Branch Davidians were to negotiating an acceptable surrender scenario that David Koresh could make sense of within the group's own millennial framework. The inability of the ATF to take that framework seriously had tragic consequences. Wessinger concludes that religious groups are usually able to reinterpret and adjust their views in response to events. A group's potential to be violent can, therefore, escalate or deescalate depending on their interaction with law enforcement agents. This being the case, agents should seek to understand the worldview of the group in an effort to provide the believers with a way out that fits with the adapted version of their theology. "The manner in which all of us interact with members of new religious movements helps to determine the potential for volatility," Wessinger writes.

Adam English raises an interesting question as to whether Christian Reconstructionism should be considered an NRM. Like many other groups, Reconstructionists have a millennial message, but, unlike those Wessinger discusses, they are postmillennial. That is, they believe not in an imminent end to history but in a long process whereby eventually America will be ruled by Old Testament law. Unlike David Koresh and others, Reconstructionists are for the most part content to wait patiently for Americans to become so distraught with the moral decline of a libertine society that they will actually embrace a theocratic alternative that will come to pass in a peaceful and evolutionary way. In the meantime, Reconstructionists write books (tomes, really) advocating their position. As Adam English's chapter shows, the coming of the new millennium loomed large for Reconstructionist Gary North but in a very different way than it did for some premillennialist Christians. For him, the impending crash of computers and resulting chaos were anticipated as the opportunity to start rebuilding a new theocratic society based on God's divine law. The new millennium was to be a new beginning, not the end. Of course, as I write this introduction on a computer and ready it to be e-mailed to a colleague for further editing, we are all reminded of the failure of North's anticipated great failure, but he is sure that ultimately Christian Reconstructionism will triumph.

In a chapter where the stakes are considerably lower than was the case at Mount Carmel or in the millennial predictions of North, Derek Davis addresses the many church-state problems inherent in President George W. Bush's initiative to fund Faith-Based Organizations (FBOs). While neither western civilization nor the lives of American citizens are threatened, this is nevertheless an important topic for the landscape of church-state relations and religious liberty. Davis focuses specifically on how such a program might affect NRMs. He shows that NRMs are as divided as the rest of America in their responses to the Bush initiatives, but even more instructive is his argument that if discrimination lurks in the details of government funding for FBOs, NRMs will be the most likely victims.

The final two chapters were not part of the original conference but have been added in this revised edition of the book because they present important case studies of two groups that have experienced discrimination. Chuck Smith explores anew the fate of Jehovah's Witnesses in West Virginia during the 1940s. Jehovah Witnesses have been around long enough now that they probably no longer qualify as a NRM, but in the period Smith covers they did, and they were considered offensive and dangerous by mainstream American society. Smith's chapter is timely because he analyzes the ways in which Jehovah's Witnesses cases affected four different areas of legal thinking. This is important in an era when the federal government's relaxing of Establishment Clause regulations on the funding of FBOs, and the Supreme Court's standard of general applicability laid down in the *Smith* decision of 1990, seem to signal that the time has passed when the federal courts alone can be relied upon to adequately protect religious liberty and nonestablishment. Vigilant protection of religious free exercise will therefore require a broadened approach that will include the use of state constitutions, federal and state legislation, and even administrative law.

Persecution of Jehovah's Witnesses and their efforts to claim First Amendment rights played a significant role in the expansion of free exercise protection in America, leaving us to ponder what role NRMs in the twenty-first century might play in keeping the courts and legislatures alert to violations of religious liberty. Among the candidates for doing in the twenty-first century what the Jehovah's Witnesses did in the twentieth are the Wiccans, the subject of Catherine Cookson's chapter. Cookson argues that the two main challenges facing Wiccans are misperception and intolerance, the second often a result of the first. (Oddly, one example mentioned in passing has Jehovah's Witnesses engaged in intolerance against Wiccans.) Cookson shows how private examples of intolerance can give way to subtle legal maneuvers such as zoning, tax laws, and actions of government officials intended to restrict the exercise of Wiccan beliefs. There is no single or easy remedy here, but informative essays like Cookson's, and the eternal vigilance she advocates, provide a start toward improving religious liberty protection.

This brings us back to the thread that holds this book together and the reason it is being published in this revised and expanded edition. The state of religious liberty in America should not be measured by how well Baptists, Catholics, Episcopalians, Methodists, and Presbyterians are doing, but by the plight of Wiccans, Scientologists, Davidians, and other unpopular and misunderstood NRMs. In other words, religious liberty should be evaluated by how well things are going on the margins of the religious landscape. The majority hardly needs the protection of the Free Exercise Clause of the First Amendment; legislatures will see to it that the interests of the mainstream are well served. NRMs have little or no voice and must be protected by constitutional and other legal provisions that treat them fairly and equally alongside the traditional groups that make up the majority. The courts must continue to play a major role in the protection of religious liberty, but given the state of constitutional law presently, legislatures and regulatory agencies need to be informed and sensitive as well. The editors of this book, and the authors of its individual chapters, hope to contribute to the conversation by suggesting that religious liberty protection must expand to meet the needs of NRMs and other religious minority groups.

Chapter 1

Controversial Christian Movements
History, Growth, and Outlook

Timothy Miller

We humans have a tendency to think that we are living in unique times, and often we are disinclined to look at our past as a help in understanding the present. In the case of new religions, their appeal, and the controversy surrounding them, some might locate their origins in the frantic pace of modern life, or in the access to the exotic that modern communications and transportation afford, or, from a more theological point of view, in the chaos that precedes the great millennial events that many anticipate in the very near future. From a historian's point of view, however, what we see is neither new nor particularly unusual. Religious innovation and the controversy surrounding it goes as far back as history can see. Some of the controversies have accompanied the rise of new religions in the past, especially in the American context. I am restricting my focus to variant forms of Christianity that have caused great stress among the mainstream faithful who are not at all happy to see the rise of heresy and heterodoxy.

HISTORIC CHRISTIANITY

Such a survey of Christian history might do well to begin with Christianity itself. Like any religion, it was new and controversial in its first three centuries

9

or so, to say the least. The early church was troubling to both of the relevant prevailing centers of power, the Jewish temple leadership, whose authority was diminished by the Christian precept that the Kingdom of God was at hand and would replace the current order, and the Roman government, which always faced insurrections in its outlying provinces and viewed radical movements of all kinds with considerable suspicion. Such movements at worst were regarded as treasonous, and at best as ignorant superstitions. The very term "Christian" was at first used derisively by the movement's opponents who scorned the contention that this Jesus fellow had actually been the Jewish Messiah. We all know well that the church suffered persecution for hundreds of years, until a great reversal occurred in the early fourth century by the edict of Constantine. Christianity was then tolerated and soon became the official religion of the Roman Empire.

The improved official status of Christianity hardly meant the end of religious persecution. The human race, in its fallen perversity, seems to be addicted to various kinds of intolerance, and the type of Christianity that became ensconced in government was more than eager to persecute its Christian competitors. All kinds of Christian movements and points of view that have gone down officially as heresies, from Gnosticism to Montanism to Manichaeism to Arianism, could be more plausibly regarded as victims of persecution than as propagators of error, or, as the popular argot would have it today, dangerous cults. Had the ruling faction in Rome, and then Constantinople, not had considerable political and military force behind it, Christian history might have worked out quite differently.

A millennium after the time of Jesus, the Eastern and Western branches of Christianity formally separated amid excommunications and anathemas and intractable doctrinal disputes. A century or two later, the Western church undertook legendarily ghastly persecution with the establishment of the Inquisition, which sought out Albigensians and other heretics. Around 1500, the Western church saw a huge challenge erupt with the advent of Protestantism. Protestantism quickly took on variant forms in different places, with Lutherans and Calvinists and Hussites and Zwinglians all having their spheres of influence and all becoming objects of the great wrath of the Roman church. But even the dominant Protestant reformers agreed with the Catholic church that the Anabaptists, the most radical of the Protestant dissidents, needed to be eliminated. The persecution of the Anabaptists for their dissent was among the most gruesome episodes in the spotted history of Christianity. The devices used by the Inquisitors and the Anabaptist-hunters make such modern anticult techniques as deprogramming look about as serious an intrusion as a telemarketing phone call.

SEVENTEENTH CENTURY

It is a sad irony that those early British settlers who came to our shores for religious freedom did not themselves prove at all tolerant. The early Puritans, so called because they originally sought to "purify," meaning decatholicize, the Church of England, had themselves suffered plenty of persecution in England, particularly at the hands of William Laud, Bishop of London and later Archbishop of Canterbury, so much so that they began to flee the country, at first in small numbers to the Netherlands, and then in larger numbers to the new world. But once they had established their holy commonwealth in New England, they were as determined as any of their predecessors not to suffer the outrages of heretical doctrine and practice. The founding of Rhode Island was one outgrowth of that persecution, as refugees from Massachusetts made it their haven. Roger Williams went to Massachusetts as a minister for the church in Boston, but upon arrival refused to serve because the church had not formally separated itself from the Church of England. He compounded his problems with other heresies, including the patently outrageous idea that the settlers should not be stealing land from the Indians, as well as a set of convictions that amounted to a belief in the separation of church and state. By 1635, Williams was sentenced to deportation, and he responded by fleeing into the wilderness in 1636, heading south and eventually founding Providence. There he founded the first Baptist church in America, and, of course, he has become a great Baptist hero now that he is more than three hundred years dead and nobody actually has to deal with him any more. As an aside, one cannot help but wonder whether the current Southern Baptist leadership has ever looked at what its founding hero actually had to say, i.e., what a strong advocate he was for church-state separation.

Two years later Anne Hutchinson was similarly expelled from Massachusetts for her challenges to the Massachusetts ministers and especially for her defense, in what was essentially her heresy trial, in which she committed the cardinal error of claiming that she had received special revelation, direct communication from God. Woe be to anyone to whom God speaks directly! She and her supporters similarly found themselves starting life anew in the wilderness of Rhode Island.[1]

The early New Englanders also had an especially intense dislike of the Quakers, who in their early years were zealous promoters of their own brand of Puritanism, which differed from that of the New England majority. The Quakers were among the most radical of the Puritans, vigorously opposing hierarchy and sacraments and seeking an intensively personal and individualized spirituality. They had their origin with George Fox, who in 1648 began to speak publicly of his faith, especially of his belief that one could have a direct revelation of Christ, indeed a direct, personal connection with God. He suffered persecution, but persevered and in 1652 organized a group of spiritual seekers in

Lancashire. Quakers did indeed pose a threat to the established order, what with their disdain for ritual, their minimizing of the importance of ordained clergy, their giving up of visible sacraments, and, perhaps above all, their tremendous zeal to spread their faith.

In 1656, the first Quakers landed in Massachusetts Bay Colony. Quakerism was not illegal in Massachusetts at the time, but the provincial authorities knew about this new body of belief and detained the two new arrivals, Mary Fisher and Ann Austin, searching their belongings, seizing their books, and even stripping them and inspecting them for signs of witchcraft. They were deported, but a mere two days later another ship docked, this time with eight Quakers. They were immediately imprisoned and then deported, but even as prisoners they managed to spread their message sufficiently to make one convert. The colony then adopted a series of laws against the Quakers that among other things provided that any Quaker arriving in the colony would be whipped and deported before he or she could talk with anyone. But that hardly made the Quakers give up; they simply settled in Rhode Island, which by that time had been established as a colony that would be open to people of all religious persuasions and which was a perfect beachhead for forays over the border into Massachusetts. The Bay Colony made its laws ever more stringent, and in 1658 made Quakerism a capital crime. Four Quakers were actually executed for their convictions.[2]

The story eventually ends more happily, of course. The Quaker convert William Penn established his colony in 1681 and in what was known as the "Holy Experiment" proclaimed toleration for all who believed in God. Quakers, among many others, came in droves, and eventually took the place they occupy today as a small but well-accepted religious school of thought.

Pennsylvania with its vaunted toleration attracted a host of non-mainstream believers, including various strains of Anabaptists. These most radical of the Reformation-era believers are usually traced to the early 1520s in Switzerland, where they dissented from the new Reformation Calvinist and Zwinglian orthodoxy with such doctrines as nonresistance to evil, separation of church and state, and pacifism. The first to arrive in America came in 1683, and many more followed. Although they had their detractors, and were repeatedly persecuted, even killed, in Europe, they generally did not experience the level of persecution that many other groups suffered in America. Nevertheless, their acceptance in American society has been mixed, and they have especially suffered as pacifists in wartime. One of the most overt persecutions involved the Hutterites, the wing of the Anabaptists that practices communal living in Canada and several north central and northwestern states in America. During World War I, their pacifism was so unpopular in South Dakota, where they all lived at the time, that they closed all but one of their colonies, selling them at distressed prices, and moved to Canada. By that time they had suffered extreme verbal persecution and even occasional mob violence and vandalism. Two of their young male members, arrested and incarcerated at Fort Leavenworth, died from what may fairly be called official torture. More recently they have been the focus of legal attempts, especially in Canada, to have their ability to buy and own land restricted. Life has not always been easy for Anabaptists in North America.[3]

EIGHTEENTH CENTURY

More than a century after the arrival of the Quakers, another group provided a textbook case in religious persecution and eventual toleration. In 1774, a group of members of the United Society of Believers in Christ's Second Appearing, better know as the Shakers, arrived in New York under the leadership of Ann Lee. After some very quiet early years, they gathered near what is now Albany, New York, and began to live communally. From that base they undertook a series of preaching missions and began to make converts, but as their visibility increased, so did their persecution. The Revolutionary War was still going on at the time, and the Shakers, who refused military service, were suspected of being British agents. But soon other charges emerged as well. One of the first bitter anti-Shaker diatribes came from one Valentine Rathbun, who joined the movement in 1780 but later dropped out and began to accuse the Shakers of practices that might now be called deceptive recruitment and even brainwashing. They greeted visitors "with many smiles, and seeming great gladness," Rathbun wrote, and fed and entertained them. But all of their seeming goodness was actually part of their strategy of developing "absolute dependence" among members.[4]

Such criticism, and sometimes physical persecution, was to hound the Shakers for many years to come. Ann Lee and several others undertook an extensive missionary tour in New England from 1781 to 1783. Although some were persuaded by the Shaker message of holy living and millennial hope, the Shakers experienced verbal abuse and, in quite a few cases, beatings and other physical abuse everywhere they went. In Harvard, Massachusetts, in January 1782, the militia drove the Shakers out of town. Shakers were whipped and beaten repeatedly, and stones were thrown and bullets fired at the houses where they were staying. Some believe the death of Ann Lee and her brother William in 1784 was the result of the abuse they had suffered.

One inevitable part of a religious movement's growth is a growth in apostasy. New members may join, but invariably some disaffected individuals leave, and sometimes harbor great hostility toward the group to which they were formerly committed. That was certainly the case with the Shakers. Mary Dyer was the most formidable of the nineteenth-century Shaker apostates, and she made a life-long career of her activism against the believers. She had joined with her husband, who stayed behind when she left and kept their children with him in the community. Her activism, fueled by a desire to get her children back, sometimes went beyond propagandizing to participating in mob violence. She and other apostates and opponents constantly contended with the Shakers by issuing manifestoes, making public speeches, and filing lawsuits.[5] All the while the Shakers had plenty of nonapostate opponents as well, including the literary luminary Nathaniel Hawthorne, who originally had a favorable opinion of the group, but eventually denounced them bitterly. In 1851 he wrote, "The fact shows that all their miserable pretence of cleanliness and neatness is the thinnest superficiality; and that the Shakers are and must needs be a filthy set. And then their utter and systematic lack of privacy; the close function of man with man, and supervision of one man over another—it is hateful and disgusting to think of; and the sooner the sect is extinct the better —a consummation which, I am happy to hear, is thought to be not a great many years distant."[6] And so it went throughout much of Shaker history.

After the middle of the nineteenth century, Shakerism started a serious decline. By the early twentieth century, it was but a shadow of its former self. Somehow the controversies of earlier years fell by the wayside. Lovers of the arts and shrewd investors began buying up Shaker furniture, which became so renowned that one of the late-era Shakers, Mildred Barker, used to exclaim that she did not want to be remembered as a chair. Today the Shakers are remembered in the warmest and fuzziest of terms, and the few survivors in Maine have a staunch support group of loving admirers and no controversy at all. The current attitude may best be summed up in the Ken Burns film called "The Shakers," which idealizes them exquisitely. Nice pieces of Shaker furniture fetch prices in the hundreds of thousands of dollars, especially since well-heeled collectors like Oprah Winfrey can bid choice items up to astronomical levels.

NINETEENTH CENTURY

Another communal Christian group had a history that in many ways paralleled that of the Shakers, and persecution was again a major part of the story, although again it has been largely forgotten as the believers have become retrospectively idealized. The Harmony Society, created and led by George Rapp, had its origins in German Pietism in the eighteenth century. Pietists criticized the state church as coldly formal and intellectual, and instead stressed deep personal religious experience and holy Christian living. Rapp was one of the most vocal and radical of the Pietists, and he took to denouncing the established church in the strongest terms. He attracted thousands of followers, and his conflict with the state became greater and greater. In 1804, hundreds of Harmonists sailed to Pennsylvania, where they founded a communal village called Harmony north of Pittsburgh. They built up a pleasant community for a decade, then moved en masse to Indiana, where they founded New Harmony, and built it up as a truly exquisite town, one that survives as one of the country's premier museum villages today. Finally, after another decade, they undertook one last move, this time back to near where they had started in Pennsylvania. There they built the sumptuous village of Economy, where they lived for the rest of their history, gradually declining after Rapp's death in 1847 but hanging on in diminished fashion until the early years of the twentieth century.

Like other groups, the Rappites underwent plenty of persecution. Groups practicing community of goods are often inherently suspect of undermining traditional American values, and the Harmonists were celibate, which did not endear them to most Americans. Their relations with their neighbors were ambivalent at best, and in 1820 a physical battle between Harmonists and their antagonists erupted right in the streets of New Harmony. There were always internal tensions as well; whatever else can be said about the society, George Rapp was a despot who ruled with an iron hand. When a charismatic visitor arrived in 1831 and was eventually rebuffed by Rapp, upon departing he took about 175 disaffected Harmonists with him. Those leaving made some bitter charges against Rapp and the Harmony Society. They alleged that Rapp believed that he was God and beyond all human rules, that community property was actually a plot by Rapp to own and control everything, that Rapp refused to let them learn English to keep them unaware of their options, and that those who left the community were forced to set out penniless.

And so it went. Like the Shakers, the Rappites had their vigorous opponents, and found themselves verbally castigated and on the receiving end of lawsuits that alleged much the same things that anticultists allege today—mind control, coercive and powerful leadership, and so forth. The Harmonists did manage to withstand the onslaughts and finally died with a whimper, after a new member joining late in the game looted the treasury and shut the movement down.[7]

Of all of the movements that have been persecuted in American history, none have been more abusively treated than the Latter-day Saints, or Mormons. From their very founding in 1830 until well into the twentieth century, they were widely regarded as outlaws, lunatics, and perverts. Although the main Mormon church has finally become well accepted in polite society, some of the fringe groups that maintain old Mormon traditions faithfully continue to feel the brunt of a great deal of public abuse today.

Mormonism was formally born in 1830 with the publication of the Book of Mormon and the organization of what was originally called the Church of Christ. The founder, a young man named Joseph Smith, Jr., had had visionary experiences since his early teenage years, and by the late 1820s was engaged in "translating" what some called Joe Smith's Golden Bible. Smith claimed that he had been directed by an angel to a buried set of golden plates on which had been inscribed the history of some of the ancient peoples of the Americas. He was miraculously given the power to translate the mysterious characters on the plates, and the translation was called the Book of Mormon, after the ancient historian who was said to have written the account that ended up on the plates.

From its beginning, Mormonism was the object of a good deal of derision, not only for its seemingly preposterous claims about the "Golden Bible," but also for the grand claims that Joseph Smith was soon making that he was a prophet of God—indeed, the prophet of God with a special pipeline to the divine, unique in all the world—and that his church was the one and only true church, a reconstruction of ancient apostolic Christianity. Soon the movement moved to Kirtland, Ohio, where it experienced enormous growth and began to run into its first round of serious hostility, not at the hands of outraged outsiders so much as from apostate members, who became numerous as the church grew rapidly. One violent attack occurred at Kirtland, directed at Smith personally; it has been recounted thus by Fawn Brodie, Smith's biographer:

> A gang of Mormon-baiters . . . fortified by a barrel of whisky . . . smashed their way into the Johnson home on the night of March 24, 1832 and dragged Joseph from the trundle bed where he had fallen asleep. . . . They stripped him, scratched and beat him with savage pleasure, and smeared his bleeding body with tar from head to foot. Ripping a pillow into shreds, they plastered him with feathers. It is said that Eli Johnson demanded that the prophet be castrated, for he suspected Joseph of being too intimate with his sister, Nancy Marinda. But the doctor who had been persuaded to join the mob declined the responsibility at the last moment, and Johnson had to be content with seeing the prophet beaten senseless. [Sidney] Rigdon [a prominent church member] likewise was beaten and dragged into unconsciousness over the frozen ground.[8]

As the account suggests, Smith may have begun practicing polygamy in Ohio, and polygamy eventually became the biggest obstacle to the Mormons' acceptance by the larger culture. Meanwhile, problems mounted and a serious financial crisis developed for the financially strapped Mormons. By the late 1830s, they moved to Missouri, where they had established an outpost as early as 1831 and where Smith announced a revelation that the town of Independence would be the site of the Second Coming of Christ, a doctrine to which all of the branches of the Latter-day Saint movement subscribe today. But life was hardly easier for the Mormons in Independence than it had been in Ohio. Indeed, it was worse, in part because Missouri was a border state dominated by pro-slavery forces who viewed with suspicion all Yankees as possible abolitionists. The saints were hounded from one county to another and suffered mob violence, incarceration, and confrontations by the local militia. Historians still refer to that episode in Missouri as the "Mormon War"; and at its worst it was something of a real war, with armed activities on both sides.

All of the persecution and violence led the Mormons to migrate yet again, this time to Illinois. There, on the banks of the Mississippi River, they took over an all-but-abandoned town called Commerce. Smith renamed it "Nauvoo," which he said meant "beautiful city" in Hebrew. There the Mormons achieved their greatest early success, building up what was for a time the largest city in Illinois with perhaps fifteen thousand inhabitants, more than Chicago in those days. They built buildings and economic institutions, and, determined to defend themselves against their seemingly intractable enemies, founded a private military unit, the Nauvoo Legion, that had two thousand soldiers by the beginning of 1842.

Nauvoo has a rich history all its own, but the beginning of the end came in 1844, when Smith suffered the most severe persecution of all when he was killed by a lynch mob. As elsewhere, the Mormons had fierce enemies in the Nauvoo area, many of whom feared that Mormonism was a dictatorial theocracy that was threatening the American way of life. They also had quite a few apostates living in the vicinity, some of whom told lurid tales of violence and corruption and sexual misbehavior among the Mormons. Polygamy, although it had not yet been publicly announced, was being practiced in Nauvoo and naturally provided sensational fodder for the Mormon antagonists.

The immediate cause of the final events of Smith's life came with the publication of the one and only issue of the Nauvoo Expositor on 7 June 1844. Among other things, it spoke openly of polygamy, surely information that would be sensational both among church members who had not been told about the new doctrine and among the many anti-Mormons in the vicinity. Smith responded by ordering the Nauvoo Legion to destroy the newspaper by smashing the press and scattering the type. That resulted in his arrest, and shortly thereafter, on 27 June 1844, a mob entered the jail and killed Smith and his brother Hyrum.

That was not the end of persecution of the Mormons. After Smith's death, they migrated to Utah and in 1852 finally announced publicly their practice of polygamy. That set off decades of conflict, which peaked in the 1880s with the federal government scouring the Utah countryside for the "cohabs," as polygamists were called. Church president John Taylor spent most of his term of office in hiding and remained in hiding until his death in 1887. Faced with intractable official opposition, the church finally gave up and abandoned the practice of polygamy in the 1890s and 1900s as a requirement for statehood, although as a doctrine it has never been repudiated.

However, quite a few Mormons were distressed that the church had abandoned a practice that was, after all, the will of God, a doctrine received by a divinely-inspired prophet of God. Once the church got serious about ending polygamy, the stalwarts withdrew into their own splinter organizations and continued the practice of plural marriage. And so things continue today, with tens of thousands of Latter-day Saints living in polygamous households in the intermountain West. And they, like their forebears, suffered plenty of persecution. The largest single polygamous enclave, now known as Colorado City, Arizona, has suffered three major raids by law enforcement authorities, the last in 1953. Those actions, however, have not stopped them from practicing what they believe to be the will of God. Today, Colorado City has over five thousand citizens and is a thriving desert town, its polygamy not at all hidden.[9] But a new conflict over polygamy is in the wings; anti-polygamy activists are currently trying to get new laws enacted, and old ones more stringently enforced, in order to wipe out the practice. Intense conflict seems inevitable.

The Mormons have not been the only believers whose unconventional sexual practices led to persecution. One of America's most famous historic communal societies, the Oneida Community, was finally hounded out of existence because of public opposition to its practice of free love. Oneida was founded and led by John Humphrey Noyes, who in the 1830s began preaching radical perfectionism—that he was free from sin and others could be too. Among other things, Noyes taught that the Second Coming of Christ had already occurred, and that because we were now living in the millennial dispensation, a whole new order of human society was called for. Perfect humans needed to overcome egotism and possessiveness, and that expansive spirit extended to marital relations. Simply put, the Oneida Community was the largest group marriage in American history, with nearly three hundred members at its peak and every male member considered married to every female member. The community had unusually harmonious internal relations and an excellent economic base, first with its production of the nation's best animal traps and later with silverware. It lasted for several decades, and might have gone on longer had not outside pressure intervened. It is not hard to imagine that vigorous opposition to such flagrant sexual irregularities did finally arise in Victorian America. Criticism grew, and Noyes became fearful. Eventually he fled the country, fearing criminal charges. Complex marriage, as the system was known, was discontinued, and in 1881 the community was formally dissolved.[10]

During the heyday of the Oneida Community, another religious movement arose that would suffer a good deal of persecution. The movement now known as the Jehovah's Witnesses had its beginnings in the 1870s among Christians who had been involved in William Miller's Adventist movement that had trailed off in various directions following the failure of the Second Coming to occur on 22 October 1844, as Miller had predicted. Charles Taze Russell, undeterred by the problems that date-setting had posed for the Millerites, set a date of his own: the great end of time would come in 1914. Despite the obvious problems that date has posed, the movement has managed to reinterpret things and continue to grow worldwide, but it has not done so without controversy.

What has caused opposition to the Witnesses, other than their unorthodox theology? Perhaps most prominently it has been their unwillingness to serve in the armed forces. During times when the country has had a military draft, the Witnesses have generally been unwilling to register as conscientious objectors because they are not opposed to war in any form, as conscientious objection requires. Indeed, they will be on the front lines when the climactic war of Armageddon arrives. Their objection is that they are not citizens of any earthly nation, but of the kingdom of God, and that the only army they will march for is the Lord's. Similarly, they are controversial for not saluting the flag, which, as far as they are concerned, amounts to an act of worship and fealty to an earthly government, which by definition is a false government; therefore the flag salute violates the Ten Commandments at Exodus 20:3-5. Yet another problem that has appeared repeatedly involves their unwillingness to accept blood transfusions, a position that stems from a point of biblical interpretation. We are commanded by the Levitical regulations not to eat blood, and they take that to mean any ingestion of blood. To their detractors such a position is ridiculous in any case, but especially reprehensible when it involves children. For their heartfelt beliefs and practices, the Witnesses have suffered enormous opprobrium. Thousands of them have gone to jail for refusing military service, and many more have wound up in court over their refusal to approve of blood transfusions. Their position on the flag salute went to the Supreme Court twice, and the second time they were victorious, although plenty of their detractors still condemn them for their disdain for worldly governments. In the United States and abroad, the Witnesses have been among the most controversial and persecuted of all religious movements. At the peak of their persecution, during the early years of the Second World War, they were so reviled that John T. Noonan in his book on American religious freedom has called the episode "the greatest outbreak of religious intolerance in twentieth-century America."[11]

TWENTIETH CENTURY

One enduring and sad human characteristic seems to be disdain for the new, and that seems to be behind the reception that Pentecostals got when their new religion first burst upon the American scene exactly one hundred years ago. Pentecostalism had its origins in Topeka, Kansas, on 1 January 1901, when Agnes Ozman and then other students of the faith-healing Holiness minister Charles Parham began to speak in tongues. Because they believed that the out-pouring of the spirit that they experienced was a sign that the millennium was at hand, they rushed headlong into missionary activities, trying to get as many people as possible on the gospel train before it pulled out of the station for the last time, so to speak.

But everywhere they faced ridicule. People were overwhelmingly not impressed with the great spiritual fervor that the fledgling Pentecostalists exhibited; they simply thought this group had gone loco. Derision and disdain met them at every turn. Gradually the movement began to sputter out, and it might well be a mere historical footnote had not William Seymour endured outrageous racism in Texas to learn about Pentecostalism and then go to Los Angeles to lead a revival there that turned the odd phenomenon into a worldwide movement. For many years, however, derision from the better-established churches continued to be the order of the day. These people who sometimes manifested physical effects in their religion were dismissed as "holy rollers." They were laughed out of their churches, and the reason that we have a series of independent Pentecostal denominations today is that the believers formed them essentially out of self-defense. For nearly two-thirds of a century the stigma remained; Pentecostals were marginalized and still often ridiculed.[12] It was not until the 1960s, when a new wave of Pentecostalism began to appear in the Episcopal, Catholic, and other churches that speaking in tongues became fairly widely accepted as a legitimate Christian alternative. Even so, some related practices remain far from general acceptance. Faith healing of the Pentecostal-revival type, for example, certainly is not regarded at all favorably by the great majority of American Christians. From the vantage point of the beginning of a new century, the birth and fantastic growth of Pentecostalism is the most significant religious story of the twentieth century, but for the majority of that century its practitioners were religious outcasts, and their full acceptance may still be in the future.

With the great historical upheaval in the 1960s came many new versions of Christianity. Several of them, like their predecessors, came in for a good deal of derision and ridicule. One group that received a great outpouring of criticism, so much that its opponents started what has become the modern anticult movement, was the Children of God, now known as the Family, founded in California in the late 1960s by David Berg. Berg was an evangelical minister who began working among the hippies and forged a movement that was in its early days best known for its dramatic denunciations of the evils of modern society. Members would dress in biblical-style robes and hurl denunciations at passers-by in public places. Soon they also began to found communes, and of course that is often suspect–people wonder, why would they want to go off by themselves? They must have something to hide–as if the monasticism of the past fifteen hundred years in Christianity represents something sinister. Eventually the controversy between members and their critics, often including their parents, became so intense that they largely withdrew, in many cases leaving the United States. For quite a time they were essentially invisible. Over time they did some unusual things, perhaps most famously "flirty fishing," in which attractive female members would essentially seduce men, telling them while making love that this act symbolized the love God had for human beings. Although flirty fishing is now a thing of the past, and in fact the group says it has outlawed all sex between members and nonmembers, a liberal sexual outlook admittedly remains, and members do have relations with members other than their spouses as the desire strikes them and they believe the circumstances warrant. It is fair to say that the Children of God had vehement critics thirty years ago, and the Family still receives plenty of criticism today. Full acceptance by mainline Christians and by society at large still seems a fair distance away.[13]

Another group roughly contemporary with the Children of God also came in for a good deal of criticism not too many years ago. The Way ministry was founded by Victor Paul Wierwille as "Vesper Chimes," a radio ministry, in 1942. Its main growth came with the grass-roots Jesus People movement of the late 1960s and early 1970s, and with growth came controversy.

Many Way members were subjected to deprogramming, but most of the complaints against the group seem pretty flimsy or just matters of opinion. Per the norm, the movement was accused of engaging in brainwashing and mind control, but it could never be discerned that it was any more intense than any number of other evangelical Christian movements. They also were accused of amassing an arsenal, but the only basis for that charge seems to be that some students at the Way College of Emporia (Kansas) once took a gun safety course. Beyond that, one is left with only theological errors. It is true that the Way was unconventional in its Christology, denying the divinity of Christ and therefore denying the existence of the Trinity. It is also true that Wierwille believed that the original text of the New Testament was written in Aramaic, not Greek, and that, as a result, he pushed ancient-language studies. The movement was Pentecostal and members spoke in tongues, although that is hardly worth noting. But those kinds of theological and biblical ideas, while mildly unconventional, do not seem to justify the outpouring of opposition that The Way experienced. After all, denial of the Trinity occurs in quite a few bodies of Christians, the most numerous of them, like the Way, of a Pentecostal persuasion. It may not matter much any longer, since the Way seems to be in serious decline following a good deal of internal turmoil that began in the 1980s. But it remains a rather puzzling case of persecution.[14]

Perhaps the most persecuted of all Christian-related groups of the last thirty years or so has been the Unification Church, founded in 1954 and still headed by Sun Myung Moon, who grew up in a Presbyterian home in Korea. Moon's parents had been converted by missionaries, and as often happens when a faith is exported to another country, their Presbyterianism reflected their own culture as well as that of Euroamerican Presbyterianism. Thus the religion that Moon said had been communicated to him in a series of divine revelations had a Christian core, with a strong emphasis on the biblical stories of the creation and the fall, but also had elements of Asian traditions, including Taoism and Korean shamanism.

Moon's first missionary came to the United States in 1959, but it was not until the 1970s that the movement began to get much public notice. When it did, it soon became just about the most reviled of all alternative religions, the very epitome of a "dangerous cult." Followers were depicted as glassyeyed zombies, their minds utterly controlled by an evil genius who sought world domination. They took in hordes of new members by outright deception, and members lived in crowded housing under conditions of sleep deprivation and near-malnutrition, it was said.

Calumny was heaped upon the Moonies from all sides. Mainline churches condemned them as heretics. Jews accused them of trying to undermine Judaism by converting large numbers of Jews to membership. Parents were convinced that their children were in mortal danger and in many cases spent tens of thousands of dollars for deprogramming to get them out. When Moon was convicted of tax evasion and served a year in prison in the mid-1980s, his critics felt vindicated, although quite a few more conventional religious organizations rallied to his defense because what he was convicted of was not unlike what they were doing as well.

The controversy has settled down somewhat in recent years. Moon's early recruits have aged and had families of their own, and the zealous young bands of church members are no longer visible. Perhaps most importantly, Moon has made overtures to the American political right wing, and now has good relations with certain elements of the conservative activist community. The newspaper he underwrites, *The Washington Times*, has become a conservative favorite. The Unificationists have not taken a regular place at the American mainstream religious table just yet, but they seem to be moving slowly toward some kind of acceptance. The enormous vituperation of the early years, in any case, has abated.[15]

One more group rooted in Christianity deserves mention for the opposition it has aroused. The International Church of Christ, also known as the Boston Movement or the Crossroads Movement, has its roots in the traditional Churches of Christ but soon developed a direction of its own. It was founded in 1979 near Boston and became visible in the 1980s and 1990s as an unusually demanding faith, one in which members had to give enormous dedication to the church and its projects, among other things making many evangelizing contacts daily. Perhaps its most controversial feature is its system of discipling, or shepherding, in which every member has a direct supervisor who has very considerable involvement in a believer's life. The discipler teaches the Bible according to the ICC's interpretation of it, and supervises the disciple's life to make sure that the disciple is living righteously. That supervision can be intense and personal, going right into a member's bedroom, in the sense that the sex life of even a married couple constitutes behavior for which one is accountable to one's discipler. The critics of the ICC are outspoken, and the church has met firm resistance, including being banned from a number of college campuses. Stay tuned, because here is a movement still very much on the front burner.[16]

There are many other Christian-derived religious groups that could be similarly included in this survey. One might look at the persecution suffered by snake handlers, who after all are merely following biblical advice given at the end of the gospel of Mark; or the Identity movement, a Christian racist school of thought that has gathered a small following over the last several decades. And let us not forget the Branch Davidians and their parent group, the Davidian Seventh Day Adventists, but since they have received sufficient attention in this book, it is not necessary to add them to my list of persecuted believers. In all, the history of persecution of Christian-related churches out of favor with the larger mainstream groups is extensive and unpleasant.

CONCLUSION

When alternative forms of Christianity in the American past are compared with those of more recent vintage, many respond with skepticism. "The Shakers were just sweet, harmless people who went off and built beautiful museum villages and manufactured nice furniture and sang pretty songs, but Moonies? Well, that's different. Moonies are zombie slaves of a power-mad dictator." These things are actually largely a matter of point of view and of historical perspective. There seems to be a human tendency to idealize things safely in the past and to demonize things that are closer to us, ideas that are just slightly different than our own. It seems to me that we would do well to follow the counsel provided by Gamaliel in Acts 5:38-39: "If this undertaking is of human origin, it will fail; but if it is of God, you will not be able to overthrow them. You might even be found opposing God!"

Chapter 2

The Cult Awareness Network and the Anticult Movement
Implications for NRMs in America

Anson Shupe, Susan E. Darnell, and
Kendrick Moxon

On 23 October 1996 at 9:30 a.m., the Cult Awareness Network (CAN), a Chicago-based national anticult organization claiming to be purely a tax-exempt informational clearinghouse on new religions, closed its doors amid bankruptcy proceedings and its assets were auctioned off. The precipitating, but not lone, event that hastened its demise was a civil suit brought against both CAN and a trio of coercive deprogrammers who unsuccessfully tried to remove a legal adult, Jason Scott, from a United Pentecostal congregation. Scott was violently abducted, physically abused, and forcibly detained at a remote Washington state location for almost a week. While CAN was at the time suffering many other lawsuits for alleged deprivation of the civil rights of members of minority religions, the Scott case became its Waterloo.

The jury was quite clear in its decision to award compensatory and punitive damages to Scott.[1] CAN's primary activity, this case and others have revealed, was to provide false and/or inflammatory opinion in the guise of "information" about minority religions to the media and other inquirers. All or virtually all of such "information" was derogatory, consistent with CAN's goals of "educating" the public that various new religious movements (NRMs) are "destructive cults," that all of the members thereof are "cult victims," are "brainwashed," and are therefore at risk, possibly needing "rescue." The jury's decision, under the definitions provided in Washington law, was that CAN was truly an organized hate campaign. CAN described its activities in a euphemistic manner to make its activities seem less outrageous from a civil liberties perspective. The reason CAN even became involved in the Scott lawsuit was that, consistent with its organizational pattern, it served as a conduit for referrals to deprogrammers (later termed by CAN "exit counselors") who would, for a fee, abduct and during detention harangue family members into religious apostasy.

As Philip Jenkins documents in his book, *Mystics and Messiahs: Cults and New Religions in American History*, charismatic, world-transforming-portending leaders and their attending flocks have been legion in North American history. So also have been their opponents. Jenkins emphasizes the continuities of both "cult" and "anticult" phenomena in American history, including the present era. He observes that "there is no period, including colonial times, in which we cannot find numerous groups more or less indistinguishable from the most controversial movements"[2] and, on the "normality" of NRMs, Jenkins adds, "far from being a novelty, cults and cultlike movements have a very long history on American soil. Extreme and bizarre religious ideas are so commonplace in American history that it is difficult to speak of them as fringe at all."[3]

Likewise, opposition movements are as much a predictable fixture of religious pluralism as are the NRMs themselves.[4] This fact has not always been obvious to those caught up in the fray. Each age, as Jenkins maintains, thinks it is uniquely being overrun by menacing, anti-social, questionable religious groups and, for similar reasons, "reinvents the wheel" of religious alarm.

There is an irony in this latest wave of NRM/ACM conflict that neither side would have appreciated several decades ago. Two veteran chroniclers of the controversy, looking back over a quarter century, report that neither side expected this protracted protest against new religious movements to last: either because a damaging image of the anti-cult movement as an intolerant, anti-constitutional, vigilante movement would have been successfully promoted by its opponents; or because, thanks to the ACM's mobilization of public officials and law enforcement agencies, health professionals, academics, and public opinion, the "innovative" NRMs would have been broken up, prosecuted, and deported.[5]

This report utilizes recently acquired new data on CAN in order to shed light on the maturing nature of the anticult movement since its inception in the early 1970s. For reasons of space limitation, the extensive social science literature on NRM is not reviewed. Elsewhere a detailed historical/organizational analysis of the ACM up to the end of the 1970s has been presented.[6] The chronicle is basically one of regional and local grassroots "mom-and-pop" groups' struggles to (1) acquire sufficient financial stability to allow them to spread their message of "destructive cults" subverting American society, (2) maintain a shifting membership base together long enough to lobby, publicize, and mobilize opposition to NRMs, and (3) establish a national unified organizational prominence with political clout. There were a number of false (i.e., unsuccessful) starts, but by the mid-1980s there were two prominent national-level groups—the Cult Awareness Network and the American Family

Foundation.[7] In the beginning (the early 1970s), most ACM groups' membership consisted of senior family members distraught at their offsprings'/junior relatives' deviant religious choices. Over time, however, the mantle of ACM activism and leadership passed to degreed behavioral science moral entrepreneurs who made ACM involvement an important, and sometimes lucrative, part of their careers.

METHODS

We rely on two sources of information. The first source consists of a large number of court transcripts and sworn testimonies in court records, depositions, and affidavits from ACM leaders, deprogrammers, ex-NRM and current NRM members, and deprogrammees gathered in the course of civil liberties litigation against primarily CAN by various attorneys (including the third author) during the legal process of "discovery."

The second source consists of approximately four hundred boxes of CAN files assigned as assets to a Chicago, Illinois bankruptcy court trustee. There is evidence that during a total of more than fifty-one pending lawsuits against CAN and its directors and during discovery inquiries (all during the early-to-mid 1990s) select documents were being destroyed by unknown persons at CAN. After the surviving boxes were secured by the court and auctioned off to a private individual, they were donated to the Foundation for Religious Freedom (based in Los Angeles, California) where they were catalogued and made available to the public (i.e., researchers such as ourselves and to representatives of a variety of NRMs) for inspection and photocopying. After the Fall of 1999, most boxes were then donated by the FRF and moved to the Special Collections section of the library at the University of California at Santa Barbara. However, a total of thirty-two boxes containing purely financial records (e.g., cancelled checks, ledgers, lists of donors and expenditures, copies of audits, and telephone files) remained until 2002 in our possession. These files are also now at the University of California, Santa Barbara.

CORPORATE CRIME AS CAN POLICY

This report deals only with financial aspects of CAN and the implications thereof for religious pluralism. Thus, evidence for the existence of what criminologists refer to as *corporate crime*, i.e., performance of illegal, harmful criminal behavior as standard operating policy for administrators will be pursued. Other interesting aspects of CAN *modus operandi* —such as coercive deprogrammers' not unheard use of illegal and legal drugs before and during deprogrammings and even the use of sexual intercourse with deprogrammees, details of which can be found elsewhere, or of the 1505 NRMs and quasi-religious groups on which CAN indiscriminately kept running files—must be omitted.[8]

CAN was incorporated in 1986, originally an offshoot of the earlier Citizens Freedom Foundation—Information Services, at the time the largest ACM group in the United States. CAN claimed to be a humanitarian information clearinghouse on NRMs and publicly claimed no association with deprogrammers. This is now known to be patently false. The evidence points to coercive deprogrammers as an important lucrative source of CAN income. Deprogrammers were also regular attenders at CAN annual conferences as speakers and solicitors of clients and in regular communication with CAN leaders.[9]

Deprogrammer Kickbacks and Money-Laundering: The Inner Sanctum of NARDEC

Journalist Nora Hamerman, in writing about the Dobkowski deprogramming fiasco, referred to CAN as "a clearinghouse for kidnap-for-hire rings."[10] This is an apt description. There was a corporate crime basis for CAN's continuance and funding, as suggested earlier.

Various background informant sources speak to a deprogrammer kickback/money laundering scheme by which deprogrammers received continued referrals from CAN in exchange for "repayments" or donations (i.e., commissions) funneled back to national CAN headquarters. In one newspaper article, former deprogrammer Jonathan Nordquist "alleges that with each referral to a deprogrammer, a 'kick-back' is sent to CAN in the form of a 'donation' to ensure that the referrals continue."[11] If so, such claims would establish a financial symbiosis between CAN and coercive deprogrammers. John M. Sweeney, Jr., past head of CFF as it turned into CAN during the early-to-mid 1980s, recounting how deprogrammers charged thousands of dollars per case, testified:

> Because of the large amounts of money they make due to referrals received from CFF members, deprogrammers usually kick-back money to the CFF member who gave the referral. . . The kick-backs would either be in cash or would be in the form of a tax deductible "donation" to the CFF. . . . Adrian Greek, who was the national chairman of CFF at the time that I was its national director, had an adult daughter in the Unification Church. Mr. Greek was very cheap and didn't want to pay money to have a deprogramming. He then attempted to get a deprogrammer to deprogram his daughter in exchange for Mr. Greek's future referrals of clients to the deprogrammer.[12]

Deprogrammer Mark Blocksom (see n. 9) alludes indirectly to this reciprocity. CAN's last executive director, Cynthia Kisser, gave the following evasive responses under legal examination. While vague, they are suggestive of such a corporate policy:

Q. Whether CAN National during the period of 1987 to 1989 to your knowledge received donations, pleads, or funds of any sort from deprogrammers?

A. I would say given the definition I gave of deprogramming, yes, they very well could have.

Q. To your knowledge from 1987 to 1989 have any families who to your knowledge hired deprogrammers subsequent to referrals from CAN made any donations to CAN National?

A. I would have no way of knowing on a first name basis, if that was their reason for giving.

Q. So, to your knowledge some families have given, but you don't know what their reasons were?

A. Thousands of people have given. I don't know what their reason may have been.

Q. Well, to your knowledge have families who in fact hired deprogrammers and made that known to you, made donations to CAN?

A. I don't know if specifically between '87 and '89 there were families who had hired deprogrammers who did also give money to CAN during that time period. I just do not know. It's possible they could have.[13]

The attorney in cross-examination was chipping away at the possibility that deprogrammers "discounted" the price of a deprogramming if the families (not the deprogrammers) made the donation directly to CAN. That this practice existed appears likely. Notes on donor index cards for NARDEC contributions (see below on NARDEC) in CAN desk rolodex files comment frequently on donors' family members' present or past membership in NRMs (e.g. COG, CUT, UC, HK, BCC, Alamo) and sometimes if the deprogrammings referred were successful or unsuccessful (and conducted by which deprogrammer—see CAN Box 249, "Rolodexes"). However, a more direct answer can be found in other testimony and in CAN records themselves. CAN staff member Marty Butz, who admitted to have made around five hundred deprogramming referrals, was asked in a deposition:

Q. Have any of the people that you made referrals to for deprogramming since you've been in CAN made any donations to CAN, any monetary donations?

A. I know that [deprogrammer] Carol Giambalvo has been a Nardeck [sic] member. That's the only extent of my knowledge of any contributions going CAN's way.

Q. What does "Nardeck" mean?

A. I don't know. I don't know what Nardeck represents.

Q. Nardeck members are people that make substantial monetary contributions to CAN isn't that correct?

A. Yes. [Butz suddenly remembers.]

Q. There's a—that's kind of the select people that are the primary financial supporters of CAN?

A. I believe what it is is a commitment for three years donating a thousand dollars.

Q. A year?

A. I can't say that's where CAN's primary support comes from.

Q. How much money has Miss Giambalvo donated to CAN since you've been involved in CAN?

A. I have no idea.

Q. At least $3,000?

A. If she's been a Nardeck member more than once, quite possibly more than $3,000.

Q. She's the person you've made the largest number of deprogramming referrals to, correct?

A. Yes.[14]

The court recorder had the subgroup of CAN spelled incorrectly —not Nardeck, but rather NARDEC: National Resource Development and Economic Council. This was the heart of deprogrammers' money-laundering operation and a key area of financial support for CAN. Its referral-in-exchange-for-a-kickback-of-deprogramming-fees is why CAN deprogrammer Rick Ross, in a "slump time" for business after having "paid his dues" to NARDEC, wrote CAN activist Priscilla Coates in a huff:

> Have not received one really solid referral, C.A.N. included. I don't know why. Perhaps summer, "turf" issues, or lack of desire to deal with fundamentalists. Phil and Annie have called from N.Y. and Annette is trying, but some parents are so cheap they prefer to let their kids "bang the Bible" than pay.[15]

Ex-CAN executive director Cynthia Kisser acknowledged the existence of NARDEC deprogrammer contributions in a deposition:

Q. Do you know of any donations that have been made to CAN by deprogrammers?

A. Let me just take a minute to look at some of the people that you've identified as deprogrammers to let me answer that question. Yes.

Q. Who?

A. Steve Hassan, Carol Giambalvo, and . . . Randall Burkey.[16]

Formed in the mid-1980s, by 1987 NARDEC had become institutionalized as a special unit within CAN. Ronald M. Loomis, CAN president, wrote in a 26 June 1987 form letter to all CAN affiliates and newsletter subscribers:

> We are grateful to those of you who responded to our appeal for contributions with the February meeting. The number of persons who have become members of the National Resource and Development Council (NaRDec) by pledging $1,000 per year for three years continues to grow,

but we need that level of commitment from many more persons. Based on your generous support in 1986, we determined that we could afford to commit ourselves to the full time salary of an Executive Director for the future. A letter from our Finance and Development Chair . . . together with a pledge card, is [sic] enclosed. It will be a real challenge for us to continue in 1987 what we in 1986. Please do what you can to sustain that effort. Remember that we cannot expect anyone to support the cult awareness effort unless we provide *the first level of support.*[17] [Italics ours.]

Apparently deprogrammers (renaming themselves "exit counselors") understood the message. Under the NARDEC aegis they began to organize within CAN. In the Preliminary Program of the Portland, Oregon 1987 annual CAN conference there was scheduled a Wednesday, 19 October special evening meeting for exit counselors (and added below that announcement: "will not post on hotel meeting sign or brochure.") On Saturday, 22 October at the same convention there was also a special NARDEC breakfast.[18] NARDEC also had special 7:30 a.m. breakfast meetings at the 1989 CAN annual conference (program noted: "NARDEC members only") and at the 1990 annual CAN conference NARDEC members met in conjunction with the CAN advisory board. Referring back to earlier sections of this chapter where CAN officials tried to distance themselves on paper and in legal testimonies that CAN in no way encouraged deprogrammings, an examination of real CAN activities belies that claim. It would appear that "exit counselors," formerly deprogrammers, were invited (literally) to sit at the CAN table.

Of course, not all contributions to CAN and NARDEC were from deprogrammers or persons who favored vigilante actions over educational goals. CAN donors each received identification numbers and were listed/enumerated in files. An inspection of such lists would include, for example, a 25 July 1988 contribution of $2,000 from the Grainger Foundation to a more modest 21 July 1995 contribution of $35.00 from evangelical Christian (counter-cult) sociologist Ronald Enroth (ID# 912). However, many were from known deprogrammers (and their sympathizers), such as Carol Giambavlo, Paul Engel, Janja Lalich, and David Clark.

Inspection of NARDEC contributions by month for 1988-95 shows a fairly stable pattern: yearly totals averaged between $40,000 and $54,000, always strongest in January (around $7,000 for that month) and then leveling off to less than $4,000 per month. (NARDEC's contribution to total CAN revenues was about one-third.) However, it appears likely that under-the-table deprogrammer referral kick-backs made up a substantial proportion of NARDEC funds. (NARDEC had its own CAN account number, 4080, as opposed to the general fund, 4000, or CAN's mail order "bookstore" selling tracts, tapes, and books, 4020.) Apparently some deprogrammers did not use this traceable account for "donations." Examining monthly NARDEC contributions for the 1990s, for example, they *rarely* approached the reported monthly total contributions in CAN and *never* approached the reported annual totals. Cash receipts for April 1992, for instance, show a total that month of one $1000 contribution. October 1992 shows the same. In other words, NARDEC fund totals in any given year cannot be explained by cash receipts or recorded individual contributions (which, as numerous boxes of rather tediously studied files show, were quite meticulously detailed).

In fact, many recorded NARDEC contributions were in "nickel-and-dime" modest amounts: $30, $50, or $150. Some donations to CAN were even split between other funds and NARDEC; for example, $50 donated by an individual in 1993, $30 to go to NARDEC and $20 into CAN's general fund. Such are the minutiae of the CAN files. There were some perennial NARDEC stalwarts who were family relatives of present or previous NRM members (and some deprogrammers). But NARDEC had a serious problem if it is assumed all monies taken in are reflected in the books eventually shown to outside auditors. There were many donors who welched on their pledges, decreasing overt NARDEC revenues: in 1992, 59 persons pledged $1000 or more, but 26 reneged; in 1993, 30 persons pledged the $1000 minimum but 14 reneged; in 1994, 23 of 27 persons reneged; and in 1995, 38 of 50 persons reneged. Towards the waning days of CAN there was a strong, last-ditch resurgence of giving to help. January 1996 checks (from a very small, "select" group of persons) of $1000 to NARDEC totalled around $10,675. But by then CAN was struggling amid many lawsuits, having lost the Jason Scott deprogramming civil suit, and had squandered an insurance settlement thereof on pointless litigation—much of which it ultimately lost or conceded.

So where did NARDEC make up the difference if recorded dollar totals do not square with meticulous, computerized receipt statements?

Two separate rolodex lists of NARDEC donors and general contacts in media, law, industry, and social sciences (marked "Major Gifts and NARDEC: comments to be included when required") include a *Who's Who* of dozens of coercive deprogrammers' names, telephone numbers, and addresses. We suggest a triangulation of evidence from: (1) deprogrammers' testimonies; (2) former CFF/CAN officials' testimonies; (3) the obvious accounting lacunae in CAN financial records; and (4) the "Cash-only" nature of deprogramming fees. (Deprogrammers typically did not take credit cards or provide receipts, so complained families who felt taken advantage of by expensive, ineffective deprogramming interventions.) Our opinion and conclusion is that systematic records of the kick-backs that went on in CAN's offices during its last days were never kept in the first place, or were perhaps destroyed. The shoddy bookkeeping of CAN, and the likelihood of white-collar crime committed by certain CAN leaders, to which we now turn, are part of the NARDEC story.

Evidence of Mismanagement of CAN Finances and
Violation of Fiduciary Responsibility

CAN president Ronald M. Loomis was especially pleased in Spring 1987 when an executive director search committee recommended Cynthia S. Kisser of Woodstock, Illinois after six months of deliberations and interviews. He wrote effusively to the CAN affiliates and newsletter subscribers about her business credentials (aside from her academic credentials): "Her professional background includes four years as a business manager with responsibility for general ledger, payroll records, tax reports, monthly billing and company financial matters. She has supervised staffs, set up computer operations and resolved hardware and software matters. . . . She has taught Business Communication for a community college."[19]

Yet, problems that had plagued the top levels of CFF-as-it-turned-into-CAN continued. Kent E. Vaughn, CFF Board of Directors member, 1982-84, had come to the disturbing conclusion that there was an "inner board" of CAN with an agenda beyond CAN's public pronouncements (see n. 8). In 1981, the earlier national director of CFFI-IS, John M. Sweeney, Jr., saw economic problems in the board's behavior. While he resigned for a number of reasons, including CFF's rejection of a deprogrammer's ethics code while simultaneously heavily involved in often illegal, coercive, expensive, and often ineffective "rescues," he was also unhappy that the group had failed to reimburse him on occasion and considered a collection suit against CFF-IS. However, his final complaint was that something untoward was occurring in CFF's management of money. He met a stonewall of silence when called for an inspection of these issues. He voiced his frustrations: "Why has the CFF-IS Board done all in its power to prevent an audit of the corporate books? Why has over $20,000 worth of donations been buried in an interest bearing CD account (did the Board approve this action?) or in a checking account? Why was not this donation money stipulated for use in anti-cult projects? Why was money freed up so easily to finance an all expense paid trip to Dallas for the Board for an unnecessary meeting yet legitimate bills could not or would not be paid on time? I have records of threatened phone cutoff and late payment notices due to C——'s inefficient method. To protect my reputation and credit rating the WATS and SPRINT have been disconnected because they are in my name."[20]

Ironically, CAN had the same troubles during its existence and demise in 1996. For example, when CAN executive director Kisser came into office in 1987, she appears to have made some radical changes in CAN financial management. In essence, she consolidated its finances, with minimal executive office accountability to members. According to one informant knowledgeable about the group:

Kisser changed the financial lines of the Cult Awareness Network. Kisser demanded that all Cult Awareness Network chapters send all of the donations they received, including uncanceled checks, to her at the national office in Illinois. Kisser then cashed the checks, kept the amount of money that she wanted and then mailed the remaining money to the affiliated chapters as she saw fit [see n. 11].

Ex-deprogrammer Jonathan Nordquist, having met Kisser at a CAN convention, remembers:

Shortly after, [Mary] Krone told me that once Kisser fully learned how to do her new job, that Krone would no longer be working at the national offices. . . . Additionally, I recall an incident that occurred while I was riding in an elevator during the [CAN] convention in Pittsburgh. Also present in the elevator were Mary Krone, Krone's son, John, Cynthia Kisser and Rachel Andres. Mary Krone was talking about the finances of the Cult Awareness Network when Kisser stated to her: "If the cults ever get a hold of our books we'd be in trouble" [see n. 11].

Having expended its insurance money on fruitless appeals of the Jason Scott/Rick Ross/CAN deprogramming case that awarded Scott over $4 million, and having wasted funds on other lawsuits, as its income decreased CAN began to default on its phone bills (all the while continuing to pay director Cynthia Kisser $3000 per month plus lesser amounts to CAN staff).

There are several serious financial implications to these operations: All not-for-profit organizations are required to follow standard ethical and legal protocol particularly with respect to financial management. Complete detailed records must be consistently maintained, then supported by both internal and external audits to ensure both accuracy and propriety. The operations and cash flow must conform with generally accepted accounting standards. A painstakingly extensive review of the alleged complete court-ordered financial records of CAN confirms blatant impropriety. CAN was classified as a 501(c)(3), not-for-profit, tax-exempt organization with the Internal Revenue Service. To qualify and comply, certain measures of practice and accounting are required; the organization is accountable by federal law. The organizational test is a mandate that specific conditions be met and maintained for tax-exempt qualification according to the IRS code. To qualify for 501(c)(3) status the organization must be formed exclusively for literary, charitable, religious, educational, or scientific purposes; the manner of operation must be described in detail. Furthermore, the articles of the organization must appropriately limit the organization's purpose, regulate the allocation of contributions, and foster the best interests of everyone concerned. CAN's admitted affiliation with deprogrammers as confirmed in the Scott trial, among other places, appears to conflict with the IRS limited purpose constraint as well as in the express powers clause [7.8.2] 3.3.4 (02-231999), titled Express Powers that Cause Failure of Organizational Test, which provides:

An organization does not meet the organizational test if its articles expressly empower it: To have objectives and to engage in activities which char-
acterize it as an "action organization" (Reg. 1.501(c)(3)-1 (b)(3)(iii)); To
carry on any other activities (unless they are insubstantial) which are not
in furtherance of one or more exempt purposes (Reg. 1.501(c)(3)
1(b)(1)(i)(a)).[21]

By affiliation, CAN cast, at minimum, a shadow on these two IRS provisions. Given the records and documented activity of this organization, it might
be said that CAN acted in multiple violations of its IRS classification.

One initial and standing concern is that of missing or duplicated documents. The general condition of the financial records is deplorable.
Documents are not in chronological order or in keeping with standard bookkeeping practice, making tracking a monumental feat. There are substantial
gaps and pertinent items, statements, canceled checks, audits, and so forth that
are missing. The list is significant. There are no itemized journals or ledgers of
income or expenditures (standard accrual accounting), merely sporadic incomplete lists. The financial records are highly questionable and are at best profes-
sionally sloppy.

Cash flow is abundantly problematic and highly critical. In mere illustration, a petty cash withdrawal of $1,500 was observed. The established, accept-
able norm for an organization of this size would be to maintain a generous $300
fund in total. Of greater concern, a review of cash receipts reflects numerous
and substantial checks issued by CAN (National) to CAN itself with no indication or record of who received said funds, nor of the generating purpose. To
illustrate, a $12,000 check issued 3/25/94 by CAN to CAN lists an account
category #4250 for which there is no correlating account description. The canceled check #184 is not present among those in that series, nor is it ever listed
as an expenditure. Interestingly, similar documentation and lack of canceled
checks occurs with numerous other like entries.

Or another example: on 1/19/95 two checks (#5876 and #5877) were issued
to J. Gordon Melton and Anson Shupe, respectively, for $600 each. Given their
extensive study in this field, both men are known critics of CAN and would
certainly not be on its payroll (i.e., certainly not "anti-cult apologists"). This
time period ties in to the Lippmann/Scientology lawsuit against CAN with neither party involved beyond personal academic interest and neither party
deposed by CAN as part of the lawsuit. (Depositional checks to professionals
are rarely made out before depositions are taken.) Neither scholar has any
knowledge of the existence of these checks. The checks were then processed as
stop payments—Melton's the same day, Shupe's not until April—yet the funds
($1,200) were never reentered into the CAN account to offset the would-be
stop payments. Both checks were physically located, reflecting stop payments,
yet the bookkeeping does not appropriately correlate. Uncannily, Shupe discovered these particular entries personally while examining financial data in the
CAN boxes. Why were bogus checks issued, who retained the $1,200, and,

more importantly, how many other orchestrated entries lie within the records of CAN and to whose financial gain?

Moreover, while not unheard of, not-for-profit CAN maintained a steady and healthy separate account with the Merrill Lynch firm housing an extremely active money market account with no correlating income relationship and with certificates of deposit averaging $40,000, far exceeding the standard required reserve. Despite these investments, letters and audits indicate financial distress. According to records, CAN was unable to pay concurrent Sprint network telephone bills, netting numerous final disconnect notices. These concerns led to a recommendation issued by Virginia Hulet, CAN Treasurer (resigned October, 1989) asking that all Sprint credit cards be returned. From whom? Phone records indicate substantial use by deprogrammers of CAN phone lines, calling from CAN's national office. We ask again, was this careless mismanagement or diverted attention?

In 1987, Cynthia Kisser, CAN's executive director, directed all chapters' funds to be generated directly to the national office. While there was noted board objection, this practice was implemented, allowing the national office complete control of funds with minimal accountability.

Peat Marwick (KPMG), a respected certified public accounting firm, was procured by CAN to conduct its annual audits. Auditing correspondence consistently expressed numerous concerns regarding the need for improved accounting principles, further suggesting accrual accounting. They cited concern with the lack of internal audits indicating neglect of Auditing Standards No. 50 as previously posed. In the face of rising litigation expenses, no allotments were made to accommodate this clear necessity appropriately. Finally on 1 June 1994, a letter signed by KPMG Peat Marwick expressed serious concern regarding CAN's solvency. In a letter dated 8 June 1995, KPMG indicated an imbalance between the general ledger and the bank reconciliations that had existed since July 1994. In a final communication, KPMG elected to withdraw its affiliation with CAN in the face of growing financial concerns.

Countless fringe questions arise when analyzing the CAN boxes: why do CAN records contain an inordinate amount of letters of dispute (i.e., a $26,228.76 disputed conference balance with the Crown Plaza Hotel in White Plains, N.Y., November 1995)? Why were multiple financial accounts simultaneously active (i.e., 4/9/96 when Cynthia Kisser requested NBD Bank of Skokie to transfer remaining funds to an account titled Cult Awareness Network Corp AKA CAN D.I.P.)? Why would an organization of good intent be faced with fiercely escalating litigation (i.e., in 1994 there were fifty-one lawsuits in various states of settlement as presented to KPMG for completion of 1994 audit)? Finally, why did Kisser and several staff members continue to receive their salaries (Kisser $1500 every two weeks) beyond the filing of bankruptcy? More importantly, what became of CAN's final funds in the midst of dissolution?

These examples serve only as a small segment of a greater deluge of seeming impropriety currently under scrutiny within the CAN financial records. Two outside veteran auditors, when questioned regarding potential innocent explanations for these issues, stated that this appears to be a case of "money laundering" or of "looting the assets" (their words). Again we ask, is this a case of atrocious bookkeeping or instead calculated misappropriation? Neither option is acceptable per standard auditing and IRS protocol.

We have evidence of substantial malfeasance throughout the documents purportedly representing the complete fiscal records of this organization. The "why" remains yet to be addressed, the leaders and trustees are yet to be held accountable. This preliminary finding is just that: a highlighted report of what we believe to be a much darker indication than that of poor record-keeping. A Brownie troop with a naive, inexperienced leader might maintain such records and be accused of poor bookkeeping. For an organization with the capital, the influence, and the magnitude of CAN, such explanations are inexcusable and suspect.

At the time of this presentation, the exploration of CAN documents continues as additional discoveries unfold. Are these findings the result of gross negligence or of something much more untoward? Our final assessment will appear in a much more extensive book treatment forthcoming.

CONCLUSIONS ABOUT CAN OPERATIONS

This report is part of a work in progress. The CAN files will take years to thoroughly comb for data. Thus, we continue to find new evidence of CAN's criminal involvement the further we delve, despite evidence that toward the end Kisser and/or CAN operatives deliberately shredded/destroyed important files dealing with CAN's telephone calls and likely selected cancelled checks.[22] In this chapter, we have dealt only with CAN, not its sister ACM organization, the American Family Foundation, although we will be examining that group in the future.

We offer five reasonable propositions about the operations and philosophy of America's formerly most activist anti-cult organization:

Proposition 1: Despite public claims otherwise, CAN had as its operating corporate policy the routine referrals of inquirers to coercive deprogrammers. As has been shown, this proposition is supported by a variety of sources: testimonies of deprogrammers, testimonies of CFF-CAN officials, CAN records, and Federal Bureau of Investigation wiretap surveillance.

Regarding the last source, it has recently been discovered that the FBI, learning of certain deprogrammers conspiring toward, among other things, the kidnapping of a young heir to the duPont estate who had become involved in Lyndon LaRouche's organization, and learning of those deprogrammers' involvement with CAN, in 1992 conducted wiretaps of CAN telephone con-

versations and certain deprogrammers' telephone conversations. FBI Special
Agent Daniel Murphy presented an affidavit dated 19 July 1992 to the U. S.
Federal Court, Eastern District of Pennsylvania, in which he stated:

> As a result of my personal participation in this investigation, my knowl-
> edge of reports made to me by other FBI agents . . . there is probable cause
> to believe that Donald Moore, Galen Kelly, Edgar N. (Newbold] Smith,
> and others unknown, have been, or continuing to, and will be committing
> offenses againt the United States including conspiracy, in violation of 18
> U.S.C., Section 371, and kidnapping, in violation of 18 U.S.C., Section
> 1201. There is probable cause to believe that communications concerning
> said offenses will be obtained through the interception of wire communi-
> cations, authorization for which is herein applied.[23]

The transcripts of over a half dozen reels of tape reveal coercive deprogrammers in frequent (and casual) contact with CAN and CAN's executive director,
Cynthia Kisser, on how to harass the LaRouche organization and simultaneously protect themselves legally from prosecution after the deprogramming.
Such transcripts may be one logical reason that Cynthia Kisser had thousands
of CAN phone sheets destroyed around the 1992-93 period. For brief examples:

Edgar Newbold Smith calls former deputy sheriff-turned-deprogrammer
Donald Moore about suing his own son, Lewis duPont Smith, a duPont for-
tune heir and a follower of Lyndon LaRouche:

But the only problem with suing Lewis, having CAN sue Lewis, is *that they
know that we contributed to CAN* [italics ours.] So you're going to get the biggest
bunch of goddamn bunch of squawk going on down there involving us. . . .
Now maybe one of the things you ought to talk to Cynthia about is why not
include Lewis in your depositions?[24]

Or: Moore's answering machine for 7/15/92:
> This is Cynthia Kisser for Don Moore. I'm in Chicago. My number is
> 312/267/7777.

Or this conversation in early August, 1992:
> Donald Moore: Hello.
> Cynthia Kisser: Hi. Is Don Moore there?
> Moore: Yes.
> Kisser: Hi, Don. It's Cynthia.
> Moore: How are you doing?
> Kisser: Good. Good. Um, listen, um, I still have not talked to um—
> Moore: Galen? [Galen Kelly, once head of security for CAN conferences
>   and convicted of kidnapping in the Dubkowski case.]
> Kisser: Yes.
> Moore: That is, uh, you are not alone in that effort.
> Kisser: Okay. Now do you think that Newbold is at his office today or at
>   his home?

Moore: He should be at his home today. And I talked to him less than an hour ago.

Kisser: Yea. I want to give him a try. Thanks.[25]

Or a call from deprogrammer Moore to CAN headquarters in Chicago:

Moore: Yes, this is Don Moore calling from Virginia. Is Cynthia Kisser there?

Female voice: No, she's on a week's vacation.

Moore: Ouch.

Female voice: And, uh, her assistant though comes in at nine o'clock and it's ten to nine. Maybe she can help you?

Moore: All right, well, uh, I, basically I don't need help as far as that goes. I'm one of the folks that work for her as far as the LaRouche case goes.[26]

One of the FBI tapes captured a conversation between Kisser and later convicted Donald Moore on 15 July 1992. Moore was retained by Newbold Smith to work with former private investigator-turned-deprogrammer Galen Kelly on the abduction of Smith's son. On the tape, Kisser informs Moore that she has filed her suit against [various Scientologists] and states:

Kisser: I think the timing is right for me to go back and try— even if I'm not going to hear from Galen, to go back and approach Newbold to talk to him a little bit now that I've got the suit filed. I want to get him a copy of it. I want to talk to him about it. I want to, uh, talk about it.[27]

The point of these sample bits of conversation is that (1) the FBI was very aware of CAN's involvement in coercive abductions, and (2) CAN's highest eschelon was engaged in corporate criminality, coordinating legal strategies with deprogrammers. Destruction of CAN's phone sheets permanently removed written notes and comments that we are certain contained details of CAN-deprogramming conversations:

The phone sheets contain the caller's name, address, number, subject of call, information provided to the caller, and notes regarding the call. . . .The sheets are used for the sending out of materials and tabulation of statistical information about calls. . . . [Ms. Kisser] affirmed that use of phone sheets was a standard office procedure. . . Kisser estimated that CAN received from 60,000 to 80,000 phone inquiries and 20,000 to 40,000 mail inquiries from 1987 to 1993, Between 53,000 and 56,000 total phone and mail sheets were created during 1991, 1992, and 1993, most of which are phone sheets. Thus, subtracting the 15,000 that remained in existence in March of 1994, at least 38,000 phone and mail sheets have been destroyed. . . .[28]

Rolodex files from the desks of CAN officials and staff members (Box 249 labeled "Rolodexes"), however, were not destroyed and also reveal CAN's familiar connection to deprogrammers. Along with the names, addresses, telephone

numbers, and business cards of attorneys, American Family Foundation offi-
cials, xerox repairmen, sympathizers like comedian Steve Allen and actor Mike
Farrell, and others, are entries (apparently for referrals) for deprogrammers like
Ted Patrick, Joe Szimhart, Newbold Smith, Gary Scharff, Rick Ross, Galen
Kelly, Shirley Landa, Ann Greek, Carol Giambolvo, Wendy Ford, Randall
Burkey, and David Clark, among others.

Proposition 2: CAN was a money-laundering scheme in that coercive
deprogrammers were expected to "kick-back" or donate, directly or indirectly,
portions of the fees they charged families to CAN in exchange for continued
referrals. The testimonies of various CFF-CAN officials, deprogrammers, and
circumstantial CAN records (i.e., the NARDEC contributions from deprogrammers and the irregular movements of cash within CAN) strongly point to
this conclusion. In this sense, CAN conforms to a judgment rendered by
Franklin H. Littell, president of the Philadelphia Center on the Holocaust,
Genocide, and Human Rights:

> CAN and its staffers encourage distraught parents to take actions that fur-
> ther alienate young people. CAN conspires to destroy the liberties of indi-
> viduals and groups that have religious [beliefs] and worldviews different
> from the rest of us. It deserves to be put in the dock with the individuals
> the FBI has exposed and the courts are now trying for criminal acitivity.[29]

Proposition 3: There were sufficient irregularities in the handling of CAN
finances and cash flows to suggest that some CAN officials may have enriched
themselves significantly at the expense of the CAN organization and its mission
without members' general knowledge. The CAN financial documents are gross-
ly problematic in numerous ways. Direct examination of the records as released
by CAN pose the following non-inclusive concerns: tax exempt violations,
incomplete and inappropriately duplicated records, pertinent required items
missing, unaccounted fund appropriations, an improper petty cash allotment,
contribution discrepancies, a questionable reserve and CDs, unacceptable
accounting and management of funds, and auditor findings resulting in termination of association.

Our preliminary findings of these staggering discrepancies, combined with
the clear affiliation to deprogrammers, points to a cash flow from deprogrammings. Are the gaping omissions in the financial records a coverup? The systematic destruction of selective pertinent financial records seems to indicate a
pointed attempt at eliminating potentially incriminating evidence. In the final
days of CAN's existence, why were Kisser and other anti-cultists so frantic to
purchase the CAN records, as evidenced in the bidding for such which occurred
during the bankruptcy sale of goods hearing 10/23/96?[30]

A final burning question rests in the reason behind the bomb threats made
towards the final shipment of the CAN documents once procured, en route to
a secure storage site. Such drastic measures only serve to arouse curiosity and to
stimulate this investigative study.

Our conclusion is that a reasonable description of CAN, as it existed in the period 1986-1995, views it as a criminal organization organized against new religious movements (and other groups) in large part for profit to certain actors, and hypocritical and deceptive in its public persona.

IMPLICATIONS FOR RELIGIOUS PLURALISM

We may seem to have been unkind to CAN. Certainly it must be embarrassing to rank-and-file CAN supporters, and perhaps threatening to former CAN leaders, all of whom never expected to have their financial secrets and personal correspondence put on display before knowledgeable critics of the ACM. But CAN was not what it claimed to be. It was a corrupt kick-back referral scheme for coercive deprogrammers and likely an avenue of enrichment and possibily even embezzlement for some leaders.

What does the CAN example say, first, about the development of the ACM, and second, about the state of American religious pluralism? First, it seems well-nigh inevitable in hindsight that in a capitalist society whose citizens are often entrepreneurial that the grassroots familial motives of love and concern, which fueled the earliest ACM leadership, would be supplanted by persons who saw financial opportunity in the controversy. Some academics and a number of deprogrammers (most untrained in any behavioral science discipline or mental health practice) climbed on the ACM bandwagon for this reason. Just as degreed "high education" drove out "low education" among many ACM spokespersons, the profit potential of the NRM/ACM controversy occured to many who came to assist or even replace the original volunteer activists. Deprogramming and/or anticultism essentially became a growth industry for a number of persons in this movement. To put it bluntly, not only will antic-ultisms normally arise out of the controversies over NRMs, but almost inevitably there will also emerge persons trying to "make a buck" out of the sit-uation. Earlier ACM examples from anti-Mormonism and anti-Catholicism can be found in American history.

Second, American religious pluralism is distinctive because it operates in a relatively unrestricted religious marketplace. Thus, with no official state reli-gion, there are also no specific state protections for NRMs, so offenses against them (i.e., violations of religious liberty for members) take longer to receive attention by state prosecutors. Hence the task of defending any NRM or its members often falls to private attorneys in civil suits where both NRM and ACM advocates argue over such issues as NRM members' "mental stability," NRMs' alleged deceptive fundraising, and so forth. In other words, defending the religious freedoms of unconventional groups is often left to private individ-uals and groups, not government.

Religious pluralism, therefore, sets the context for groups like CAN to emerge and operate. But pluralism also contains the seeds of anti-ACM back-lash, which in CAN's case eventually resulted in unremitting lawsuits by angry ex-deprogramming victims and their NRM advocates, on one hand, and bankruptcy, on the other.

Something similar to the current controversy, in cyclical fashion, ought to be expected again in the future.

Chapter 3

A Contemporary Ordered Religious Community[1]
The Sea Organization[2]

J. Gordon Melton

Most major religious traditions have made room for and encouraged the development of organizations and associations which provide a structure in which its most committed members may give their full-time effort to the deepening of their commitment through purely religious activities and offer their life in service to humanity, the larger religious community of which they are a part, and the divine as they conceive it. These associations are usually structured as intentional and ordered communities though their actual organization varies widely from the Eastern Orthodox monastic community on Mount Athos in Greece to the wandering sanyassin ascetics in India. Many ordered communities are celibate, while others admit married members. Some reside in intimate relationships in tightly structured centers, while others are rather loosely dispersed with members engaged in various service enterprises.

Members of such committed structures have been generally known for a range of practices including the assumption of special tasks and disciplines not expected of the rest of their parent community. Entering the special status of the organization usually begins with the taking of an oath of long-term commitment analogous to marriage vows. Many members of religious communities, for example, live a scheduled existence in which obedience to earthly superiors is a high virtue. Within the Roman Catholic tradition to obedience, monastic vows generally also add poverty and chastity. The Eastern Orthodox Church selects its leadership from among its monks, as do Tibetan Buddhists.

Monks and nuns commonly adopt different sexual mores, wear clothing marking their special role in the community, and form an intimate relationship with their fellow sisters and brothers that compete with, if not entirely replace, their previous familial attachments.[3] Sanyassins, for example, once having assumed their new name and status, often refuse to talk about or consider their prior life and identity.

Even among groups that largely abandoned, even denigrated, the monastic life, some accommodation to disciplined community emerged. Protestantism immediately comes to mind. Protestants rejected the celibate priesthood and during its formative period closed the monasteries and nunneries only to have them reappear several centuries later. Protestant history is replete with accounts of, for example, pietist communal groups such as the Ephrata Community and the Oneida Perfectionists, the Deaconess movement in the Lutheran[4] and Methodist[5] churches, modern experiments such as the Chicago-based Ecumenical Institute,[6] and the hippie communities associated with the Jesus People movement of the 1970s, the largest and most successful being Jesus People, U.S.A.[7] Among Protestants, intentional communities frequently became, for all intents and purposes, a new denomination with a few such as the Hutterites growing into large international organizations.[8]

Western Esotericism, the surviving remnant of the ancient Gnostic tradition that emerged in the seventeenth century as Rosicrucianism, produced a series of ordered communal expressions from the German Rosicrucian group that established itself on Wissahickon Creek in Germantown, Pennsylvania[9] in the 1690s, to the contemporary Holy Order of MANS.[10] Among theosophists, communal life flourished in the early twentieth century[11] and Gnostic bishop George Burke has built a community of monks in present-day Nebraska.[12]

Given the ubiquity of ordered religious communities, it is no surprise that various New Religions have developed their own variations on monastic life. Among the more interesting of these new ordered communities is The Way Corps, the committed community within The Way International;[13] The Esoteric Section of the Theosophical Society;[14] and the subject of this paper, the Sea Organization, founded in 1967.[15] The Sea Org took its name from its origin aboard a fleet of ships, most prominently the Apollo, where L. Ron Hubbard, the person around whose thought the Church of Scientology[16] emerged, and a number of associates had located in order to continue the development of the teachings and practices of the church, most prominently what are today known as the Operating Thetan or OT Levels. In 1971, the Sea Organization assumed responsibility for the ecclesiastical management of the Scientology churches in addition to its other duties. In 1975, the Sea Org largely transferred its activity to church facilities on land, and Sea Org members were present and active during the reorganization of the church following the trauma it experienced in 1979-80 with the arrest and conviction of a cadre of its leaders associated with the Guardian's Office (GO). The GO was a special office established in 1966, its stated purpose being to deal with attacks upon the church so that the main body could continue with its spiritual work apart from the distraction of public controversies.

BEGINNINGS

To understand the Sea Org, it is necessary to understand the particular belief system of the Church of Scientology and its development through its first decade.[17] Scientology is an esoteric Gnostic system based upon the belief that the true self, called the Thetan, is trapped in MEST (matter, energy, space, and time), the visible world. Freedom from that entrapped state to total freedom is accomplished in a series of steps that involve both awareness of one's state and taking action to detach oneself from the encumbrances that hold the Thetan to the material world. In Scientological terms, one crosses "The Bridge" to "total freedom" one step at a time.[18] The process of moving up The Bridge is analogous to the degrees or levels of accomplishment familiar to anyone who has studied Esotericism.[19]

Important to Scientology is a belief that the Thetan has, over the millennia, been embodied on many occasions, a belief commonly called reincarnation, though Scientologists generally avoid the term.[20] They also eschew any idea of transmigration, i.e., the belief that the Thetan would incarnate into any animal form less than human. In the first stage of Scientology, one concentrates on removing from the Thetan some encumbrances acquired both in this life and in past existences. These encumbrances called "engrams" are described as aberrations attached to the self that produce dysfunctional behavior patterns. The completion of this initial work is symbolized by the acceptance of the status known as "Clear." Once one has reached that plateau, one is now ready to begin exercising one's free life operating as a Thetan. The upper levels of Scientology offer the secret wisdom, the *gnosis*, necessary to continue removing the additional encumbrances from one's past lives and experiencing total freedom.

Scientology's essential contribution to Esotericism has been the wedding of technological precision to the process of spiritual progress. This technology is expressed most prominently in the use of an instrument called the E-meter as an assist in spiritual counseling, coupled with the demand that the processes and format of counseling, called auditing in Scientology, be followed with a high level of exactness. Technological preciseness is equivalent in Scientology to adherence to orthodox belief in conservative Christianity. Thus deviation from that precision, i.e., alteration of standard tech, is considered a serious matter within the church.

By 1966, Hubbard had largely set in place the process of reaching the state of Clear, but was aware that there was more. Through that year, he explored the first of what would become the advanced realizations of the church and released the material associated with OT I and II in August and September respectively. Then, in September 1966, he resigned his role as administrative leader of the church, and turned over its management to a number of trusted associates. This resignation did not mean abandonment of the movement and organization he had founded, but it did mean that he redirected his activity to the further development of the OT levels and the associated activities. He moved aboard a series of the ocean-going vessels, illustrative of his own love of the seafarer's life, which served as his laboratory for experiments and consideration of the implications of what he observed and the experiences reported to him by those who first shared the life of an Operating Thetan. A common element in these experiences was what was termed exteriorization, more commonly designated the out-of-body experience. According to Scientologists, the Operating Thetan begins to have short periods in which it experiences itself outside the physical body with a goal of lengthening the stay.[21]

Aboard the *Apollo*, the flagship of the Scientology ships, Hubbard attracted a cadre of older, more committed Scientologists, most of whom had no experience aboard such a ship, and who had to learn from scratch the various tasks from navigation to engine repair to cooking meals for the crew. Several structures were established to concentrate on the vocational training of the crew including the Pursers Project Force and the Stewards Project Force. The idea of on-the-job training became integral to the development of the Sea Org, which recruited only a minority of people with prior training in the various areas in which they would be called to operate. Life aboard the *Apollo,* and its sister vessels, the *Diana* and the *Athena*, became the crucible in which the Sea Org was initially tested.

The Sea Org was actually established in 1967 by a small group of Scientologists, all of whom had reached the state of Clear, and some of whom had completed the previously released OT I and II levels. (OT III was released in September 1967; OT IV, V, and VI were released in January 1968.) The Sea Org membership would soon encompass all who worked on the three ships, though these were by no means all Clears.

The impact of what was occurring quietly aboard the Apollo began to be felt within the larger community of Scientologists in 1968 when the first Sea Org members left the ships to establish the initial Advanced Organizations at which the material relative to the OT Levels were released to then relatively small number of designated Clears. At the time there were approximately five hundred such individuals, though the number was rapidly expanding. The Sea Org itself expanded through the first half of the 1970s and in 1975 experienced its first dramatic change when life aboard the ships was abandoned and what was termed the Flag Land Base was established in Clearwater, Florida, which would become the spiritual center of the faith.

Meanwhile, the leadership of the movement (the organization of the church above the local church centers) had been placed in the hands of the Executive Council Worldwide. However, in 1971, it was thus determined that the Council was not doing its job adequately. It was disbanded, and its duties (primarily the management of the church's continental and national offices and its publishing facilities around the world) were assumed by the Sea Org.

Through the end of the 1970s, the Sea Org was in charge of the administration of the church internationally and three additional Scientology structures. First, the Saint Hill Organizations (named for the center in East Grinstead where Hubbard lectured while in England) specialize in the advanced training of auditors. Thus the Saint Hill Organizations are the Scientology equivalent of seminaries and graduate schools. Saint Hill graduates are deemed the most efficient and qualified auditors within the church. While the basics of auditing training may be acquired in any local Scientology church, those who wish to pursue a career as an auditor or audit people during their more advanced sessions at the OT levels would seek Saint Hill training.

Second, the initial Advanced Organizations (AO) were established in 1968 to deliver the OT Levels. The first AOs were opened in Los Angeles and Edinburgh (the latter soon moved to London and then East Grinstead). Today, there are two additional Advanced Organizations in Copenhagen, Denmark, and suburban Sidney, Australia.

Third, the Flag Service Organization offered all of the curriculum of the AOs, but also became the first center to offer OT Levels above OT III. Following the release of the OT IV-VI Levels, OT VII was initially made available in 1970. Prior to the establishment of the Flag Land Base, these higher levels could be accessed only aboard the ships and at the two Advanced Organizations.[22]

In the process of pursuing the OT Levels, church members are given access to a set of confidential materials that include the instructions for the spiritual exercises to be followed to gain the particular benefits of that level as well as the most complete statement of the religious myth underlying all of Scientology (a myth that is required for making an overall evaluation of Scientology's place on the large religious landscape).[23] This presents an obstacle for any outsider who wishes to understand the Scientology worldview.[24] Fortunately, with the continued publication (in both audio and literary formats) of Hubbard's many lectures, all of the elements of the myth have been made available and can be accessed by anyone without reference to the confidential documents, though some diligence is required as the references are scattered in a variety of sources.[25]

THE TRAUMA OF 1979

In 1979, the church began to experience a trauma of immense proportions, analogous on a smaller scale to the Counter Reformation that hit the Roman Catholic Church in the sixteenth century. After decades of complaints that the church had become corrupt at the highest levels, and following a major schism by those seeking its reform, the Roman Catholic Church finally called a church council and instituted widespread reforms that dominated the institution into the twentieth century.[26]

The Guardian's Office (GO), once formed, was headquartered at Saint Hill Manor in England. It also began to reproduce itself and soon most local churches had one or more of its representatives on its staff. The GO operated somewhat autonomously and in addition formed an Intelligence Bureau, which operated in secret from all but the GO's higher officials. The Guardian's Office also competed with the Sea Org for hegemony within Scientology. Once the problems in the Office became known, the internal process of investigating and dealing with them took several years.[27]

As the criminal trial of the church officers in the United States proceeded, the church launched its own internal review of the GO management. Based upon its assessment, a complete reorganization of the church at the national, continental, and international level was begun in April 1981 with the first preliminary investigations of the facts. In July, Mary Sue Hubbard, the wife of L. Ron Hubbard, was asked to resign. Action in line with internal church policy was begun against eleven senior Guardian's Office officials, all of whom resigned their church posts in October. Through 1982, the investigation expanded resulting in a number of those involved in what was considered improper conduct being released from their position in the church and a few being expelled entirely from the church. Still others chose to leave the church at this time. It was eventually decided that the Guardian's Office was unsalvageable as a church agency and in 1983 it was totally disbanded and its functions assigned to a variety of new agencies.[28] Also in 1983, the international headquarters of the church was relocated to Los Angeles, where it remains.

Meanwhile, as the investigation of the Guardian's Office proceeded, three important new structures were also created. The Church of Scientology International was established as the new "mother" church (using a model not unlike the Mother Church in Christian Science) to have direct oversight of the movement's otherwise autonomous local churches. A significant part of the Guardian's Office's previous functions was assigned to the Office of Special Affairs, a division within the Church of Scientology International. A second organization, Scientology Missions International, was formed to oversee the local Scientology missions (proto-churches not yet large enough to provide all the services that a "church" provides). Both of these structures were then placed into the hands of the members of Scientology's ordered community, the Sea Organization.

The most important new organization was the Religious Technology Organization, a rather unique ecclesiastical structure. RTC was established to ensure that the "technology" of Scientology is properly administered (i.e., orthodoxy and orthopraxis is followed) and remains in its intended hands (i.e., remains in the control of Hubbard's appointed successors). Hubbard assigned all of his Scientology-related trademarks to RTC and it is through its control of and ability to license said trademarks that it exercises its authority.

The actual operation of each of these new organizations (and a few other additional organizations such as the International Hubbard Ecclesiastical

League of Pastors) is an interesting subject in itself, but far beyond the scope of this essay. The important point is that all of these new organizations were placed in the hands of the Sea Org. Their creation amounted to the complete reorganization of Scientology and the assumption by Sea Org members of the leadership role at the national, continental, and international levels. Scientology's organization is thus quite analogous to the placement of the Roman Catholic Church, and especially the Eastern Orthodox Church, in the care of the clergy and the members of its ordered communities. For Scientology, the changes of 1980-81 were as significant and as far-reaching as were the reforms instituted by Pope Gregory VII were for Roman Catholicism.[29]

The reorganization of the church was not well received by all Scientologists, especially those most affected by the disbanding of the Guardian's Office. Several of those who left the church in the early 1980s went on to write of the change in authority structures in a somewhat hostile fashion, and a few who broke with Scientology at this time went on to become some of the church's most hostile and committed critics. They carried with them the knowledge of the actions of the office and have used that knowledge freely to attack the church during the last two decades. Their revelation of events was supported by the opening of the Guardian Office's files by the Federal Court.[30]

Today, two decades after the reorganization of Scientology internationally, the administration of the movement above the level of the local church remains the business of the Sea Organization. Sea Org members hold all policy and administrative posts in each of the corporations mentioned above as well as the Celebrity Centre in Los Angeles, a church established to respond to the special situation of those in the artistic and entertainment industries.[31] The new organization is the Flag Ship Service Organization based on the *Freewinds*, an oceangoing vessel that operates in the Caribbean, where members go to participate in OT VIII and other advanced course material.

THE SEA ORG TODAY

During the more than thirty years of its existence, the Sea Org has grown (as of the summer of 2000) into a dedicated community of some 5,800 members, a relatively small number of church members given the scope of Scientology's activities internationally.[32] It is the dedicated core of members who have chosen to devote their lives to the spread of Scientology. The largest number of members reside at the church complexes in Los Angeles, Clearwater, Copenhagen, London and Saint Hill (in the UK), and Sydney. Smaller Sea Org centers can be found in Johannesburg, Toronto, Budapest, Madrid, Milan, and Moscow, and individual Sea Org members can at any moment be found elsewhere as their services are needed.

The process of joining the Sea Org has become somewhat institutionalized. In most instances, it begins with a public meeting in a Scientology church facility in which a Sea Org representative presents a profile of the work of the organization and invites interested attendees to consider joining. Those who attend such meeting are usually already familiar with the Sea Org from leaflets that are freely distributed in most church facilities, as well as articles in different church periodicals.

At the close of the meeting, those who express an interest in the Sea Org are invited to consider making an initial commitment in the form of signing what has come to be known as the billion-year "commitment."[33] This brief document is actually a letter of intent of offering oneself for service in the Sea Org and to submit to its rules. To be a part of the Sea Org is not just to join the fraternity, but an agreement to enter into full-time employment by the church and to go where one is needed. However, it closes with the statement, "I commit myself to the Sea Organization for the next billion years." This symbolic commitment of the individual beyond their present earthly existence is appropriate to a community that believes in reincarnation. It is also somewhat reminiscent of Mormon sealing ceremonies during which a person is sealed to a spouse beyond this earthly life for "all eternity."

After the signing of the commitment document, which is largely of symbolic import, the individual is given a period of time to consider their decision, but more importantly, to clear up any impediments to their joining the Sea Org. For example, many new Sea Org recruits are already serving in the church at one of its local centers. In those cases, they must complete any unfinished tasks with their current position before continuing with the process of joining. Others leave the meeting with a belief that their destiny belongs to the Sea Org, they may have even signed the "billion year commitment," but they are not yet ready to actually join. I have talked to members who waited as long as three or, in one instance, even six years before taking the next step which is to report to the Sea Org's induction program, called the Estates Project Force (EPF).[34] Beginning the EPF usually means a change of residence to one of the large Sea Org centers at Los Angeles, Clearwater, East Grinstead, or Copenhagen.

The completion of the EPF program takes from two weeks to several months, (as it includes a self-study program that is completed at different rates by different people). Included in the program is a rigorous daily routine of work and study that introduces people on an experiential level to the nature of the commitment being asked of them. It also introduces them on a cognitive level to the various options for service, the goals of the Sea Org's activity, and the rules by which they must abide. As the church will invest much in the Sea Org member's training, and in common with most ordered communities, it wishes to filter out those with a lesser or superficial commitment. The EPF attempts to ensure that each recruit is making an informed and heartfelt assent to the overall vision of what they are entering. Integral to explaining the Sea Org is a set of lectures given by Hubbard in 1969 to the fledgling group of original members struggling with their new life on a ship. Though most Sea Org members are not working on a ship, the principles articulated are deemed to have universal value.

Following the completion of the EPF program, the recruit makes a final decision to continue, church personnel make a final assessment of the recruit's worth to the organization, and the person is accepted into the Sea Org. If the person has not already done so, he or she now participates in a formal swearing-in ceremony that includes the reading of the "Code of a Sea Org Member," sentence-by-sentence, and his or her verbal ascent to each clause. The code reads as follows:

1. I promise to help get ethics in on this planet and the universe, which is the basic purpose of the Sea Org.

2. I promise to uphold, forward and carry out, Command Intention.[35]

3. I promise to use Dianetics and Scientology for the greatest good for the greatest number of dynamics.

4. I promise to do my part to achieve the Sea Org's humanitarian objective which is to make a safe environment where the Fourth Dynamic Engram[36] can be edited out.

5. I promise to uphold the fact that duty is the Sea Org's true motivation, which is the highest motivation there is.

6. I promise to keep my own personal ethics in and uphold beyond all contemporary honor, integrity and true discipline that is the Sea Org's heritage and tradition.

7. I promise to effectively lead, care for and train those under my charge and to ensure they keep their own ethics in and if that fails to take action with fair and legal justice.

8. I promise to take responsibility for the preservation and the continued full and exact use of the technologies of Dianetics and Scientology.

9. I promise to exemplify in my conduct the belief that to command is to serve and that a being is only as valuable as he can serve others.

10. I promise to improve my worth to the Sea Org and mankind by regularly advancing my knowledge of and ability to apply the truths and technologies of Dianetics and Scientology.

11. I promise to accept and fulfill to the utmost of my ability the responsibilities entrusted to me whatever they may be and wherever they may carry me in the line of duty.

12 I promise to be competent and effective at all times and never try to explain away or justify ineffectiveness nor minimize the true power that I am.

13. I promise at all times, to set a desirable example in appearance, conduct and production to fellow Sea Org members and the area in which I operate.

14. I promise to demand that my fellow Sea Org members not fall short of the purpose, ideals and spirit of the Sea Org.

15. I promise to do my part to protect and further the image of the Sea Org.

16. I promise to come to the defense of the Sea Org and fellow Sea Org members whenever needed.

17. I promise through my actions to increase the power of the Sea Org and decrease the power of any enemy.

18. I promise to make things go right and to persist until they do.

Each Sea Org member reaffirms that acceptance in a formal ceremony annually on 12 August, the anniversary of the founding of the Organization.

Once accepted as a member, the individual is assigned to a position in the church and living quarters. Single members live in a dormitory-like facility and married couples in modest apartments. Most meals are taken communally in a Sea Org managed dining facility. Following a period of training, members work a full day (five days a week) and then have several hours each day for their own spiritual development in personal study, auditing, or course work. Sea Org recruits come from all levels of progress in the overall Scientology program.

Generally, one day a week (Saturday), members will leave their regular job (which may be anything from translating texts, writing legal briefs, or assembling E-meters) and join with the local grounds crew on the upkeep of the buildings or grounds. The Sea Org has shown a pattern of buying rundown property and refurbishing it, and the work of renovation usually involves some form of physical labor from laying brick, installing plumbing or electrical outlets, to planting shrubbery or painting walls.[37] On the other hand, at various points when the church is preparing for a major event or making a big push to accomplish a particular goal, Sea Org members may work extra long hours (overnight shifts being occasionally reported) for a short period.

It is interesting to compare the daily life of the Sea Org member with that of a Roman Catholic monk or nun. In many respects they are quite similar, in that both include a preprogrammed routine that includes work and time for spiritual development. They differ somewhat in that in many of the older Roman Catholic or semi-cloistered orders the life is much more ascetic. For example, the day of a member of the Cloistered Nuns of Perpetual Adoration begins at 5:30 each day. It is punctuated with times of prayer at 11:30 a.m. and at 2, 4, and 7:45 p.m. The sisters retire at 8:45 but rise for the Midnight Office at 12:00 a.m. and then return to their room until a new day begins at 5:30. The Carmelite Nuns of Our Lady of Divine Provence rise at 5:40 each day. Their day is marked by Morning Prayer at 6 and mass at 7:30. Their schedule then follows with prayer times at 11:40, 2, 4, 7:30, and 9:30. They retire at 11 p.m. each evening.[38] Monks/nuns integrate a variety of activities as penances as part of their spiritual growth and effort to deal with human sinfulness. These penances are frequently of a kind that an outsider might consider to be of a humiliating or degrading nature. As one writer on her observation of cloistered nuns noted, "Mortification was considered an essential part of most cloistered life, and common penances included frequent fasting, kneeling during meals, and praying for extended periods of time with arms outstretched.[39]

On Sunday, most Sea Org members attend a weekly worship service, and then perform their normal tasks for a halfday (they may take every other Sunday off). They have the rest of the day to attend to personal needs such as shopping, cleaning their personal space, and washing clothes. Members receive a modest allowance that covers their personal needs. The church also arranges for medical care. Most Sea Org members dress in uniforms mildly reminiscent of the group's origin aboard the ships in 1967, though what is considered uniform clothing has become increasingly tailored to the local environment and/or duties of the office.

Married couples in the Sea Org attempt to have a normal married life within the context of their mutual commitment to Scientology. Some choose to have children; many do not. Beginning in 1986, couples that chose to have children were granted a leave of absence from the Sea Org[40] and usually assumed a staff position at a local church until such time as the child was six years old.[41] After they return to staff, the children are raised and schooled communally, and visit with parents on the weekend until they are of age. It is currently the case that a number of children of Sea Org members have reached adulthood and have joined of their own accord. It is among the basic rules that members may not marry anyone who is not a Sea Org member nor may they engage in extramarital sexual relationships.

The Sea Org is described as having no formal organization itself. In fact there is no person designated as head of the Sea Org, nor is there a Sea Org hierarchy as such.[42] However, concurrent with Sea Org membership, one also develops a service relationship with one of the church's organizations that requires most of its staff to be drawn from the Sea Org membership. Thus, each Sea Org member is assigned to a post with a particular structure be it CSI, one of the Advanced Organizations, a Saint Hill facility, a continental organization, one of the church's publishing or recording subsidiaries, or one of any of the additional church facilities.

From that point they develop a relationship to the church through the facility that officially engages them for the church. Each facility is run according to the general organizational structure delineated by Hubbard and each Sea Org member can locate him/herself on the prominently posted organizational chart. On a practical level, the local church corporation, rather than the entire Sea Org as such, has primary responsibility for the individual member.

After a period of time at any given post, a person may be asked to assume a new position in the church or may decide that they would rather engage in some other activity or at some different task. In the latter case, they may apply for any openings about which they have become aware, but upon acceptance must finish any incomplete tasks and find a replacement for their post before moving to the new position. In every church facility, an organizing board is posted showing every job position, and the person assigned to it. The organizing board will also show any positions that are currently unfilled.

THE ROLE OF ETHICS

As the first clause of the "Code of the Sea Org Member" implies, ethics is of primary concern to the life of the fraternity, both the upholding of ethics by the individual member and the spread of ethics, as understood within Scientology, through society as a whole. That being the case, the integrating of the ethical system laid out in Hubbard's volume, *Introduction to Scientology Ethics*, is basic to becoming a Sea Org member.[43]

On an abstract level, Hubbard built his ethical system (as the whole system of Scientology) on the principle of survival. The urge to survive is, Hubbard believed, the dynamic principle of existence, and he observed, "The goal of life in this universe may be easily and generally defined as an effort to survive as long as possible and attain the most desirable state possible in that survival."[44] Hubbard also saw the universe in terms of what he described as eight urges or drives in life, the eight dynamics. That is, humans express the urge to survive in eight arenas:

Self
Creativity (including family and children)
Groups (from a circle of friends to the nation)
Species (humankind)
Life forms
Physical Universe of MEST (matter, energy, space, time)
Spiritual
Infinity[45]

Ethics refers to those actions that an individual undertakes in order to accomplish optimum survival for him/herself and others. Harking back to John Stuart Mill, he proposed that the highest ethical decisions were those that "brought the greatest benefits to the greatest number of dynamics."[46] Based upon their contribution to survival in the different arenas, one can judge actions as good or bad. Moral codes express the experience of the race as to what has proven at any given moment to be the actions that produce survival as opposed to those that counter it. Ethical conduct includes the adherence to the codes of the society in which one lives.

The person pursuing a course that is counter survival is operating "out-ethics."[47] A person who begins to operate out ethics first becomes self-destructive, but eventually the actions will become visible on several dynamics. When the actions of an individual negatively affect the group, it will react. Justice is the name we give to the system any society develops to protect itself from the anti-survival actions of the individual.

Hubbard suggested that when an individual performs a counter-survival act, he or she attempts to correct it. However, these efforts usually fail due to a lack of knowledge about what is occurring and ignorance of the means of becoming an ethical person (i.e., unfamiliarity with the Scientology tech on ethics). At the moment, the ethics technology operates only within the Church of Scientology, and the most complete attempt to apply it has occurred in the Sea Org.

The effort to establish Hubbard's ethical system is done, of course, within the context of the overall development of the spiritual life advocated by the church. Each individual Scientologist is seen as being on a spiritual journey. Ideally, that journey involves intensive self-examination, the confrontation with and removal of all of the negative influences that are seen as having attached themselves to the Self, and the learning of a new means of operating without such influences. The new Scientologist encounters what Hubbard called "engrams" and learns that dealing with engrams at various levels of reality is considered an essential element in traveling up the Bridge to the highest levels of Scientology.

When one becomes concerned with the ethical question, a second emphasis is added, the concern with present moment acts of commission or omission that transgress the moral code of the group, in this case the Sea Org. Such acts are called *overts*. An overt is an act (or failure to act) that leads to the injury, degradation, or reduction of the self or others. Overts often lead the person committing them to cover them up. The act of not revealing or talking about an overt is called a *withhold*. The withhold is seen as an act of dishonesty to the self and one's colleagues. Within the Sea Org, a primary ethical concern is with handling overts and any resulting withholds. It is the duty of a Sea Org member to report their own overts and withholds or any committed by others of which they become aware to their unit's ethics officer. Typical overts might involve negligence at one's assigned task, theft of church funds, or illicit sexual activity.

Overts, seen as having an origin in one's past, are usually dealt with in counseling (auditing) sessions. However, if they become serious, they are seen as harming the group, and the individual has to deal with the unique justice system that operates within the Sea Org. That system is based upon other beliefs of Hubbard, possibly the most important one being that handling misdeeds by punishment is ineffective. It simply leads to a worsening of the sequence of overts while at the same time degrading the individual. Thus the Scientology justice system replaces the imposition of punishment with action that seeks to remove the cause of the overts and hence prevent them in the future. That action involves the individual's willingness to confront and accept responsibility for their life, and through the technology remove the underlying cause of the overts.[48]

When the ethics officer within the church becomes aware of serious overts committed by a person of the particular organization over which they have jurisdiction, they initiate a process of fact-finding to determine the truth of any accusations. This process may, depending on the severity of the actions under discussion, involve a Board of Investigation and a Committee of Evidence. In the more serious cases, the Committee of Evidence will weigh any mitigating circumstances in the situation and make recommendations by which the person may make restitution for any harm done and take action to prevent the repetition of such acts in the future. There is also a system of appeals by which a person who feels that the initial finding against them has been wrong, can seek redress.

In the most extreme cases, when a Sea Org member has lost faith in Scientology, has actively taken actions to harm the church, and has no desire to realign with the church, the committee may recommend expulsion from the Sea Org or even the church.[49] In several instances, individuals expelled from the Church have gone on to engage in long-term public opposition to Scientology. In other cases, also deemed severe, but in which the individual has not intended direct harm and wishes to remain a member of the Sea Org, Hubbard created a program by which the person may deal with their overts and withholds in a comprehensive manner, make restitution to the group, and return to their post in good standing. The program is called the Rehabilitation Project Force (RPF). Though founded in the 1970s, this aspect of the Sea Org was virtually unknown until the 1980s when it began to be discussed in anti-Scientology writings and was introduced into several court cases. It subsequently became one of the more controversial aspects of the Church of Scientology.

THE RPF[50]

As most religions have created ordered intentional communities, so those intentional communities have created systems whereby those who break the rules may make recompense and be integrated back into the life of the community. The most famous system operating in the West is possibly that created by St. Benedict for the Benedictine order. The section on rule breaking begins:

> If a brother is found to be obstinate, or disobedient, or proud, or murmuring, or habitually transgressing the Holy Rule in any point and contemptuous of the order of his seniors, the latter shall admonish him secretly a first and second time, as Our Lord commands. If he fails to amend, let him be given a public rebuke in front of the whole community. But if even then he does not reform, let him be placed under excommunication, provided that he understands the seriousness of that penalty; if he is perverse, however, let him undergo corporal punishment.[51]

Among the Trappists, anyone seen breaking the rules would be reported to the "Chapter of faults, which would in turn announce these actions at the next meal after which the superior of the order would pronounce a suitable punishment. For example, . . . a monk might be ordered to lie in the doorway of the refractory while the other monks stepped over him on their way to a meal."[52]

Within the Roman Catholic Church, there is a set of general laws that all orders follow. Each order then adopts additional rules peculiar to its special purpose and mission. Canon law operating within the Roman Catholic Church notes that a monk or nun under perpetual vows may be dismissed from their order for what are termed "grave external reasons." It is the duty of the person's immediate superiors to admonish them in hopes of correcting the situation, and may in that endeavor impose various punishments. If the person proves incorrigible, he or she is informed that he or she risks being terminated as a member and is asked for a defense of the questioned behavior. If the situation remains serious, it is presented to the proper authority, the local bishop or superior of the order, who passes it to the Congregation of Religious in Rome. It is ultimately the decision of the pope formally to order the dismissal.[53]

In the Eastern world, one soon runs into the *Patimokkha* section of the *Vinaya-pitaka* that lay out the rules for Buddhist monks.[54] Among the important admonitions for the monk or nun are to refrain from sexual activity, avoid secular work, and not attempt to create a schism in the sangha (monastic community). There is also a prescribed code of etiquette, which anyone who has been present at a Buddhist gathering that included monks and nuns has witnessed. The Vinaya also prescribed rules for disciplining rule breakers. There are a set of rules that if transgressed leads to the immediate expulsion of the member from the group. Lesser rules may be handled through the imposition of punishments after a confession or other determination of guilt.[55] In The Korean Chogye tradition (the majority tradition in Korean Buddhism), there are four deeds that will lead to immediate dismissal from the monastic community, sexual relations with a woman, stealing, killing, and telling lies, especially making a false claim about one's state of enlightenment. The Sea Org's system differs from that of both the Roman Catholic and Buddhist systems in that it offers a means for those judged guilty of expulsion offenses to redeem themselves and be reintegrated into the community.[56]

The RPF, the Sea Org's program for those who have committed serious violations of ethical policy, was created in January 1974 while the center of the Sea Org was still aboard the ships. The program grew out of the recognition that some people either could not or did not wish to adapt to life aboard the ships. Originally such persons were put off the ship, the equivalent of being dismissed from the Sea Org. Then in 1968, Hubbard created what was termed the "Mud Box Brigade." Those on board the ship who were found slacking off their duties or misbehaving (which in some cases on board the ship could place the lives of the crew and passengers in danger) were assigned to clean the "mud boxes," the place where mud collected from the anchors, and the bilge, the rather foul water that collects in the bottom of any ocean-going vessel. While the average person looking at such a structure might see it as punishment, Hubbard understood it in terms of making retribution to the people who had been harmed by the nonperformance or incorrect performance of one's assigned tasks. This rather stop-gap measure, however, was replaced in 1974 with RPF, a more systematic structure for handling misbehavior that was more fully integrated into Hubbard's understanding of ethics. The RPF also served additional purposes beyond those served by the Mud Box Brigade.

The new Rehabilitation Project Force program was designed with multi-goals, though the basic one was providing a situation in which individuals who had been negligent in their posts could be isolated from the group (thus preventing further immediate harm). They were also assigned a period each day to work on themselves using Scientology tech, considered a necessary step to their being reintegrated into the larger group. As Hubbard described it in an early Flag Order, "The RPF is in actual fact a system of recruiting by taking people off the lines who are blocking things and then not letting them back on lines until they are a valuable operating staff member."[57] The RPF was also designed as a work force in which the members spent five hours a day working upon their own inner condition using the resources available in Scientology technology, and the rest of the day engaged in physical labor of the kind that involved coordinated work with others as a team. While learning to work with others, one could make restitution for the harm done through contributions to the physical facilities in which the Sea Org and the church are housed. As each project is completed, RPF members feel rewarded, usually with a sense of accomplishment.

Assignment to the RPF can begin in one of several ways. Often it starts with a realization by an individual that his/her behavior is out of line with expectations. With a number of people I interviewed, their realization came during or shortly after their ending an illicit extramarital affair. In some cases, the affair began to affect their work, but in others the fact that their performance at work was judged superior allowed them to keep the affair unknown to their colleagues. In most cases, however, problems with performance at their assigned work over a period of time was noticed and reported. Following an investigation, the individual was offered the option of pursuing the RPF program or leaving the Sea Org. In one case, the person I interviewed had misappropriated a considerable amount of church money for personal use.

Once a person is informed of the basics of the RPF option, understands what is involved, and chooses it, he or she signs a document noting his/her agreement to join the program. The new RPFer then generally moves quickly to one of the RPF centers that are located in the Sea Org complexes in Los Angeles, Clearwater, London, or Copenhagen. The largest number is in the LA RPF (in 2000, when this study was done, more than half of the approximately 350 currently participating in the program were in LA. Slightly less were in the Clearwater RPF, and by comparison, the RPF at Copenhagen had less than 20). Choice of location is determined by several factors including space available and the presence of another person at approximately the same level on The Bridge with whom the RPFer can work in their mutual counseling. A person, for example, who is working on his/her OT levels would not be counseled by a pre-Clear.

When the person arrives, he or she is assigned to space in a dorm-like room with others and given some orientation. That orientation includes the reading of the thirty Flag Orders pertaining to RPF. Once fully aware of the conditions under which he or she will be operating,[58] he or she chooses to proceed, and then begin a refresher course in ethics.[59] In addition, some technical training is included, especially if the new person is unfamiliar with the basics of auditing.[60] The person is also assigned to a team with whom he or she will be working. In Copenhagen, the number of options is extremely limited, while in Los Angeles and Clearwater, a variety of work assignments are available.[61]

Finally, the individual is assigned to a partner with whom she/he will work during the stay in the RPF. This partner is extremely important as one's progress in the program is tied to the partner's progress. During what will be a year or more together, the pair audit each other and are responsible for each other's success. They will finish the program together, and one criteria for graduation is the demonstration that the RPFer can help another, specifically their partner. The importance of the partner is underscored in those occasional cases in which a person drops out of the program. The person who remains will be assigned another new partner whose success now becomes his/her responsibility.

The RPF is located within the Sea Org facilities, but members dine and sleep in separate quarters. In Los Angeles, for example, the RPF space—dorm, dining hall and kitchen, and woodwork shop—are in the main AO building. In Copenhagen, they are in the basement (study space) and top floor (dorm rooms) of one of the Sea Org buildings currently undergoing renovation. In Clearwater, they are located in two separate buildings in the Sea Org residence complex. These buildings housing the RPF are on the edge of the complex and immediately outside the front door of the two buildings is a gate that opens from the inside. Any person could simply walk out of the buildings and out of the gate into the city of Clearwater.[62] Contrary to images of a concentration camp-like atmosphere, there are no locks on the doors of the RPF facilities, and at almost anytime, participants in the program could, if they decided, simply walk away.[63] In the case of the Los Angeles, Clearwater, or Copenhagen facilities, such a person could lose themselves in the city in a matter of minutes.[64]

The RPF program is rigorous by any standards. It includes eight hours of physical work six days a week that begins each day immediately after the morning muster and breakfast. Most people on the RPF come with little or no skill in the tasks required to renovate and maintain buildings (painting, plumbing, carpentry, furniture making, grounds upkeep, etc.). Thus they will be taught a trade along with being involved in numerous tasks that require little training. In Los Angeles, a number of people have been taught woodworking and the professional appearance of the walls and furniture in the church's Hollywood facilities is ample evidence of the skills that they have acquired. In fact, the overall appearance of the various Scientology buildings along Hollywood Blvd. and L. Ron Hubbard Way (off Sunset Ave.) can be credited to the RPF.

This aspect of the RPF is designed to provide a change in the usual pattern of the participant's life (which has most likely been a desk job) and involve them more immediately with what in Scientology is termed the MEST uni-verse. It is reminiscent of the work ("chop wood, carry water") that is often inte-grated into Zen Buddhist retreats.[65] There, work remains an integral part of the daily life of Zen monks and nuns, and visitors to a Zen monastery for retreats or short stays will be scheduled to participate in the workday that might include cooking, chopping wood, heating water, working in the fields, and cleaning.[66] Participants learn one or more skills, and RPF graduates with whom I have talked enjoyed pointing out particular things in buildings on which they had worked. By working intimately with a small cadre of fellow participants, they learned the value of teamwork.

Participants spend five hours each day with their individual partner engaged in study or auditing. Many with whom I talked had been in the Sea Org many years, but, although they had received auditing, they had never learned to audit anyone else. They reported that as a result of learning to counsel their partner, they had gained a heightened level of sensitivity to the needs of others in gen-eral and how their lives affected everyone around them.

The dominant program used by the RPF currently (others are mentioned in the Flag Orders) is called the False Purpose Rundown.[67] It is Scientology's understanding that overts and withholds are indicative of hidden evil (i.e., counter survival) purposes, solutions to problems adopted in a moment of con-fusion. The auditing process includes a lengthy inventory, using the immediate overts that led to the person being assigned to the RPF, of one's life, a con-frontation with and clearing-up of counter-survival purposes. The goal is to see life objectively and assume responsibility for one's present condition as the result of one's own decisions. The False Purpose Rundown is repeated until the person is considered free of evil intentions on each of the eight Dynamics. The Rundown is a lengthy process, hence the year or more required to complete it.[68]

The RPF is designed to isolate the individual and provide a time and space for total concentration on self-change. The hardest hit by the program are mar-ried couples, as they have little contact while one of them is in the program. They are encouraged to write regularly, but have only infrequent face-to-face contact. Informants in LA noted that they occasionally grabbed a few words with spouses in the brief time between the lunch and afternoon activities. The program does make allowances for family needs and a number of participants noted that they had taken a week or more break in the midst of their program to attend to different particular family obligations.

As might be expected, on occasion, the problems that landed one in the RPF can and do continue to manifest in the life of a participant during their stay in the program. In that case, there is a program, the RPF's RPF, in which people may participate for short periods of time. In this case, the offense is seen as against the RPF itself and thus the person recommended to the RPF's RPF is isolated from other participants in the program. During this time, their partner still has the task of helping the person in the RPF's RPF. The person on the RPF's RPF also performs specific tasks to benefit the RPF (the group that is considered harmed, in this case), and their manual work assignment might include such tasks as improving the RPF facilities. They may return to the RPF program only by vote of the other participants in the RPF. While in the program, their communication is further restricted and must go through the RPF ethics officer.

The RPF organization is difficult to describe, as the participants essentially run it. There is an overseer (the RPF-I/C) who is not a participant whose job is to see that the program runs smoothly. The RPF-I/C, for example, handles the money that pays for the program. Each organization of the church that assigns people to the RPF also pays for his or her stay and each month contributes a stipend to cover their food, housing, and personal needs. It is also the RPF-IC's job to liaison with those in charge of the church's facilities and to decide on the particular deployment of RPF participants by prioritizing tasks to be completed.

However, the day-to-day operation of the program is left in the hands of the participants. One of the participants who is further along in the program is designated the bosun and will have several deputies to handle various practical and technical matters, including ethics. For example, one or more people with accomplished auditing skills oversee and check the auditing as it proceeds.[69]

RPF participants are organized into work teams, and such teams proceed to their assigned tasks (and partners proceed to their auditing) without immediate and constant outside supervision. The atmosphere is much more one of an adult education class in which participants are there to get what they can out of the program than that of disgruntled individuals just putting in the time. Their success will be manifest in the finished product of their labor and in their self-reported realizations about their life acquired in auditing.[70] Testimonies of new insights and understandings concerning their life may be posted for others in the RPF to read, though they have no circulation in the Sea Org or among general church members.

Because of the relative differences in the speed that individuals work through the False Purposes Rundown, different people's stay in the program varies. One year appears to be the minimum. I interviewed one person who had been in for approximately three years.

Following completion of their program, graduates generally return to the post (or a similar post) that they held when they went into the program. Graduates indicated that they received a cordial welcome back to their post. While most of the people with whom I have talked about their previous RPF experience hold anonymous staff positions, several people have gone on to hold high positions and a few are now well known in the church internationally. People whom I have met who lead different church organizations report that staff who have completed the program become their most productive staff members.

CONCLUSION

As an ordered community, the Sea Organization is another doorway offering scholars of New Religions some further understanding of the manner in which innovative religious organizations fit into the broader picture of the religious life of the culture. The more that we know about them, the less distinct they appear relative to larger, more familiar groups. New Religions, with a few unique innovations, tend to rediscover successful modes of operation that have been utilized by the older groups through the centuries and to learn anew some of the same insights as these older groups. In the case of Scientology, they have rediscovered a means of channeling the enthusiasm of their more committed members as well as a means of reintegrating people who had experienced problems in adjusting to the particular pattern of behavior that accompanies their initial commitment. As with marriage, even the most informed person cannot totally predict his/her reactions to the living out of long-term personal commitments.

Understanding New Religions from the perspective of ordered communities also assists us in explaining a spectrum of phenomena, especially the high level of personal commitment shared by the members of some groups. In older ordered communities, both those formed within larger religious groups and those formed as separate religious bodies, we can see processes of formation, means of building and sustaining commitments, ways of problem-solving, and the means of channeling high levels of religious enthusiasm into activity deemed useful in the world. Each of these topics have been issues for discussion in our deliberations on New Religions.

There is a large body of literature on ordered communities both historical and ethnographical as well as sociological and psychological. This study of the Sea Org suggests that such literature would prove a fruitful source of data on New Religions. It is hypothesized that the behavior of people in the first generation of, for example, new Catholic or Eastern Orthodox orders would manifest many of the characteristics of the behavior patterns we have seen in the high-demand New Religions.

Chapter 4

Women in Controversial New Religions
Slaves, Priestesses, or Pioneers?

Susan J. Palmer

New religious experiments in gender roles and relations, both their excesses and their austerities, are well publicized by the media and condemned by the anticult movement. Needless to say, these stories do not contribute to the general public's tolerance of "cults." The fact that women in NRMs participate in new, religiously motivated forms of "free love," celibacy, or polygamy—and that they may renounce marriage and even their children—certainly challenges not only traditional values, but also the more contemporary ethics of feminism and individualism. Thus, new religions, branded as "cults," tend to be portrayed in anticult literature as a backlash against the twentieth century's emancipation of women.

For the researcher who adopts a social-scientific approach to studying these movements, however, a more complex and contradictory situation emerges as he/she moves from group to group. Rather than documenting women's domestic enslavement in patriarchal enclaves or degradation in charismatic leaders' sexual experiments, the researcher begins to piece together strange, hybrid patterns of marriage, family relations, and gender politics that may combine the avant-garde ideals of feminism with traditional and fundamentalist forms of patriarchy. Thus, current standards of "political correctness" are less than useful in trying to make sense of women's participation in the fictive, spiritual "families."

How and why do NRMs tend to experiment with gender and exert control over their members' sexual and familial relationships? There seem to be at least three possible theories advanced by scholars. The first is the "leader's lab" theory. This proposes the notion that founders and prophets of new religions create new social forms to compensate for or heal their own psychic wounds and that they organize their communities so that their followers "act out" the leader's unrealized desires or participate in a utopian venture.[1]

The second is the "social change" theory, which argues that NRMs are sensitive barometers responding to upheavals, tensions, and transitions occurring in the larger society. Thus, communal groups or millenarian movements with radical new gender patterns are like summer camps or workshops where more extreme versions of the experimentation already occurring in the mainstream can occur. According to this approach, the motivations that reshape women's roles and lives do not necessarily emanate from the "charismatic cult leader's" dark psyche. Rather, these alternative patterns of gender might be influenced by counter-cultural experimentation, or the ongoing redefining of gender roles that is an ongoing process in secular society.

The third theory is the well-known "commitment mechanism" model proposed by Rosabeth Moss Kanter,[2] in which she argues that in order for a commune to "succeed" (defined as surviving twenty-five years or more), members must, among other austerities, renounce exclusive personal ties to spouses and progeny in order to strengthen their ties and commitment to the whole group.

Other explanations to account for new religious innovations in gender have been proposed, but these are variations of the three outlined above, the first focusing on the leader's needs, the second on the surrounding society's influence, and the third on the new religious community's imperatives.

A TYPOLOGY OF GENDER IDENTITY

Sister Prudence Allen[3] first proposed a typology of philosophical views of gender within the Christian tradition, and I have adapted it to apply to NRMs. Allen's tripart typology is based on the two variables of equality and difference.

Sex Complementarity groups regard women and men as endowed with distinctly different spiritual qualities. Marriage is strongly recommended as a means of uniting two incomplete halves of the same soul, in order to form one androgynous, balanced, and harmonious being. The individual's gender and marriage relationship are often believed to continue on in the afterworld, and ritual weddings between the living and the dead (or spirits) may be practiced. Marriage and procreation are valued as a path to salvation or a means of assisting the birth of the New Age. An androgynous godhead is often a feature of sex complementarity religions.

Sex Polarity groups, in contrast, view men and women as quite distinct and separate in their spiritual paths and qualities. They often rule that the sexes should live separately, since they cannot help, and may hinder, the other's salvation. Moreover, the sexes are not equal, since one sex is perceived as purer, more intelligent, or closer to God than the other. As one might expect, it is usually men who are held to be the superior sex, but some NRMs such as the Osho International Commune, the Raelian Movement, Dianic Wiccans, and the Brahmakumaris, consider women to be superior to men. Sexual segregation may be based on notions of spiritual danger and pollution. In some NRMs, the sexes are permitted to engage in limited, tightly controlled relationships as a necessary phase in the individual's spiritual development, or to contribute children to the group.

Sex Unity groups regard the body and its gender as a superficial crust of false identity obscuring the immortal, sexless spirit. Thus, groups believing in the essential unity of the sexes might dress unisex and foster androgynous social personae, or they might play out traditional sex roles while maintaining an inner detachment from the role. In neo-shamanic groups or neo-gnostic groups, there is often the notion that letting go of one's attachment to the body and gender is a necessary prelude to realizing one's godhood or infinite power. Sex unity groups see gender as something that can be chosen or changed through elective surgery for Raelians, through reincarnation or conscious rebirth for Scientologists, and through metamorphosis into a higher androgynous immortal extraterrestrials for the "classmates" of the notorious Heaven's Gate.

Over time, the researcher will often find that these types do not maintain their "pure" and distinct forms. A longitudinal study of a group's history often reveals a gradual transition from one type to another or to a hybrid form of two types. A quite common development found in the more mature and successful NRMs in their second generation of membership and leadership is a new, strong emphasis on traditional family values and on stable marriages and secure parent-child bonds. Former *polarity* groups, for example, will encourage families to live together under the same roof, and their literature will place a new emphasis on the (hitherto ignored) quality of the marital relationship.

This has been occurring in the Hare Krishna movement since the mid-1990s, in response to the high attrition rate among the second generation of "gurukula kids" who complained of the neglect and abuse they suffered as the result of being separated at a young age from their parents and placed in the ISKCON boarding schools or *gurukulas*. In a similar vein, since the disbanding of the international commune, the Rajneeshee (or "Friends of Osho") have abandoned their policy of placing women (seen as spiritually more advanced) in charge over men and have been offering workshops on couples rather than emphasizing short-term pluralistic sexual relationships as a viable path to "superconsciousness."[4] In general, as new religions mature in age and seek recognition as authentic religions, they tend to downplay their more startling sexual ethics and conform more closely to mainstream family values.

For this reason, in the early phases of a NRM, one notices that a woman's role tends to be extreme, stylized, and clearly defined. A remarkable simplicity and clarity is achieved by emphasizing only *one* role (or sometimes two) at the expense of other roles. Thus, one finds women defined by the role of "lover" or "sister" or "mother" or "wife," as one moves from group to group, to the exclusion of other roles that are perceived as profane. The disciples of Rael (prophet-founder of the largest UFO religion in the world, currently numbering around 50,000) define themselves as "lovers," but reject monogamy and marriage while tending to devalue, postpone, or even proscribe motherhood. Women in Reverend Moon's church are celibate "sisters" for many years before taking on the roles of wife and mother.[5] The Children of God, now known as The Family, have evolved a more complex role in which the normally incompatible roles of lover and mother are reconciled, and, surprisingly, a high birth rate does not interfere with women's opportunity in executive and leadership roles.[6]

ECOLOGICAL AND APOCALYPTIC FEMINIST SPIRITUALITY

Whether a group espouses sex unity, complementarity, or polarity, a common thread running through their rhetoric is the notion of woman as world savior. New religious movements manifest a deep concern for ecological issues such as overpopulation, pollution, deforestation, species extinction, and the nuclear threat. In forging new spiritual solutions to these contemporary problems, they often stress the notion of the androgyne. The idea is, if men and women could discard their differences, if men could stop exploiting, oppressing, and objectifying women, then the balance between the human world and the natural world could be rectified. Thus, men should cultivate feminine qualities, and women should assume leadership positions.

J. Z. Knight, the most famous and successful channeler in the U.S., is a pretty, diminutive blonde who goes into a trance so that the dynamic, masculine personality of Ramtha, an ancient warrior from Lemuria, takes over her body and vocal chords and conducts "Dialogues," instructing his students in gnostic philosophy and shamanistic powers.[7] The Reverend Chris Korda of the cyber Church of Euthenasia, is a transvestite who preaches a radical message of human extinction through suicide and cannibalism in order to bring back the diminishing species and placate the spirit of Earth, who appeared to him in a dream.

Radical prophets like Mary Daly, the "post feminist" theologian, like Bhagwan Shree Rajneesh, the late Indian-eclectic spiritual master; and Rael, the Messianic founder of the largest UFO religion in the world, predict that only if men develop the "feminine" qualities of love, receptivity, and empathy, can future holocausts be avoided. Rajneesh in his book *A New Vision of Women's Liberation* (1987) presents a utopian vision of a new society based on women's sexual, social, and spiritual liberation.[8] Rael preaches the "sex unity" view of gender—that men and women possess identical abilities—and compares them to "biological robots" that are programmed to give the other pleasure. He argues that not only gender, but human life itself is an artificial construct since extraterrestrial scientists created us in their laboratories from their own DNA when the planet was colonized. Since cloning will soon be possible, biological reproduction is considered outmoded, and for Raelians the purpose of sex is for pleasure, a panacea for man's violent impulses and a way to promote world peace. Rael urges his male followers to be more like women, for the "Age of Apocalypse is the age of women!" Homosexuals are welcomed and prominent in the Raelian community, and Raelians participate in international gay marches every year.[9]

Thus, while the sexual experimentation that is ongoing in new religious movements—whether it veers towards celibacy, free love, or polygamy—certainly raises problematic social and ethical questions, both for the individuals involved and for outside relatives. It also provides a rich source of religious symbols, new and old. These become part of a metaphysical discourse in these groups in which some of the most serious dilemmas of our era are addressed, and various spiritual solutions are proposed.

Chapter 5

Satanism and Witchcraft
Social Construction of a Melded but Mistaken Identity

James T. Richardson

THEORETICAL INTRODUCTION

Satanism and Wicca, the latter known more popularly as witchcraft, have captured the attention of the media and the general public in recent years in the United States and elsewhere. Both are usually defined in a quite negative fashion, although there are important differences in the public definitions of the two sometimes intertwined entities. Why the current interest has developed, and the direction it has developed will be the subject of this chapter, which adopts a decidedly sociological approach in its analysis.

Before proceeding with details about Satanism and Wicca, some preliminary attention needs to be given to the theoretical perspective employed in this essay. First, one of the basic maxims of sociology, comes from W.I. Thomas: "If people define something as real, it is real in its consequences." This sociological truth seems to have special application when discussing Wicca and Satanism, both of which involve small numbers of people doing things that are usually quite harmless to themselves and others. However, the perceptions of these two entities are quite to the contrary, and both are defined as major social problems by many in the U.S. and elsewhere. Often they are quite mistakenly defined as the same social problem. This is to say that many people do not distinguish between Satanism and Wicca, although they are different in very important ways.

A social problem is something that is socially constructed, and, important-ly, the construction may have little to do with objective reality or truth. The social construction is an orientation toward putative conditions, characteristics, or activities that are defined by many people in a society as inherently immoral or unjust. The emphasis here is on the putative nature of claims being made about how things are, and how they should be.[1] Thus, Nazis defined Jews as racially inferior, and Native Americans were defined as "Red Devils" by American settlers, with both definitions leading to huge historical tragedies. Another such example of obvious relevance to this chapter is the "Burning Times," when at least a hundred thousand and perhaps more of so-called witch-es were put to death in Europe based on claims that they were a threat to Christian society.

Social problems require promotion, and often in the development of a social problem, including Satanism and Wicca, one can discern the actions of moral entrepreneurs who are interested in making sure a certain definition of a situa-tion is accepted.[2] Scholars of deviant behavior sometimes refer to such people as claims makers, meaning that they make claims about certain people or groups that, if true, would place those persons or groups beyond the pale of acceptable society.[3] They would be outcasts, and even perhaps defined as threats to normal society that should be dealt with harshly in order to protect society. Moral entrepreneurs are in the business of defining evil, and helping ferret it out, for the good of the moral order of a society.

When claims makers are especially successful, a moral panic may develop in a society.[4] The key element of a moral panic is that the perceived danger is consid-erably out of proportion to the real threat posed by whatever is of concern at the moment. A moral panic occurs when many or all segments of a society become involved in defining something as a social problem of major proportions, when in fact there is little real danger. Thus we see an inordinate amount of attention paid to the putative danger in the mass media by political figures, and in every-day conversation among the general population. The fear engendered by the par-ticular socially constructed problem becomes widespread. Virtually everyone accepts the definition of reality being promoted and is willing to take action (or to allow action to be taken) based on that hegemonic definition.

When moral entrepreneurs attempt to promote a new moral panic in a soci-ety, it is useful to pose a few questions about such efforts. First, who is making the claims? What kinds of people are saying things about the reputed danger, and what do they have in common? Second, what do the claims makers have to gain if their claims are accepted and whose interests are served by the claims being accepted? Third, what exactly is the content of these specific assertions, and what are the potential consequences if they are accepted as true by others? These questions will guide our analysis of the rise of Satanism and its perceived relationship to Wicca and witchcraft.

Something akin to a moral panic has existed in recent years concerning both Satanism and Wicca in the U.S. and some other Western societies. Many media articles have dealt with the dangers of Satanism and witchcraft, and some key opinion leaders in society have spoken about the dangers. The general public has accepted many of the claims being made, as well as efforts by government officials and others to control these dangers. Discerning the objective facts of these developments will be the focus of the rest of this chapter. First, Satanism will be examined, using the social constructionist theory outlined above.

HISTORICAL AND STRUCTURAL FACTORS CONTRIBUTING TO THE "SATANIC SCARE"

Satanism has become a major concern of many in Western societies in recent decades. Explaining why this has occurred poses a challenge for social scientists, but several scholars have made some important efforts.[5] Adopting a sociological and structural approach using the social constructionist perspective is a fruitful way to address the problem. What such an analysis reveals is that the Satanism scare movement is actually easily explained as the confluence of several related movements within a certain time, space, and cultural location.

First, it is an objective fact that some examples of Satanism do exist in contemporary society. Some small "Satanic churches" exist, especially within the U.S. Anton LaVey established the Church of Satan in San Francisco decades ago, and it received an inordinate amount of media attention from its very inception. Spin-off groups from LaVey's initial effort have also gained media attention. At least one of the "new religions," The Process, studied in detail by William Bainbridge, involved the figure of Satan, albeit a vastly redefined one from that of the LaVey tradition.[6] Media coverage of these Satan-related groups, particularly LaVey's, augmented by the involvement of some well known people such as movie stars in his group, made most people in the U.S. aware that Satanic churches existed. The inordinate amount of attention given to these groups may have made people think they were more prevalent and widespread than was actually the case.

Also, there are other activities, usually involving young people, which can be considered manifestations of Satanism. Bill Ellis calls this behavior "ostensive traditions" in his discussion of "legend trips" of adolescents, as they find ways both to upset and garner the attention of adults.[7] Acting out rituals presumed to be a part of the Satanic tradition has become a favored way for some youth to define their own identities. Usually such activities are a passing phase of behavior, but occasionally some young people get so caught up in the legend trips that tragedy results, with people being injured or even killed, supposedly in the name of Satan. When such rare events do occur, they receive huge amounts of media attention, of course, contributing to the perception that there are dangerous Satanists everywhere. The media also contribute to the odds that other youth will notice the furor and engage in such ostensive behavior themselves.[8]

A second major factor is the rise of Christian fundamentalism as a social force in the U.S.[9] This development has had many consequences, including a major contribution to the rise of the Satanism scare. The reason for this effect is that Christian fundamentalists typically believe in, and accept the reality of, Satan and Satanism. Wherever Christian fundamentalists are taken seriously, or accepted as part of the social fabric, their beliefs about Satan are a part of the cultural baggage that they bring with them into the social arena. Thus, Satan and his alleged activities and goals may be treated as "real" (and are thus real in their consequences) by people who usually would not hold such personal beliefs.

A third element is the development of a "child saver" movement in American society and elsewhere in recent decades.[10] This is the term applied by social scientists to the broad movement concerned about the welfare of children, something that is a relatively new development in Western society. This movement has spawned new laws concerning child abuse and large governmental bureaucracies charged with enforcing the new laws in order to protect children, even if this involves the assertion of hitherto unheard of rights of ownership of said children by the state.

The child saver movement is based on the premise that there are great dangers to children afoot in the land, and that children are to be protected, at nearly any cost. One of those dangers concerns Satanism, which, according to some, is rampant in day care centers in the U.S. and elsewhere, and helps "explain" why staff members of child care centers (most of whom are female) might engage in certain kinds of ritual abuse involving their charges. Supposedly, Satanism even motivates some families to abuse their children in ways involving Satanic rituals, a claim that has been especially prevalent in some areas of the United Kingdom, as Phillip Jenkins has described, but also in the U.S. as well.[11]

When allegations of Satanic abuse arise, that is, when claims are made that Satanists are operating in day care centers or families, governmental agencies developed to protect children spring into action, sometimes without carefully checking the veracity of such claims or the motives of those making the claims.[12] Thus, we may see quite secular governmental bureaucrats acting as if the claims of anti-Satanists are true, even if they do not themselves accept the reality of Satan. And others, such as media representatives, may report on such activities as if they are true, when in fact the reporting is being done quite cynically for opportunistic reasons.

A fourth element contributing to the rise of the Satanism scare is what is called the "occult survivor" or "repressed memory" movement, which is supposedly historically related to the child saver movement, but also brings in a new major element, the involvement of the psychotherapeutic profession.[13] The occult survivor phenomenon occurs when adult women recall, usually while undergoing therapy from "believing" psychiatrists or psychologists, that they were sexually abused years ago as children. The alleged perpetrator is usually the father, but sometimes the mother or other relatives are also implicated in the claims being made by the "survivor."

What makes this phenomenon relevant to the concerns of the analysis is that the "eyewitness" claims of abuse from years before often involve alleged participation in some sort of ritual abuse associated with Satanism. Sometimes the entire family is supposedly involved in a Satanic cult that uses its children in ritual activities. The initial abuse experienced by the survivor was so horrible that memories of these events were apparently repressed, only to be dredged up years later under the helpful assistance of a psychiatrist who understands that such things do occur. Such claims are important because they supposedly demonstrate that child sex abuse associated with Satanism has been occurring for decades. Also, such claims demonstrate to those accepting them that the Satanism problem is more widespread than might have otherwise been thought, and that it affects some apparently normal families or even groups of families in society.

A fifth element germane to understanding the Satanism scare is the rise of the so-called Anti-Cult Movement (ACM), a movement that has become a major social force within the U.S. and in some other Western societies over the past three decades or so.[14] The ACM has garnered considerable attention from scholars attempting to understand how new religious movements (NRMs) have come to be defined as a major social problem within American society and elsewhere.

Some scholars have noted that the ACM predated the rise of anti-Satanism concerns, but that the ACM was quick to incorporate that concern and take advantage of the interest being shown by the media and the general public in alleged activities of Satanists. Consequently, Satanism was lumped by the ACM with other quite different groups and movements such as the Hare Krishna, the Unification Church, Scientology, the Jesus People, and many other new religious phenomena defined as dangerous by the ACM. Thus Satanism was defined as a special and virulent form of the "cult menace" in society, a development that may appear more opportunistic than real, but one that has been effective with both the general public and policymakers.[15]

A sixth related development that has contributed to the rise of concern about Satanism is the rise of feminism as a powerful social movement.[16] The contribution is not as direct as that of some other movements that have been discussed, but it is nonetheless the case that feminism has played a role in fomenting concern over Satanism, as some scholars have noted. This is mainly the result of the following line of reasoning: most of the children allegedly abused in day care centers, and most of the people making claims about being sexually abused in their childhood are female. The impetus to "believe the children" (and its corollary "believe the adult survivors") who claim sexual abuse has been promoted by some (but not all) feminists, who claim that rejecting such assertions does not take seriously the women's claims, a dismissal which only exacerbates their feelings of abuse or exploitation.

So, we have the seemingly strange situation of quite secular feminists sometimes appearing to take seriously the claims being made by anti-Satanists with whom they appear to have very little else in common. Jenkins tells of a feminist scholar writing in a Marxist journal who treats quite seriously objective claims by Christian fundamentalists about the actions of Satanists in child care centers.[17] Such occurrences are illustrative of the many forces and movements that flow together to help form the Satanism scare.

A seventh development to take into account is related to several of the ones mentioned above. I refer to the spread of anti-Satanism seminars for staff in agencies established to protect children, for law enforcement personnel, and for others in the "helping professions."[18] Many professional and semi-professional staff in such occupations are required to earn continuing education credits to maintain their professional credentials. A popular way to gain such credits is to sign up for seminars offered by self-claimed experts on the Satanism threat; such offerings have been a regular part of continuing education efforts for years in the U.S. and elsewhere. These seminars thus reinforce the claims of those who say that Satanists are everywhere and gaining strength and numbers, that they are taking over the child care industry, that sex abuse was prevalent years ago in many families where children were allegedly abused by their parents in Satanic rituals, or that Satanic cults are like other cults, except maybe a little worse than most since they allegedly sacrifice and sexually abuse small children. The seminars offer a direct aura of legitimacy to those who would make such claims about Satanism. Thus they contribute to the rise of the Satanism scare.

Technology of communication and the organization of the mass media have also played a role in the spread of the Satanism scare. There has been an understandable tendency for the mass media to focus on Satanism in its normal operation involving print media and traditional television programming, because of the widespread interest in the topic within American culture and society.[19] However, the development of satellite and cable technology to transmit television more easily has exacerbated this tendency because of the increased demand for inexpensive programming to fill hours of newly-acquired airtime. The talk show motif has become prevalent in both television and radio, which means that on any given day dozens if not hundreds of different talk show hosts are looking for things to talk about that will interest potential viewers and listeners. Cults, particularly Satanic cults, meet the needs of this new media market. Self-proclaimed experts on Satanism can gain an audience on national radio or TV just by being willing to make claims about Satanism, the more colorful and audacious the better.[20]

This point was driven home to many in the media industry when Geraldo Rivera produced a television documentary on Satanism in 1988. His show, "Satanism in America," was the most watched documentary in American history with its initial showing, and was subsequently shown in a number of other countries as well. This one program demonstrated that the topic of Satanism was a powerful way to attract viewers, and many other talk show hosts soon copied it.

The outcome of these many movements and developments has been the social construction of a moral panic that scholars have dubbed the "Satanism Scare," or the "Satanic Panic." Many opinion leaders and members of the general public have accepted as objective fact some or all of the claims made about the pervasiveness of Satanic activities in society, and they have acted (or allowed others to act) accordingly. This moral panic has also been spread around the globe by anti-Satanist "missionaries" from the U.S. carrying their message and materials to other countries whose traditionally Christian cultures have made it receptive to such ideas. Thus the "Satanism scare" has become globalized.[21]

SATANISM AND WICCA LINKED

Much to the chagrin of practitioners of Wicca, there has been confusion in the minds of many about their religion, which is often linked with Satanism, although there are important differences between the two. Some in the media treat Wicca and Satanism differently, primarily (and ironically) because of the ties Wicca has with the feminist movement; the positive opinion of some in the media regarding feminism occasionally helps produce more objective coverage.[22]

Wicca has no organizational ties with the Church of Satan, and its practitioners claim historical ties with ancient Paganism, not with Christianity. Thus it is a perversion of history to claim that Wicca involves a focus on Satan, and that Wiccan rituals are Satanic. But, this claim is made and has been made for centuries, first as part of the conflict between early Christianity and Paganism, a conflict eventually won by Christianity. Later in the history of the West, claims linking Satan and allegations of witchcraft were made, to devastating effect. Hundreds of thousands of people, mostly women, were killed in horrible ways during the "Burning Times" that took place from the fifteenth through the seventeenth centuries in Europe, and also in a limited way in colonial America (recall the Salem witch trials). Today in the U.S. and elsewhere where Wicca groups have developed, opponents of Wicca claim ties between Satanism and Wicca, and many seem to accept such claims, resulting in a melding of the identities of Satanism and Wicca, much to the disadvantage of Wicca.

WICCA IN CONTEMPORARY SOCIETY

Wicca exists as a separate religious or spiritual phenomenon in contemporary society. It gained new impetus in the 1950s in England with the work of Gerald

Gardner, an English civil servant who claimed to have been initiated into the craft in the 1930s by an old woman named Dorothy.[23] Wicca practitioners such as Starhawk claim ties with ancient Paganism, although some dispute such claims and assert that Wicca is something new, that is, a product of contemporary ideas and movements.[24] The major themes within Wiccan beliefs include: (1) a rejection of traditional religion and dominant cultural values, and a willingness to engage in experimentation with other beliefs and values; (2) a focus on nature and ecological concerns; and (3) an acceptance of the values of feminism, including the rejection of the patriarchy of the major religions and dominant cultures. Note that Satan does not play a part in contemporary Wiccan beliefs, except for being rejected as part of the cultural baggage of Christianity. Thus the melding of Satanism with Wicca and witchcraft is especially problematic for Wiccans.

Some claim that between 200,000 and 300,000 people practice Wicca in the U.S., although other scholars dispute that claim.[25] Wiccan groups also exist in other parts of the world as well. Following the lead of Margot Adler's classic modern treatment of witchcraft in the U.S., Helen Berger and others have written about the recent development of Wicca within the U.S., offering insight into how the groups operate, what types of people participate in them, and how children of Wiccans are dealt with in such groups.[26] Lynn Hume writes of the development of Wicca in Australia, and the problems brought on by the fact that most Wiccan rituals were developed in the Northern Hemisphere, and were attuned to the seasons of that region, making them poorly suited for observance "down under."[27]

Wicca is accepted within the U.S. as a legally valid religion, having won some key court cases establishing that right. Thus Wiccan religious leaders can marry people, serve as chaplains in federal facilities, rent public facilities, buy insurance for their property and activities, and do other things any other religious group can do. Also, contributions to Wiccan groups are tax deductible (if the specific group has applied for and received tax exempt status). A large Wiccan group operates at Fort Hood, Texas, and does so openly and legally, given the current legal status of Wicca in the U.S.[28]

Describing the legal status and social acceptance of Wicca is not to say, of course, that the lot of a Wiccan group in the U.S. is an easy one. Wiccans are not well accepted by many in American society, in large part because of the ties that some would claim between Wicca and Satanism.

Satanic groups and Wiccans have vastly different beliefs or ideology, with Wicca stressing the importance of nature and human beings being a part of nature. Also, Wiccan groups focus on the female, rejecting patriarchy in any form (including the usually male-like figure of Satan), and being greatly influenced by the values and aims of feminism. But, in the minds of many, Wicca and Satanism are linked, and have been since the Middle Ages and the Burning Times. Witches have been defined as agents of Satan, bent on destroying Christianity and its values. This hegemonic definition justified doing terrible things to those who fell within the ambit of the Catholic Church in its crusade to establish its dominance and repress Paganism in any form.[29]

Some of the several contributing factors to the rise of the Satanism scare also can be applied to the growing concern in some quarters about Wicca and witchcraft. Some Wicca groups have attracted considerable media attention in recent years. When it is revealed that a Wiccan group is operating in a local area, this nearly always leads to publicity, usually, but not always, of a negative kind.[30] Christian fundamentalists also reject witchcraft as antithetical to Christianity. Their claims have contributed greatly to the linking of Satanism and witchcraft in the popular perception. Some concern about Wicca comes from the child saver movement, especially because children are now being raised as a part of Wiccan groups, as noted by Helen Berger. The Anti-Cult Movement also contributes to anti-Wiccan sentiment by lumping Wicca with other "cults" and over-generalizing about their activities in a quite negative fashion, as is its usual practice. The anti- Satan seminars contribute, as well, when those operating them for professionals do not distinguish between Wicca and Satanism. Talk show hosts on television and radio often are not careful in making important distinctions, and indeed may quite cynically link the two just for added interest among potential audiences. Thus, many of the same factors that contributed to the Satanism scare have also played a role in linking Satanism and witchcraft.

CONCLUSION

This analysis has presented a sociological explanation for the rise of concern about Satanism in the U.S. and elsewhere. A number of factors have contributed to the moral panic concerning Satanism, mainly because a proclivity exists to accept such claims within Western culture, and this tendency has been exacerbated in recent times by the several movements and developments described above. Thus, some areas of American society have major concerns about Satanism, leading to consequences beyond what would appear to be warranted by the actual facts of Satanism in contemporary society. Wicca and witchcraft, a growing "new religion" in its own right, has been linked to Satanism by some of the same movements and developments, although the linkage has not always been complete. However, the forced melding of the identities of these two movements has led to difficulties, especially for Wiccan groups. Regrettably, it would seem to be the case that this mistaken melding of identities, and the consequent difficulties, will continue for the foreseeable future.

Chapter 6

A Critical Analysis of Evidentiary and Procedural Rulings in Branch Davidian Civil Case[1]

Stuart A. Wright

On 14 July 2000, a jury in the Branch Davidian wrongful death lawsuit returned a verdict finding no fault with federal agents in the disastrous siege and standoff at Mt. Carmel in 1993. The federal actions precipitated the deaths of eighty sect members. Government attorneys praised the verdict, saying it was a vindication of federal law enforcement. Lead co-counsel for the government, U.S. Attorney Michael Bradford, boasted after the verdict: "What this shows is that the responsibility for the tragedy that happened at Waco is with David Koresh and the Branch Davidians." He added, "It's time to put this to rest and move on." But few scholars and observers think this verdict will put the Waco incident to rest. There are far too many lingering and disturbing questions about the civil trial.

The most troubling aspect of the trial is the discretionary authority exercised by Judge Walter Smith in limiting evidence and crafting procedural rulings that handcuffed plaintiffs' attorneys. Indeed, Davidian attorneys waged an unsuccessful battle to have Judge Smith removed from the case for over a year prior to the trial. Based on Smith's rulings in the earlier criminal trial of Davidians in 1994, the plaintiffs believed they could not receive a fair hearing in Judge Smith's court. Perhaps in response to the expressed concern, Smith empanelled an "advisory" jury in Waco, even though federal civil trials do not require a jury and the court is not bound by its verdict. Some observers suggested that by appointing an advisory jury, Smith was attempting to deflect criticism of bias arising from problems surrounding the earlier criminal trial. These concerns and criticisms appear to have some validity.

The criminal trial of eleven Branch Davidians in San Antonio in 1994 was fraught with controversy. Judge Smith took the unusual step of issuing to the initial jury pool an 80-item questionnaire to screen potential jurors.[2] Some of the questions appeared to be entirely inappropriate.[3] For example, there were ten items on religion, including questions on frequency of church attendance, degree of religiosity, extent of organizational participation, and formal religious training. One item even asked if the respondent had ever belonged to a "non-traditional" religious group. There were also eleven items on gun ownership. Here, one item asked if the respondent had ever belonged to the National Rifle Association, and another asked if the respondent had ever attended a gun show. The questionnaire was used to eliminate 216 jurors, leaving the attorneys with a group of 84 screened individuals from which to choose. Smith also suppressed efforts by defense attorneys to introduce self-defense evidence. Despite these obstacles, the jury acquitted all defendants of the more serious charges of murder and conspiracy to murder. Five defendants were convicted on the lesser charge of aiding and abetting manslaughter of a federal officer. Confounded by Judge Smith's instructions, however, the jury also convicted on a weapons count, assuming it was tied to the manslaughter charge. Technically, the charge of carrying a firearm during the course of a crime was tied only to the murder charge. Faced with the inconsistent verdict, the judge set aside the verdict, but then, at the behest of the prosecutors, changed his mind and reinstated the convictions. Prosecutors successfully argued that perhaps the jury was split, some wanting a murder conviction and some wanting an acquittal. Smith failed to ask the jurors their intent (jurors later filed sworn statements to the effect that the confusion arose from the instructions, not a split decision). The judge ruled that the weapons used in the commission of a crime were machine guns, and he sentenced the five Davidians to forty years each, the maximum allowed by federal sentencing guidelines. On appeal, the U.S. Supreme Court unanimously reversed Smith on the sentence enhancements, finding that the district court improperly decided during sentencing that the firearms used were machine guns. According to the court's ruling, the type of firearm used should have been determined by presentation of evidence during the trial.

Another indication of Smith's prejudice appears in the sentence findings and opinion in the criminal trial. Incredibly, Smith referred to the deaths of the federal agents as "homicide," and boldly asserted that the Davidians "engaged in a conspiracy to cause the deaths of federal agents."[4] Smith's written opinion blatantly ignored the verdict, riding roughshod over the findings of the jury that acquitted all the defendants of murder and conspiracy to murder.

Given the history of Smith's rulings in the criminal case, it was hardly surprising that Davidian attorneys sought to have the judge removed from the civil proceeding. Actually, up until August 1999, it seemed likely that the civil lawsuit would be dismissed altogether. But things changed dramatically in early

August when it was revealed that the FBI had lied about discharging pyrotechnic devices in the CS gas assault on the Davidian settlement that might have caused the conflagration. After six years of official denials about using pyrotechnic or "military" rounds, investigators for plaintiffs' attorneys discovered the devices in the evidence storage room in Austin. It was later learned that the FBI also failed to turn over audiotapes and written documentation that would have revealed the use of pyrotechnic rounds. The mishandling or concealment of evidence and the false statements made by government officials suggested a cover-up. Pressured by government missteps and the new evidence, Judge Smith was compelled to allow the Davidian lawsuit to go forward.

This promising development, however, did not mean that Davidian survivors and their kin would get a fair trial. As an observer in the courtroom during the civil trial and one who has studied the Branch Davidian tragedy for seven years,[5] I want to address some of the problems surrounding the proceedings that I believe contributed to a flawed verdict. Specifically, I contend that the federal trial in Waco failed to deliver a just verdict because evidentiary and procedural rulings handicapped the plaintiffs and prevented the jury from hearing all the evidence.

KEY EVIDENTIARY AND PROCEDURAL RULINGS

To begin with, Judge Smith granted a "discretionary function" exemption to federal officials granting them immunity for "bad judgments" in actions taken against the Branch Davidians. The intent of the discretionary function exemption is to protect law enforcement agents from being secondguessed in situations requiring urgent decision-making in the course of their duties. But how this exemption is applied is left to the judgment of the court and can be interpreted broadly or narrowly. Judge Smith chose the broad interpretation.

A similar claim, of course, was made by the government in the Randy Weaver case when FBI sniper Lon Horiuchi shot and killed Weaver's wife, Vicky, during a standoff which occurred less than six months before the Waco incident.[6] Horiuchi was part of the FBI's Hostage Rescue Team (HRT), the same unit that was in charge of the standoff at Waco. Mrs. Weaver was standing at the door of her cabin holding her infant child when the .308 caliber bullet pierced her neck, severed her carotid artery, then exited, ripping away most of the left side of her jaw and half of her face. The debris from the gunshot showered her children with blood and bits of skull. Prosecutors in Boundary County, Idaho filed murder charges against Horiuchi. But officials from the Justice Department filed a motion claiming that Horiuchi had immunity from prosecution based on the discretionary function exemption. The trial court agreed and in a 2-1 decision, the U.S. 9th Circuit Court of Appeals upheld the lower court's ruling. In a sharply worded dissenting opinion, however, Judge

Alex Kozinski criticized the sniper's action as unprovoked and indefensible, declaring that the court's opinion "waters down the constitutional standard for the use of deadly force by giving offenders a license to kill even when there is no immediate threat to human life."[7]

In the Waco case, a Justice Department official confirmed that the government enjoyed a distinct advantage as a result of this ruling before the case ever went to trial. In an Associated Press wire service report on 15 July, Department of Justice spokesman Thom Mrozek was quoted as saying, "Even before we got to trial, the case was whittled down significantly to relatively narrow legal issues, in large part because a lot of things we did are protected by the nature of discretionary function."[8] Was this evidentiary ruling critical to the case? Did it create an uneven playing field, giving the advantage to the government? It appears that it did.

There were at least three "bad judgments" that were excluded from jury consideration. The first was the decision by ATF to engage in a dangerous, high-risk, paramilitary assault on a residence housing infants, children, pregnant women, and elderly persons in order to execute a search and arrest warrant for a single individual. It is clear that David Koresh could have been arrested away from the Mt. Carmel property, thus avoiding the reckless endangerment of 130 people who were not charged in the warrants. The second was the decision by the FBI to abandon *conciliatory negotiations* with the sect only ten days into the standoff in favor of a "psychological warfare" strategy, which according to CIA documents is a counter-terrorism tactic developed by the military designed to induce fear, emotional and psychological instability, sleep deprivation, distrust, dissension, and hopelessness in the mind of the enemy.[9] The third was the decision to assault the complex with CS gas—a chemical weapon that is banned by international treaty for use even in wartime against our worst enemies—and using tanks to crush and demolish the building. Each of these so-called bad judgments were protected by discretionary function exemptions and contributed to the disastrous outcome at Waco.

The second of the three "bad judgments" just mentioned (FBI decision to abandon conciliatory negotiations) is of particular interest. After the 1995 U.S. House of Representatives hearings on Waco, Congress mandated that the FBI overhaul the HRT to improve internal communication and give negotiators more voice and power in future hostage-barricade incidents. Following the debacle at Mt. Carmel, negotiators complained that they were ignored and undercut by the tactical unit, making the negotiations ineffective (which was then used as a rationale for the CS insertion). The FBI was told by Congress to develop an advisory group of experts on unconventional religious movements whom they could consult in similar incidents should they arise in the future. I was asked to serve on the advisory group of experts to the renamed Critical Incident Response Group (CIRG). One of the first things I sought to determine was the soundness of existing hostage-barricade protocols. Did the feds do their homework, incorporating grounded theory and research in psychology, sociology, and communications to develop crisis negotiations? To my surprise, available materials were well-grounded in scientific research. They were excellent. The only problem was that they were entirely ignored in the Waco standoff. In the 1999 summer issue of the international *Journal of Terrorism and Political Violence*, I published an extensive analysis of the FBI's crisis negotiations during the 51-day standoff.[10] Using materials culled from the FBI's own curriculum to teach law enforcement agents from all over the world how to conduct hostage-barricade incidents, sixteen violations at Mt. Carmel were identified. Space does not permit a full examination of these violations. Instead, the focus below concerns just one.

A key principle in crisis negotiations is reducing the stress of the hostage-taker or the barricaded subjects. According to a crisis negotiations manual authored by two veteran negotiators, "one task of the negotiator is to reduce stress. . . . If the negotiators want themselves or the hostage-taker to come up with new ideas, they need to reduce stress levels as much as possible."[11] "(H)igh levels of stress interfere with negotiators performance. . . . Stress affects the hostage-taker's decisionmaking skills. Stress elevates emotions, speeds physiological processes and interferes with cognitive processing. The ability to make decisions is hindered or even ceases."[12] If the negotiator is effective, stress levels will dissipate and provide an atmosphere conducive to a peaceful resolution: "With time, the negotiator can reduce stress, calm the hostage-taker, improve decision-making skills and fulfill most need states. The hostage-taker feels better and works to resolve the incident."[13]

So what did the FBI do? The HRT's response plan in Waco after March 17 was referred to as a "stress escalation" program in the Department of Justice log.[14] By stress escalation, the plan refers to the intensification of physiological and psychological pressures. "The constant stress overload," according to Dr. Alan Stone who was asked to review the actions of the FBI at Waco, "is intended to lead to sleep deprivation and psychological disorientation. In predisposed individuals, the combination of physiological disruption and psychological stress can also lead to mood disturbances, transient hallucinations and paranoid ideation."[15] The stress escalation strategy also entailed the alternation of conciliatory and hostile gestures to confuse the target (carrot and stick approach sending mixed messages), the deployment of high-powered stadium lights at night, combined with amplification of recorded sounds of rabbits beings slaughtered, dentist drills, and chanting. Stone reports that the recorded sounds deployed exceeded 105 decibels that could produce nerve deafness in children as well as adults. The use of debilitating light and sound were deployed as psychological irritants to induce sleep deprivation.

Dr. Robert Cancro, another expert asked to review the FBI's actions at Waco, was confounded by this approach. He stated, "From a behavioral science perspective it is not clear what benefits were expected from imposing sleep deprivation on the members of the compound. If anything, this was likely to make their behavior more erratic and less predictable."[16] Nonetheless, the

Justice report states that around this same time, special agent in charge, Jeff Jamar, decided that it was time to increase the pressure. Stone notes that "By March 21, the FBI was concentrating on tactical pressure alone."[17]

The psychological warfare program also utilized the threat of force—using tanks to demolish the children's toys (bicycles and motor bikes), crushing automobiles, driving CEVs over the graves of buried Davidians outside the complex, and encircling the buildings with tanks and helicopters to "tighten the noose" as the Justice report documents.

This is the most obvious and defiant breach of fundamental hostage and barricade protocol evidenced by the government. It is virtually impossible to reconcile a *stress escalation* strategy with the principle of *stress reduction*. No amount of government spin can erase the inexplicable and inexcusable contradiction. The only rationale for the stress escalation plan was that it would result in "driving a psychological wedge between Koresh and his followers," in the apparent hope that group fragmentation would occur. Tragically, the strategy produced the opposite effect, bonding members together against a perceived common enemy, a basic sociological axiom. All sixteen violations were of this nature. Bad judgments? More likely, it would seem, the violations were too systematic and uniform to be accidental. In any case, the jury never got to hear any of this evidence.

Judge Smith also restricted presentation of evidence to the fifty-one days between the initial ATF raid on 28 February and the final conflagration on 19 April. Why was this important? Since the jury was being asked to determine whether the ATF used excessive force in the execution of the warrants, it stands to reason that facts and events leading up to the raid were crucial to a complete understanding of the excessive force issue. The use of a high risk, "dynamic entry" is brought into relief when one considers that the ATF had less lethal and far less dangerous options that it did not exercise. Indeed, the whole plan of operation by the ATF was castigated by the Treasury Department report and Congressional investigations on Waco. Consider the summary conclusions in the final joint report by the House Committee on Government Reform and Oversight and the Committee on the Judiciary regarding the ATF raid on Mt. Carmel:

> The ATF's investigation of the Branch Davidians was grossly incompetent. It lacked the minimum professionalism of a major Federal law enforcement agency. While the ATF had probable cause to obtain the arrest warrant for David Koresh and the search warrant for the Branch Davidian residence, the affidavit filed in support of the warrants contained an incredible number of false statements. The ATF agents responsible for preparing the affidavits knew or should have known that many of the statements were false. David Koresh could have been arrested outside the Davidian compound. The ATF chose not to arrest Koresh outside the Davidian residence and instead were determined to use a dynamic entry approach. In making this decision ATF agents exercised extremely poor judgement, made erroneous assumptions, and ignored the foreseeable perils of their

course of action. ATF misrepresented to Defense Department officials that the Branch Davidians were involved in illegal drug manufacturing. As a result of this deception, the ATF was able to obtain some training from (military) forces which would not have otherwise provided it. . . .

The decision to pursue a military style raid was made more than 2 months before surveillance, undercover, and infiltrations efforts were (even) begun. The ATF undercover and surveillance operation lacked the minimum professionalism expected of a Federal law enforcement agency. Supervisors failed to properly monitor this operation. The ATF's raid plan for February 28 was significantly flawed. *The plan was poorly conceived, utilized a high risk tactical approach when other tactics could have been successfully used,* was drafted and commanded by ATF agents who were less qualified than other available agents, and used agents who were not sufficiently trained for the operation. Additionally, ATF commanders did not take precautions to ensure that the plan would not be discovered. The senior raid commanders, Phillip Chojnacki and Chuck Sarabyn, either knew or should have known that the Davidians had become aware of the impending raid and were likely to resist with deadly force. Nevertheless, they recklessly proceeded with the raid, thereby endangering the lives of the ATF agents under their command and the lives of those residing in the compound. *This, more than any other factor, led to the deaths of the four ATF agents killed on February 28.*[18]

The jury never heard the findings of the official report because it fell outside the time frame that Judge Smith would permit the jury to consider evidence.

Finally, Judge Smith revealed a pattern of bias against the Davidians and their attorneys in a number of bench decisions. For example, the interrogatories given to the jury were so specific and narrow that one could have found substantial fault with the government but answered in the negative to the interrogatories. In the first interrogatory, the jurors were asked to decide if excessive force was used. But jurors were only allowed to consider the question in terms of whether agents fired 1) indiscriminately into the complex, and 2) without provocation. The question, as worded, clearly ignores Texas state law that says excessive force may exist in the form of a threat, even before a shot is fired. The applicable law, cited below in its entirety, allows for a citizen to forcibly resist an arrest or search if, before any resistance is offered, he or she reasonably believes a peace officer is using or attempting to use greater force than necessary. We will return to this argument momentarily.

Smith also lumped all Davidians into a single group, not allowing the jury to consider that some sect members, such as the children, were innocent victims of aggressive government actions. This was done despite the fact that during voir dire (jury selection), Smith specifically asked potential jurors if they could consider each of the plaintiffs *individually.* Plaintiffs' attorneys were led to believe that the judge would give the jury this charge in their deliberations. The Davidian attorneys built their case on this presumption. When Smith reneged, Michael Caddell, the plaintiffs' lead counsel, was outraged and publicly accused the judge of trying to "engineer a verdict." In an eighteen-page motion filed after the trial, Caddell alleged that Smith showed a "deep seated prejudice" towards his clients.[19] In one instance, the motion stated that Smith referred to one videotaped defense witness, Livingston Fagan, as a "lying, murdering son of a bitch." Elsewhere in the motion, it stated that Smith referred to plaintiffs' transcripts of government surveillance recordings as "bullcrap," even though it was later shown that their transcripts were more accurate than those submitted by government lawyers. The motion also stated that the judge admitted that he had not read some evidence introduced by the Davidians. In one other instance, Mr. Caddell's motion said the judge acted improperly by shaking the hand of a government lawyer during a recess and congratulating him for "a good job" after a grueling cross-examination of Davidian Clive Doyle. The government attorney conducting the cross-examination, Jim Touhey, viciously attacked and ridiculed Mr. Doyle's religion and belittled his belief that Koresh was a prophet. Mr. Touhey's performance invoked frightening images of the Medieval Inquisition and the Salem witch trials. The government's challenge to the legitimacy of Davidian theology was a broadside against constitutionally protected, albeit unconventional, religious belief. Perplexing was the fact that plaintiffs' attorneys failed to object to this line of questioning. When asked later why he did not raise objections during the cross, Michael Caddell responded that he thought the tactic would backfire and that the jury would see through it. It did not, and they did not.

As an observer, I noted that Smith barked and snapped at plaintiffs' co-counsels, Ramsey Clark and James Brannon, showing notable contempt and sending less-than-subtle messages to the jury. Smith lost patience with Clark on several occasions, evidently irritated by Clark's slow and methodical style of questioning witnesses. In one exchange, Smith's face turned bright red as he yelled at Clark, demanding that he quicken his pace and "get to the point." Smith interrupted both Clark and Brannon routinely, demanding explanations for questions posed to witnesses, challenging their competency and credibility with the jury. Overall, this left me with the impression that the irascible Judge Smith harbored considerable disdain for plaintiffs' attorneys.

In the end, justice was not served in Smith's court. The finding that excessive force was not used in the initial ATF raid is particularly troubling. If Waco does not rise to the standard of excessive force, one could reasonably conclude the standard is a legal fiction. Texas state law clearly defines excessive force and the rights of citizens to protect themselves under these circumstances. The *Texas Penal Code*, in Subchapter C. Protection of Persons, section 9.31, states

> The use of force to resist an arrest or search is justified: (1) if, before the actor offers any resistance, the peace officer (or person acting at his direction) uses or attempts to use greater force than necessary to make the arrest or search; and (2) when and to the degree the actor reasonably believes the force is immediately necessary to protect himself against the peace officer's (or other person's) use or attempted use of greater force than necessary.

Did the Davidians exercise reasonable belief that ATF officers in the initial raid were "using or attempting to use greater force than necessary?" Specifically, could a paramilitary assault by eighty armed agents in camouflage and full combat gear, including Kevlar helmets and flak jackets, wielding MP-5 submachine guns, semi-automatic AR-15s, Sig Sauer 9MM semi-automatic pistols, .308-caliber high power sniper rifles, shotguns, and concussion grenades rushing a residence housing infants, children, pregnant women, and elderly persons, with only an arrest and search warrant for a single individual, be grounds for a reasonable belief that the officers were using or attempting to use greater force than necessary? If allowed to hear all the evidence, what jury would completely exonerate federal agents of such charges?

In the 1994 criminal trial of eleven Branch Davidians, Judge Smith declared that he would "not allow the government to be put on trial."[20] Judging from the proceedings of the recent civil trial, he still will not. In September 2000, Davidian Attorneys Michael Caddell and Ramsey Clark announced plans to appeal the verdict in the civil case. Based on the earlier motion filed by Caddell, it would appear that attorneys will attempt to convince an appeals court of an appearance of bias or impropriety by the trial judge. Federal courts, however, are very reticent to overturn decisions based on the alleged bias of the trial judge. The case will now go to the U.S. 5th Circuit Court of Appeals in New Orleans, thought by many to be the most conservative in the country. In all likelihood, the Davidians will not find relief in the appellate proceedings, closing the final chapter of legal redress available to the surviving sect members and their families.

CONCLUSION

The annals of American law will show that the government prevailed in all its legal challenges. But one must ask, at what price? Historically, no religious sect has ever been more brutally victimized by the U.S. government. Scholars have already made comparisons to the Oglala Sioux at Wounded Knee.[21] Waco is now a permanent part of our culture and serves as a symbol of raw state power and control. In the end, what was achieved in legal victory pales in comparison to what was lost in civility, confidence in public officials, and belief in our system of justice.

Chapter 7

New Religious Movements and Conflicts with Law Enforcement

Catherine Wessinger

A conference at Baylor University in Waco, Texas, with its proximity to Mount Carmel Center, the site of the 1993 Branch Davidian tragedy, is a fitting place to highlight the lessons that can be learned from that case concerning conflicts between law enforcement agents and members of new religious movements. The Branch Davidian incident and the conflict involving the Randy Weaver family at Ruby Ridge, Idaho in 1992, both watershed events in the history of conflicts between American law enforcement agents and religious believers, illustrate that the *quality of the interactions* between law enforcement agents and believers is crucial in determining whether or not lives will be lost. In both cases, law enforcement agents and believers died unnecessarily. If we can understand the causes of these and other significant conflicts between law enforcement agents and religious believers, then perhaps tragic deaths can be prevented in the future.

Randy Weaver and his family were Identity Christians who had retreated to the Idaho countryside to find a refuge from the conflicts that they expected would lead to Armageddon. Federal marshals were engaged in surveillance when they got into a gunfight with Sammy Weaver, age 14, and Kevin Harris, a Weaver family friend, after the marshals shot and killed the Weavers' dog. Deputy U. S. Marshal William Degan and Sammy Weaver were killed. Subsequently, members of the FBI's Hostage Rescue Team (HRT) surrounded the Weaver cabin, but did not announce their presence and did not ask the

Weavers to surrender. An FBI sniper fired upon Randy Weaver and Kevin Harris when they came out of the cabin, and one of his bullets passed through a door window striking and killing Vicki Weaver as she held her youngest child.[1]

In 1993, at Mount Carmel Center near Waco, Texas, four agents of the Bureau of Alcohol, Tobacco, and Firearms were killed, twenty ATF agents were wounded, five Branch Davidians were killed, and four Davidians were wounded during a raid carried out by seventy-six ATF agents on 28 February 1993. Interestingly, the shootout may have begun as a result of ATF agents shooting the Davidians' dogs. ATF agents killed another Davidian later that afternoon as he attempted to return to his family. The FBI's Hostage Rescue Team then arrived to preside over the 51-day siege of Mount Carmel Center. On 19 April 1993, fifty-one adult Davidians and twenty-three children died in the fire that erupted during the tank and tear gas assault launched by FBI agents.[2]

None of the deaths at Ruby Ridge or Mount Carmel Center would have occurred if law enforcement agents had been sensitive to how their activities were perceived by religious believers, if they had undertaken more ordinary measures to investigate the possibility of criminal activity, and if they had taken more moderate steps to enforce the law.

Violence involving religious groups is the result of the *interactions* between believers and people in mainstream society. The manner in which law enforcement agents, reporters, social workers, concerned family members, apostates (disgruntled former members), and citizens *interact* with members of a religious community either heightens conflict or promotes dialogue and mutual understanding.[3]

A common pattern has emerged in my comparative study of violence involving new religious movements: ritualized acts of violence can increase in scope and thus build up to a large explosion of violence in which many lives are lost. Law enforcement agents as well as religious believers can participate in rituals of violence that can escalate.[4]

Sometimes religious believers engage in acts of coercion and violence that can escalate into a large-scale culmination, such as a mass suicide or an assault against society, as in the group suicide and murders involving members of Peoples' Temple in Jonestown, Guyana, on 18 November 1978, or the release of sarin gas on the Tokyo subway by members of Aum Shinrikyo on 20 March 1995.[5]

Coercive discipline and punishments had been carried out in the Peoples' Temple both when it was a church in California and after the relocation of most of its members to Guyana in 1977. There had been suicide rehearsals in Jim Jones's inner circle since 1976. At Jonestown, the committing of a collective "revolutionary suicide" had been discussed in the community for at least a year as a means to preserve the group's ultimate concern, which was maintaining the cohesiveness of their community. The Jonestown residents had practiced carrying out group suicide in "white night" drills. The mass suicide in which 909 people died in Jonestown as a result either of drinking Fla-Vor-Aid laced with cyanide and tranquilizers or being injected with the poison included 294 children under the age of eighteen. Prior to the group suicide, men from Jonestown had opened fire on the party of Congressman Leo Ryan, which was departing with some long-time members of the Peoples' Temple, killing five people, including Ryan and wounding ten others.

Aum Shinrikyo's violence began with the coercion of devotees to follow an ascetic lifestyle by immersing themselves in extremely hot or cold water, a practice that resulted in an accidental death in 1988, and a murder in 1989 to keep that death a secret. In 1989, Aum devotees murdered an attorney, his wife, and their baby son to prevent him from revealing information about fraudulent claims made by the Aum guru, Shoko Asahara. Members of Aum Shinrikyo who wanted to leave the group were coerced, tortured, and drugged. Various individuals in Japan were attacked with poison gases because they had been identified as enemies of the group. On 27 June 1994, Aum devotees released sarin gas in the town of Matsumoto with the intention of killing three judges who were to decide an upcoming court case involving Aum. Six hundred people were injured and seven died in Matsumoto. The 20 March 1995 sarin gas attack on the Tokyo subway that injured over five thousand people and killed twelve was intended to prevent imminent police raids from being carried out on Aum communes. Aum devotees believed that their violent actions were helping to create a Buddhist utopia built by the grace of their infallible Buddha, Shoko Asahara.

The Branch Davidian tragedy illustrates that law enforcement agents can likewise engage in coercive and violent acts that can culminate in a large number of deaths and injuries. Branch Davidians who came out of Mount Carmel Center during the FBI siege were arrested and paraded in prison clothing before television cameras. Every time that adult Davidians came out, the remaining Davidians were punished by an act of coercion or psychological warfare. The electricity was cut off, bright spotlights were shone at the residence at night, and high-decibel sounds were blasted at them. The agents in the tanks made obscene gestures, mooned, and cursed the Davidians. The tanks crushed the Davidians' vehicles, which amounted to destroying evidence that was relevant to the question of whether the Davidians or the ATF agents did most of the shooting, the tanks crashed into the building from time to time, and repeatedly ran over the grave of a Davidian. These ritualized acts of violence culminated in the tank and tear gas assault on 19 April 1993, in which CS gas, which is banned for use in international warfare, was inserted into a residence containing civilians, including twenty-one children and their mothers, two pregnant women, and elderly people. The demolishing of the residence by the tanks killed Davidians, eliminated escape routes, and created conditions in which a fire could spread rapidly through the building. Regardless of whether the fire began accidentally, was ignited by pyrotechnic devices used by FBI agents to deliver the CS gas, or was set by Davidians, it would not have occurred if the FBI had relied on negotiations instead of coercion to deal with the Davidians.

Repeated acts of violence take on a ritualistic nature and can escalate into an explosion of violence. *Both* religious believers and law enforcement agents can participate in rituals of violence. In all three cases, Jonestown, Aum Shinrikyo, and the Branch Davidians, the believers were enmeshed in a net of conflicts with apostates, concerned relatives, reporters, and government and law enforcement agents of various types. The way that people in mainstream society *interact* with believers is important in determining a group's potential for volatility.

One of the most important factors in promoting conflict with a religious group is to call it a "cult." "Cult" was originally a word used to refer to an organized system of worship focused on an object of worship. Worship in a Christian denomination, according to this definition, is a "cult," and in jest we speak of people devoted to particular movies and games as "cults." Since the 1970s, "cult" has become a pejorative word to refer to religious groups that people do not like or understand, and, therefore, fear. The word "cult" now conveys a stereotype that the members are "brainwashed," whereas research has demonstrated that new religious movements typically utilize the same recruitment tactics as other evangelical and missionary religions.[6] The "cult" stereotype implies that the leader has total control over followers, although in fact no leader gains any power over people without the complicity of followers. The "cult" stereotype implies that unconventional religions are dangerous and violent, which encourages people to forget that believers in mainstream religions fight wars, torture and kill people, and often commit acts of terrorism, and that religious leaders in every tradition have emotionally, sexually, and financially abused believers. The "cult" stereotype implies that all unconventional religious groups are the same, when in fact they are vastly diverse in their characteristics, and most of them do not break the law or commit violent acts. "Cult" is a four-letter word that conveys hatred and prejudice just as much as racial, anti-Semitic slurs, and the various ugly words for women and gay people. Applying any pejorative label to a group of people can dehumanize them, make it appear to be legitimate to discriminate against them, deprive them of their civil and human rights, and kill them.

The application of the word "cult" and its corresponding stereotype to religious groups by law enforcement agents creates a situation in which law enforcement agents may be motivated to utilize excessive force. When law enforcement agents label a religious group a "cult," as was the case with the Branch Davidians, conflict between the agents and the believers is exacerbated. Law enforcement agents can avoid falling into the trap of the anticult mindset by consulting *bona fide* experts on religion, religious studies scholars, and sociologists of religion, instead of the self-styled "cult experts" who usually have no credentials in the study of religions. Given that violence involving religious groups is determined by the *quality of the interactions* between law enforcement agents and believers, law enforcement agents have the challenge of determining the best way to proceed in enforcing the law in relation to unconventional religious groups. To assist in this task, I will offer some conceptual categories for understanding religious groups and violence, and then offer some indicators for risk assessment.

MILLENNIALISM AND VIOLENCE

New religious movements are extremely diverse, ranging from Christian and Bible-based groups, to Asian and African derived religions, to UFO believers. The leader of a new religious movement may be regarded as having access to a spiritual source of authority. Believed access to an unseen source of authority is termed "charisma" by religion scholars. Charismatic leadership of a religious group can contribute to the potential for volatility, because there are fewer checks on the whims of the leader than in a group that has institutionalized offices.[7] It must be noted that charismatic leadership is socially constructed, and if there are no believers in a person's claimed access to an unseen source of authority, then there is no charismatic leader. Leadership in a new religious movement may be provided by elected officers or may be shared in some institutionalized manner. Authority in the group may be derived from adherence to a revered body of literature. Some believers may live in communities that are set off from mainstream society to varying degrees. Many new religious movements make very low demands on their members in terms of time, money, associations, and commitments. They do not ask believers to separate from their families, friends, occupations, and ordinary lifestyles.

Religious studies scholars observe new religious movements using the same methodologies that they employ when studying other religions. The assumption is that all of these groups are religions, regardless of size. I define religion as "ultimate concern," that which is the most important thing in the world for the believers.[8] An ultimate concern is the goal that believers wish to attain. An ultimate concern or goal is always about well-being. An ultimate concern is about salvation from the suffering and death inherent in the human condition. Human beings want to experience well-being in their earthly lives and continued well-being after death. Ultimate concerns of individuals and groups can change over time, especially in response to events. Since ultimate concerns are about well-being, many people will adjust their ultimate concerns if their well-being is threatened due to their religious beliefs. Alternatively, people may adjust the methods that they practice in their attempt to achieve their religious goals if former methods prove unproductive. Some believers hold on to their ultimate concerns so tightly that they may become willing either to kill or die for their religious goals.

Religious groups that have come into conflict with law enforcement authorities have often been millennial movements. Millennialism, or millennarianism, refers to certain patterns of belief, that, strictly speaking, have nothing to do with the year 2000 and the temporal millennial period just begun, although anticipation of the year 2000 appeared to increase millennial religious expectations during the 1990s. Religion scholars term these patterns of religious expression "millennialism" because the New Testament book of Revelation speaks of the Kingdom of God on earth lasting one thousand years. Millennialism is belief in an imminent transition to a collective salvation that will be either heavenly or earthly. It is a collective salvation because the millennial dream is that a group of people, called the "elect" in Christianity, will enter into a state of well-being in which suffering is overcome once and for all. While millennialists expect a collective heavenly salvation, others expect that the kingdom of God will be created on Earth.[9]

I use the term "catastrophic millennialism" to refer to the belief that the transition to the millennial kingdom, the collective salvation, will occur catastrophically; the old order will be destroyed to make way for the new order. I use "apocalypticism" as a synonym for catastrophic millennialism. I use the term "progressive millennialism" to refer to the belief that the transition to the collective salvation will take place due to a progressive creation of a just society. The progressive millennial belief is that humans working according to a divine or superhuman plan will create the millennial kingdom. The study of new religious movements demonstrates that both catastrophic millennialism and progressive millennialism may or may not have a messiah, a charismatic leader who is believed to have the power to create the millennial kingdom. A messiah is a prophet, someone who is regarded as receiving divine revelation, but a prophet is not necessarily a messiah.[10]

There is a range of behaviors associated with both catastrophic millennialism and progressive millennialism. Catastrophic millennialists include the vast majority of believers who wait in faith for God's intervention to destroy this corrupt world and create the millennial kingdom. This is the position taken by many Christians in mainstream churches. Catastrophic millennialists also include those such as the Randy Weaver family and the Branch Davidians, who arm themselves for protection during the tribulation period leading to Armageddon. They live apart from mainstream society. They do not threaten society's safety, but if they are attacked, they will fight back. Catastrophic millennialists also include those who believe that they are called by God to engage in revolutionary actions to overthrow what they regard as a satanic government and to establish God's righteous kingdom. There is a contemporary right-wing Euro-American nativist millennial movement in the United States, for example, whose very extreme members resort to terrorism. They are hoping to instigate what they call the "second American Revolution" against the federal government. They know that at present they do not have a majority of Americans willing to fight against the overwhelming power of the American law enforcement establishment.[11]

My focus will not be on progressive millennialism in this chapter, but I will say briefly that the same range of behaviors is associated with progressive millennialism. Most progressive millennialists rely on social work, personal development, and ethical living to build God's kingdom on Earth. Some progressive millennialists arm themselves for protection if they feel they are under attack. In significant cases, some progressive millennialists resort to revolutionary violence to speed progress up to an apocalyptic rate. Examples of revolutionary progressive millennialism include the German Nazis, the Maoists in China, and the Khmer Rouge in Cambodia.[12] These seemingly non-religious movements were expressions of ultimate concerns to create collective salvations on Earth.

Catastrophic millennialists who live in isolated communities are inherently in tension with mainstream society. They reject the values of society that they deem to be ungodly. They withdraw to create their own god-fearing communities in anticipation of the millennial kingdom. If law enforcement agents can interact with these believers in a respectful and even friendly manner that acknowledges their right to freedom of religion, they can go a long way towards avoiding heightened conflict that might lead to violence.

A recent article in the *FBI Law Enforcement Bulletin* recommended that law enforcement agents adopt a community-oriented policing strategy when dealing with unconventional religious groups.[13] This strategy was used successfully in 1998 with Chen Tao, a Taiwanese new religious movement located in Garland, Texas, whose leader had predicted that God would appear in his front yard on 31 March 1998 as a prelude to the predicted catastrophic destruction of the world in 1999. The Garland police established friendly personal relations with the Chen Tao leaders and members. The Garland police consulted a credentialed scholar of religion, Dr. Lonnie Kliever of Southern Methodist University, enabled him to interview and observe the Chen Tao believers, listened to his advice, and permitted him to share his expertise in religious studies with news reporters.[14] They used ordinary investigative and policing measures while protecting the safety of both the Chen Tao believers and the general public. The Garland police officers were prepared to intervene in the event the group decided to take violent actions, but their humane, practical, and nonconfrontational approach to the situation contributed to the positive interactions that Chen Tao believers had with the general public and helped create a social context in which the leader could reinterpret his failed prophecy to his followers. The wise and moderate approach of the Garland police also helped to reduce sensational news coverage of Chen Tao and protect the believers from a possible hostile public. The news coverage in the *Dallas Morning News* was especially intelligent and informed.

My comparative study of catastrophic millennial groups that have become caught up in violence shows that the potential for violence is increased if catastrophic millennialists feel persecuted. A sense of being persecuted increases the intensity with which apocalyptic beliefs are held. Additionally, an apocalyptic worldview increases the possibility that a group will interpret any amount of social opposition as being persecution. An apocalyptic or catastrophic millennial worldview involves what I call "radical dualism," a rigid perspective that sees things in stark black and white, good versus evil, us versus them terms.[15] Extremely aggressive law enforcement tactics against an apocalyptic group simply confirms the group's belief that satanic agents of an evil "Babylon" will attack the true believers. Persecution by civilians and law enforcement agents, such as that of the Mormons in nineteenth-century America, only increases the believers' theological emphasis on apocalypticism.[16] Catastrophic millennial worldviews and their associated dualisms assure believers that, in end-time events, evil people will be punished and righteous people will be rewarded. When dealing with apocalyptic groups, law enforcement agents should try to avoid making believers feel persecuted.

It is important that law enforcement agents realize that they, also, are likely to possess a worldview that is dualistic. Law enforcement agents are prone to see things through the lens of radical dualism. Law enforcement agents tend to be concerned with good versus evil, us versus them, good guys versus bad guys. When two parties are in conflict, both possessing radically dualistic worldviews, what generally transpires is akin to warfare, such as the incident at Mount Carmel Center. The only way to get out of this trap of "dichotomous thinking"[17] is to promote dialogue and negotiation in which the two parties can build trust in each other's good will and humanity.

When law enforcement agents are perplexed by the unusual beliefs and practices of an unconventional religious group, they will benefit from consulting with *bona fide* scholars with academic credentials in the study of religious movements. Individuals who promote themselves as "cult experts" usually have no credentials in the academic study of religion. Religious studies scholars can help law enforcement agents by serving as information resources and as "worldview translators."[18] Trying to communicate with believers possessing an unusual religious worldview can be compared to communication with someone who speaks a foreign language. In those cases, skilled and knowledgeable translators can promote better understanding. Religious studies scholars can explain to law enforcement agents the theology of the group as well as common sociological dynamics of new religious movements and their interactions with society. Religious studies scholars can analyze religious beliefs that motivate actions.

In 1993, two Bible scholars, J. Phillip Arnold of the Reunion Institute in Houston, Texas, and James Tabor, University of North Carolina at Charlotte, made an innovative and successful attempt at intervening in the religious critical incident that involved the Branch Davidians.[19] Unfortunately, they had to do so without the cooperation of FBI agents, whose tank and gas assault on 19 April 1993 fatally undermined the progress that Arnold and Tabor had made to persuade the Davidians to come out of Mount Carmel safely. Arnold went to Waco on 7 March 1993, to offer his services to the FBI, but was ignored by agents. On 15 March, the Davidians heard Arnold on a radio program discussing biblical prophecies. Davidian Steve Schneider asked the FBI to permit

Arnold to discuss the Bible with David Koresh, but this request was denied and FBI negotiators were instructed to ignore the Davidians' "Bible babble."

During the 51-day siege, the Davidians attempted to negotiate with FBI agents. The Davidians did not want to die, but they were not going to come out of Mount Carmel Center unless the exit process conformed to their understanding of biblical prophecies. Their ultimate concern was to achieve salvation by remaining faithful to God's will as expressed in biblical prophecies. Steve Schneider told an FBI negotiator that if Arnold could show the Davidians from the Bible that they should come out, they would come out no matter what David Koresh said.[20] As Seventh-day Adventists, the ultimate source of authority for the Branch Davidians was the Bible. David Koresh was open to revising his interpretation of biblical prophecies, but he could not come out without biblical sanction, because his authority as the Branch Davidian messiah was based upon what appeared to be his divinely inspired ability to interpret the Bible and its prophecies. Koresh had been wounded in the 28 February ATF raid and he was probably confused about how he could surrender and still make that scenario fit prophecies in the Bible.

On 1 April, Arnold and Tabor discussed the Bible on a radio show for the benefit of the Branch Davidians. The Davidians believed that as a result of the ATF assault they might be in the Fifth Seal of the book of Revelation, which says that after the agents of Babylon kill some members of the godly community, there will be a waiting period before the remaining believers will be martyred. The Branch Davidians were waiting to see what God had in store for them. In their radio discussion, Arnold and Tabor suggested that the waiting period would last more than a few months. They suggested that the biblical prophecies indicated that God wanted Koresh to come out to spread his message of salvation to the rest of the world.[21]

David Koresh spent Passover recuperating from his wounds and thinking over the situation. On 14 April, Koresh sent out a letter to the FBI stating that God the Father had given him permission to write a "little book" on the Seven Seals of Revelation. After the manuscript was in safekeeping with Arnold and Tabor, he and the Davidians would come out of Mount Carmel Center. The Branch Davidians' cheers at the prospect of coming out were recorded on a negotiation audiotape. On 15 April, the chief FBI negotiator at Mount Carmel Center told Justice Department officials that negotiations with the Davidians were going nowhere. On 16 April, David Koresh reported to negotiators that he had completed writing his interpretation of the First Seal, and the Davidians requested a word processor to speed up the production of Koresh's manuscript. The Davidians requested a word processor again on 17 April. On 18 April, the word processor was delivered to the Davidians, but the tanks also crushed and removed the remaining Davidian vehicles in preparation for an assault. David Koresh called a negotiator and asserted that the actions of the agents in the tanks contradicted the negotiators' claim that the FBI wanted a peaceful resolution. Koresh asked, "*What do you men really want?*" Koresh warned the negotiator that his ultimate loyalty was to God and that the actions of FBI agents were pushing him into a corner. On 19 April at 6:00 a.m., the tank and CS gas assault began what culminated in the fire which ignited at noon. The nine Davidians who escaped the fire included a woman who had a computer disk in her pocket on which was saved Koresh's interpretation of the First Seal.[22]

The intervention by Arnold and Tabor with the Branch Davidians had worked. David Koresh had been helped by these scholars to interpret the biblical prophecies in a manner that would have enabled the Davidians to come out safely from Mount Carmel Center. However, the FBI tank and CS gas assault probably convinced the Branch Davidians that God indeed intended for them to die at the hands of Babylon as predicted in the Fifth Seal as a major end-time event leading to Armageddon.

The careful reader will have noted that this chapter does *not* suggest that millennial groups cause religious violence. I have been saying that millennial groups or some new religious movements *become caught up* in violent episodes. Millennial groups involved in violence are not all the same. The comparative study of important violent incidents involving millennial groups reveals that they fall into three categories: assaulted millennial groups, fragile millennial groups, and revolutionary millennial movements.[23]

An assaulted millennial group, such as the Branch Davidians in 1993, is attacked because civilians and law enforcement agents regard the religious believers as dangerous. This often proves to be a mistaken judgment, as was the case with the Mormons in nineteenth-century America, the Lakota Sioux band massacred by American soldiers at Wounded Knee in 1890, and the police assault on a group of black Africans (Xhosa) calling themselves Israelites at Bulhoek, South Africa, in 1856.[24] Assaulted millennial groups are not rare.

Members of a fragile millennial group, such as the Jonestown residents and Aum Shinrikyo devotees, initiate violence because they perceive that they are failing to achieve their ultimate concern, the religious goal that is the most important thing in the world to them. Fragile millennial groups suffer from internal problems and external opposition that make the believers conclude that they are failing to achieve their ultimate concern, so they resort to violence to preserve their religious goal. In the instances of fragile millennial groups that initiate violence, the believers are likely to direct their violence both inwardly towards their own members and outwardly at perceived enemies in society. Always in these cases, *the quality of interactions* with people in society is crucial in creating a context in which the believers decide to take violent actions.

The exact balance of pressure from within the group and from outside the group will vary in each case. Jonestown suffered from *too much* hostile investigation and scrutiny from people in mainstream society; Aum Shinrikyo suffered from *too little* police investigation, and therefore, for a considerable period before the Tokyo subway attack, police overlooked the activities of Aum devotees in torturing and murdering people and acquiring weapons of mass destruction. The Jonestown residents had the goal of preserving the integrity of their community, which was endangered by the activities of aggressive apostates and concerned family members, sensational media coverage, and harassment by the Internal Revenue Service, the Customs Service, the U. S. Postal Service, and other federal agencies. The Jonestown community was also suffering from internal problems including the physical and mental decline of Jim Jones, financial difficulties, the challenge of supporting about a thousand people in the Guyanese jungle, disruptive dissidents, and long-term members giving up on the group's ultimate concern and leaving. The community was pushed over the edge by the unwelcome visit of Congressman Leo Ryan, whose party included representatives of Jonestown's avowed enemies, the federal government, reporters, relatives, and hostile former members. When some long-time members of Peoples' Temple decided to leave with Ryan, the Jonestown residents despaired of being able to maintain their community, their ultimate concern.[25]

Aum Shinrikyo's fragility was due primarily to internal stresses created by Shoko Asahara, who claimed to be a Buddha with the infallible ability to foretell the coming Armageddon. It was vital to the perpetuation of Aum Shinrikyo as a religion that Asahara's predictions not be disproved, because the guru's supernatural power and grace were believed to be the devotees' only means of achieving salvation. Although Asahara's inner circle of devotees was preparing to wage Armageddon against sinful society, the acts of violence committed against dissidents, people who wanted to leave, reporters, judges, and others in society who were seen as enemies, were designed to protect the religious organization from investigation and, therefore, protect the ultimate concern of creating the Buddhist millennial kingdom and the believed salvific authority of Shoko Asahara. When Aum devotees committed violence, Aum Shinrikyo was a fragile millennial group.[26]

In addition to assaulted millennial groups and fragile millennial groups, there are revolutionary millennial movements whose adherents commit violent acts to overthrow the current order to establish their millennial kingdom. When revolutionary millennial movements become socially dominant, they create vast amounts of suffering as World War II and the various Communist revolutions bear out. When revolutionary millennial movements are not socially dominant, their members resort to acts of terrorism.

It should be noted that these ideal types—assaulted millennial groups, fragile millennial groups, and revolutionary millennial movements—are dynamic categories. Circumstances and events can cause a group to move from one type to another. For instance, Aum Shinrikyo was preparing to become revolutionary, but police stopped its members from their violent activities before they could initiate revolutionary Armageddon. Twice federal agents assaulted the Branch Davidians, but they had the potential to become revolutionary in the future because David Koresh taught that the Davidians would go to Israel and fight on the side of the Israelis in the war of Armageddon that would occur in 1995. The ATF assault and the FBI psychological warfare waged against the

Davidians confirmed David Koresh's interpretations of biblical prophecies, so the Davidians were *not* a fragile millennial group. However, it is possible that the tank and CS gas assault on 19 April 1993 had the effect of pushing the Davidians finally over the edge to become a fragile millennial group, so that some of its members may have intentionally set the fire to make their situation conform to their understanding of biblical prophecies, thus enabling the Davidians to enter into God's heavenly kingdom by remaining faithful to God and his commands.

EVALUATING THE POTENTIAL FOR VOLATILITY

In evaluating a religious group for its potential to become caught up in violence, it is important that law enforcement agents remember that the *quality of interactions* with the group members contribute to whether or not there is potential for volatility. Any consideration of possible indicators for the potential for violence *is not predictive*. There is always the factor of human free will and there are many sociological, psychological, and even theological factors that may not be known at the time of the assessment. Szubin, Jensen, and Gregg cautioned that law enforcement agents needed to become informed about the group's worldview and that they should take their beliefs seriously.[27] The Branch Davidian tragedy illustrates what can happen if law enforcement agents disregard a group's religious beliefs. No matter how strange the beliefs appear to outsiders, the believers adhere to their religious faith sincerely because it makes sense to them. Szubin, Jensen, and Gregg advise law enforcement agents to assume that the leader sincerely believes in the doctrines that he or she teaches, even if they appear to be self-serving. It is a mistake to approach an unconventional religious group with the assumption that the leader is a con man. Likewise, law enforcement agents make a mistake if they assume that religious believers are brainwashed and cannot think for themselves. It is a *serious* mistake to rely solely on a psychological diagnosis of a religious leader when assessing a group.[28] Solely applying a psychological label to one member of a community, which may or may not be correct, does not contribute to the interdisciplinary analysis that is needed to understand fully a religious group. Insights from the disciplines of psychology, sociology, law enforcement, and religious studies, which pays particular attention to theology and worldviews, are all relevant in a good assessment of a religious group's potential to become caught up in violence.

When a religious group is suspected of breaking the law, ordinary and careful investigative measures should be taken. Whenever possible, law enforcement agents should meet with believers and cultivate positive relations with them. As long as it does not endanger law enforcement agents, it is best to give the believers the opportunity to cooperate with the investigation. David Koresh, for instance, had a record of cooperating with the investigations of law enforcement agents and social workers. David Koresh had invited ATF agents to inspect his guns and this invitation was ignored in favor of launching a no-knock, dynamic entry against Mount Carmel Center. The ATF undercover agent who had spent time inside Mount Carmel Center had reported that there was no evidence that the Davidians possessed illegal weapons.[29]

Certain characteristics of religious groups and their interactions with members of mainstream society suggest that they have the potential to become caught up in episodes of violence. A significant number of these characteristics in relation to a religious group should indicate to law enforcement agents that they should exercise even more moderate and careful methods in dealing with the group. The characteristics that cause concern can be counteracted by other characteristics that a group will not become caught up in violence.

CHARACTERISTICS THAT CAUSE CONCERN

The characteristics that cause concern can be grouped under the three headings of "interaction factors," "internal factors," and "belief factors."[30]

Interaction Factors

1. The group is labeled with a pejorative term such as "cult" or "sect" by members of mainstream society, and it is the target of a great deal of aggressive activity on the part of the media, government and law enforcement agents, concerned relatives, and disgruntled former members.
2. The group is extremely resistant to investigation, and either aggressively battles against its perceived enemies or withdraws to an isolated refuge.
3. As a result of conflict and opposition from mainstream society, the group abandons proselytizing to gain new converts, and turns inward to preserve salvation for its members alone.
4. The group has already engaged in a violent conflict with law enforcement agents in which agents have died.

These characteristics describe a group that is in strong conflict with society. The group's opponents as well as the believers possess a rigid dualistic worldview of "us versus them," good versus evil. They are locked in a battle that can accelerate. The believers' radical dualism is expressed in their excessively combative responses to their perceived enemies, or by their withdrawal from society to an isolated refuge. Because of the social opposition that they experience, the believers may decide to stop proselytizing; they resolve that salvation is extended only to current members of their group. Their social opponents dehumanize the believers by calling them "cultists." The believers dehumanize members of mainstream society by regarding them as aligned with evil forces.

The religious group is especially prone to be caught up in further violence if it has already engaged in a violent conflict in which law enforcement agents have died, as was the case with the Weaver family at Ruby Ridge and the Branch Davidians at Mount Carmel Center. Law enforcement agents need to become aware of their propensity to take punitive violent actions against a group they deem responsible for the deaths of colleagues. Both at Ruby Ridge and Mount Carmel Center, law enforcement agents magnified the threat posed by the Weaver family and the Davidians, and they failed to consider that the actions of law enforcement agents contributed to the tragic loss of life of their colleagues.

Internal Factors

5. Believers take an extremely literal approach to interpreting scriptures and other texts that are important to the group.
6. Followers are overly dependent on a charismatic leader (who claims authority from an unseen source, such as God) as the sole means to achieve their ultimate concern (salvation).
7. The leader's charismatic authority has not yet been routinized into institutional structures and decisionmaking bodies and offices.
8. The charismatic leader has set goals for the group that is in danger of being disproven by physical events.
9. The group's leader gives new identities to the followers, including new names, and drastically rearranges the believers' family and marriage relationships.
10. Leaving the group involves very high "exit costs"[31] in terms of personal identity, family and friendship associations, and livelihood.
11. The group exists in an isolated situation, so that members are not exposed to alternative interpretations of reality.
12. Acts of violence are repeated in a ritualistic manner, so that the scale and intensity of the violence increases.

Many of the religious groups that have been involved in violence, including the Branch Davidians, Heaven's Gate, and individuals associated with Christian Identity follow a literal approach to interpreting scriptures and other texts. They think they are interpreting scripture literally, when in fact they are exercising a selective reading. Their rigid manner of reading texts is not sensitive to ambiguity and subtlety in the meaning of the texts, and they take little or no account of the historical and social circumstances that produced them. This literal approach to reading "sacred" texts appears to be related to the rigid dualism that characterizes their patterns of thinking.

There does not have to be a charismatic leader for the group to be potentially violent. For instance, the Montana Freemen who were involved in an 81-day standoff with FBI agents in 1996 were Identity Christians, who threatened violence and hoped to initiate the second American Revolution, but did not have a charismatic leader. They possessed a revolutionary ideology that contained the potential to motivate the Freemen to commit violent acts.[32] But some religious communities become overly dependent on a charismatic leader as being the sole means of attaining salvation. This gives considerable scope for a leader to abuse his or her power over followers if there are no checks on the leader's authority. Again, it is important to stress that this does not mean that followers are not able to think for themselves. They can, at any time, withdraw their allegiance and hence undermine the leader's charismatic authority. An overdependence on a charismatic leader to achieve the ultimate concern can imperil the group's ultimate concern if the leader is in danger of being removed by death or arrest, which may prompt followers to resort to violent actions in order to safeguard the ultimate concern.

Charismatic leaders often make predictions that are disconfirmed by physical events. The leader then usually provides a reinterpretation that the followers find satisfying. If the group's failure to achieve goals set by the leader calls into question whether they will achieve their ultimate concern, however, then group members may resort to violent actions to preserve their ultimate concern.

There are numerous new religious movements who make high demands on followers, which do not become involved in violence. However, I regard members permitting leaders to give them new identities and to rearrange their family relationships as giving too much authority to a leader who may turn out to be unworthy or on an ego trip.

People leave high demand groups all the time. However, if leaving the group involves high costs in terms of one's identity, friendships, family associations, and economic survival, then it is possible that members might choose to die together or attack perceived enemies rather than abandon a failing ultimate concern.

The level of isolation of a community will vary. For instance, the Branch Davidians had regular interactions with their neighbors and some had jobs outside Mount Carmel Center. The Davidians welcomed an undercover agent inside Mount Carmel Center even though they had a good idea that he was a law enforcement agent. FBI agents imposed the isolation of the Branch Davidians during the siege. Jonestown was a community isolated in the

Guyanese jungle with the news of outside events controlled and interpreted by Jim Jones. Aum Shinrikyo devotees ran businesses that catered to the general public as well as lived in communes. Their isolation was self-imposed by the worldview that they adopted. The same was true of the Montana Freemen inside Justus Township who had Internet connection with likeminded believers.

I have discussed above how ritualized acts of violence can escalate.

Belief Factors

13. The group has catastrophic millennial and dualistic beliefs that expect and promote conflict.
14. The group's millennial beliefs are related to a radical dualistic view of good versus evil that dehumanizes other people.
15. The group combines apocalyptic millennial beliefs with a conviction that the group is being persecuted.
16. Belief in reincarnation is combined with catastrophic millennialism and belief that the group is being persecuted.
17. The theology expresses the view that this Earth is not the believers' true home.
18. The group members' sense of being persecuted is expressed in strong belief in conspiracy theories.

While most millennialists never become involved in violence, many religious groups that become caught up in violence have apocalyptic or catastrophic millennial worldviews. Catastrophic millennialism involves a radical dualism that expects conflict and can even promote it. This rigid dualism has the effect of dehumanizing others outside the group who are deemed to be enemies. Such dehumanization exacerbates the conflict and can sanction the murder of those who are dehumanized; they are seen as not being worthy of life.

Apocalypticism, the expectation that the world will soon be destroyed, can devalue earthly existence in the eyes of the believers. If the believers feel authorities are persecuting them, there may be greater temptation for them either to leave this sinful world through death or to commit violence against their persecutors, who in their eyes are obviously aligned with Satan. A belief in reincarnation is not usually related to violence, but the cases of Jonestown, Aum Shinrikyo, Heaven's Gate (1997), and Solar Temple (deaths in 1994, 1995, 1997 in Switzerland, France, and Quebec) suggest that the combination of belief in reincarnation with apocalypticism and a conviction that the group is being persecuted can be an especially lethal mixture, which radically devalues earthly life and can prompt some believers to commit murder, suicide, or both to prevent the failure of their ultimate concern. If the theology already emphasizes that the Earth is not the believers' true home, then this will receive heightened emphasis when there is persecution, and may be used as justification for leaving earthly life. The believers' sense of being persecuted will be expressed in a strong adherence to conspiracy theories.

Reassuring Characteristics

1. The group is not being attacked by hostile opponents such as reporters, concerned relatives, apostates, government agents, and law enforcement agents.
2. The group openly and constructively responds to questions and investigations about their beliefs and activities.
3. The believers strive to be good citizens and neighbors in their surrounding community.
4. The group is active in evangelization to extend salvation to others, but it is not preaching a hate-filled ideology.
5. The group and its leader have made clear statements against the use of violence.
6. The leader has made statements indicating a willingness to reinterpret predictions that are likely to fail, or has indicated a willingness to be flexible about the goals set for the group.

Note that the first of the reassuring characteristics involves the absence of opposition by avowed enemies of the religious group. Again, *the quality of the interactions* of people in mainstream society with members of unconventional religious groups is crucial in determining whether the group will become caught up in violence. The second reassuring characteristic is that when there is suspicion and opposition directed toward the religious group, the members respond in a healthy constructive manner to answer questions and cooperate with investigators. Correspondingly, the believers will participate as good citizens and neighbors in their surrounding context.

The believers might actively proselytize to extend salvation to others, as were the Branch Davidians, who, when their access to the public was cut off, tried to convert the FBI negotiators. This was a group that was not likely to take hostile actions against mainstream society. However, revolutionary millennialists can be very active in proselytizing, while also preaching a hate-filled ideology, such as Christian Identity or Nazism that can prompt believers to attack and kill the hated "others."

Statements against violence issued by the group and the leader need to be analyzed very carefully. For instance, Heaven's Gate posted a statement against suicide on its website, but the members defined their self-administered deaths in 1997 as an "exit" to a heavenly salvation on the mother ship instead of a group suicide.[33] It is a good sign if the group and its leader make clear statements against suicide, but it should be recalled that theological interpretations and religious methods to achieve the ultimate concern are changed in response to circumstances and events. A great deal of persecution can push the members of a peaceful group to resort to violence, either against themselves or their enemies, or both, to preserve their ultimate concern.

If the leader has made predictions that are likely to fail, it is reassuring if he or she indicates ahead of time a willingness to reinterpret. However, charismatic leaders most often make reinterpretations anyway when their predictions fail.[34] If the group is failing to achieve goals related to the ultimate concern, an expressed willingness on the part of the leader and the members to be flexible about the goal is likewise reassuring.

CONCLUSION

A religious group's theology is constantly being adjusted in response to events within the group, events in society, and the interactions that believers have with nonbelievers. Furthermore, members of a religious group will inevitably have different interpretations of the theology. Religious beliefs motivate people to take actions of various sorts, but those beliefs are often adjusted in response to events. A group can shift from being one that causes concern for its potential to be caught up in violence, to one that is not cause for great concern, or vice versa. Individuals and their social interactions are never static. Law enforcement agents, meanwhile, make a grave mistake if they think that the propensity to create violent religious incidents only resides with members of unconventional religions. *The manner in which all of us interact with members of religious movements helps to determine the potential for volatility.*

If a religious group is assessed to have a number of the factors that give cause for concern, that is an indication that a more thorough investigation is needed, and that law enforcement agents should deal with the group very cautiously, using moderate means. Law enforcement agents should avoid taking aggressive actions that make the believers feel persecuted and are likely to cause loss of life. Law enforcement agents have the challenging job of attempting to prevent violent acts by members of revolutionary millennial movements, while refraining from unnecessarily assaulting a religious group, or applying so much pressure to a group that it becomes fragile, prompting its members to initiate violence to preserve their ultimate concern.

Chapter 8

Christian Reconstructionism after Y2K

Gary North, the New Millennium, and Religious Freedom

Adam C. English

During the so-called Y2K crisis, many would-be technological prophets and prognosticators predicted a computer meltdown on 1 January 2000. The reason? For the past three decades, programmers used the last two digits of the century instead of all four when installing the calendaring function on computers. Sometime in 1997, various programmers like Ed Yourdon began to suspect that when the date rolled to "00," computers would read it as "1900" and not "2000." It was conjectured that such an error would result in widespread computer malfunction and/or shutdown. The thought of such an occurrence prompted some to consider the implications of a worldwide temporary computer failure. The results of such an occurrence were predicted to be dire. And perhaps no one was as fervent about the gravity of the circumstances as Gary North.

In 1997, Gary North launched a website, www.garynorth. com, warning the public of the imminent technological disaster. The site boasted over six thousand documents on Y2K as well as links to hundreds of other sites. It was even equipped with a "Doomsday Computer" simulator that calculated the probability of computer malfunction. According to the site:

> At 12 midnight on January 1, 2000 (a Saturday morning), most of the world's mainframe computers will either shut down or begin spewing out bad data. Most of the world's desktop computers will also start spewing

out bad data. Tens of millions—possibly hundreds of millions—of pre-programmed computer chips will begin to shut down the systems they automatically control. This will create a nightmare for every area of life, in every region of the industrialized world.[1]

Along with an uncounted number of governmental and business computers, perhaps as many as 300 million personal computers were noncompliant early in 1999 and would be subject to malfunctioning. What kind of turmoil would erupt with an unchecked Y2K crisis? According to North, months before 1 January, the world's stock markets will have crashed because everyone will have taken their money out of banks. After 1 January, all levels of orderly business both in the states and abroad will grind to a halt. Without their databases, governments will no longer be able to collect taxes because they will not be able to trace people and compel them to pay. Within a matter of time, governments will collapse due to lack of funding or anarchy, whichever comes first.[2]

A PREMILL OR POSTMILL CRISIS?

North's grim prophecies sound uncannily similar to the predictions of premillennial dispensationalists like Hal Lindsey who was popular in the 1970s. Indeed, North has always been drawn to the year 2000. As early as 1990, North had a premonition that something cataclysmic would happen at the turn of the millennium.[3] But, does that make him a date-setter? Is he just another doomsday premillennialist stoking the flames of fear and apocalyptic hype? Ironically, the answer must be "no." On first glance, it is often assumed that Reconstructionists like North are premillennialists (which involves the belief that Jesus Christ will rapture his church before a thousand-year reign of peace and final judgment). Nevertheless, Christian Reconstructionism is a staunchly postmillennial group. In fact, North often attacks premillennialists in his monthly newsletters and has even authored book-length exposés on them, including such titles as *Millennialism and Social Theory* and *Rapture Fever: Why Dispensationalism is Paralyzed*.[4] Why then was he so distressed about the Y2K situation? Why do his warnings have an end-of-the-world tenor? Y2K was to be a catastrophic event, but of the postmillennial, not premillennial type. What does this mean? Unlike the premillennialists of the past who were noted for their gloom-and-doom, end-of-the-world predictions and their mantra-like call to "Repent Now! The End is Near!," North did not see 2000 as "the end of the world."

North, and the overwhelming majority of Y2K pop-commentators, urged America to make preparations to *survive* Y2K. The question was not, "Will we still be here after 1 January?" but instead, "Will we be prepared to survive whatever is on the other side of 1 January?" A search of Amazon.com for books on Y2K turns up 209 titles, including *101 Ways to Survive the Y2K Crisis; 3 Steps to Y2K Readiness for the Home and Family; About Y2K Survival: Handbook and Guide to Practical Preparations for the Year 2000 and Beyond; Act Y2K Small Business Workbook; Action Y2K: A GrassRoots Guide to the Year 2000; Are You Ready? Y2K Challenge; Beat the Beast!—Y2K Preparedness Guidebook;* and *Building Your Ark: Your Personal Survival Guide to the Year 2000 Crisis.*[5] As is evident from this partial listing, most of the Y2K books are not pessimistic, gloom-and-doom farewells to life. They are pro-active, do-it-yourself survival manuals. As people took the advice of these manuals, they stockpiled canned food, water, guns, gasoline, and other supplies—determined to "beat the blackout." They did not, like the nineteenth-century Millerites, find a tall tree to sit in so that they would be closer to the Lord when he came out of heaven to rapture them on 1 January. It appears that the Y2K crisis, if nothing else, was certainly *not* a premillennialist crisis. Y2K never was the end of the world for North or any other Y2K prophet—far from it.

So what was the impetus behind North's Y2K scare? Besides feeling a genuine sense of responsibility to warn the world about the imminent technological, social, and political cataclysm, it seems that North envisioned the Y2K crisis as his chance for his lifelong project to reach fulfillment. It was a ray of hope for the establishment of God's theonomy (rule by biblical law) in America:

> The Y2K crisis is systemic. It cannot possibly be fixed. . . . I think the U.S.A. will break up the way the U.S.S.R. did. Call me a dreamer. Call me an optimist. That's what I think. This will decentralize the social order. That is what I have wanted all of my adult life. In my view, Y2K is our deliverance.[6]

A Y2K disaster would provide the type of worldwide breakdown needed for Christians to step forward, take the reins of leadership, and establish a biblically-based society. Yet, the "reconstruction" of society would not be from the top-down, issuing from an autocratic or oligarchic Christian government. Instead, it would be "from the bottom-up: *self-government under God.*"[7] Millions of souls would have to be supernaturally transformed so that they would submit to the government of biblical law. In what manner would this occur? Another quotation from North is appropriate:

> The postmillennialist is anti-apocalyptic. He knows that God breaks into history, but God does this by using the familiar processes of Church history: evangelism, the sacraments, Church discipline, civil justice, and family order. He will send the Holy Spirit to transform billions of individual hearts, and the regenerate then use the familiar tools of dominion to extend God's kingdom in history. This is *conquest by conversion.*[8]

Of course, 1 January 2000 came and went without the collapse of computers and government. The so-called "false prophets" of the millennium immediately became the objects of ridicule. Gary North was no exception, as illustrated by the Internet site entitled: "Gary North is a Big Fat Idiot."[9]

Understandably, many questioned his "genuineness" and honesty concerning his Y2K warnings. Concerned Christians such as Steve Hewitt of *Christian Computing* magazine surmised that the Reconstructionists were making a profit from people's fears by selling Y2K videos and books.[10] It is not unimaginable that North benefited financially from the hype, but he could easily respond that the majority of his writings on Y2K were available for free on the Internet. Indeed, one of his websites is called www.freebooks.com.

Part of the difficulty in unraveling North's stance regarding Y2K revolves around the categories "postmillennialism" and "premillennialism" (not to mention a third category, "amillennialism"). Catherine Wessinger has attempted to resolve some of the confused terminology by suggesting the more descriptive labels: "catastrophic millennialism" and "progressive millennialism." Catastrophic millennialists (i.e. premillennial dispensationalists) hold a pessimistic view of humanity and believe that the current world order must be destroyed in order for a new, millennial kingdom to enter. Progressive millennialists (presumably North) have a more optimistic view of humanity and believe that social work and divine assistance will gradually usher in a utopian world order.[11] While Wessinger's tag describes fairly accurately the Reconstructionist position, there are two reasons to resist it. First, the Reconstructionists prefer the term "postmillennialist" because it locates them within a certain tradition. Thus, Greg Bahnsen called himself a "evangelical postmillennialist," Ray Sutton "covenantal postmillennialist," Kenneth Gentry "progressive postmillennialist," and North "judicial postmillennialist."[12] While different Reconstructionists adopt different adjectival qualifiers, all use the appellation, "postmillennialist." Second, unlike the progressive millennialists, the Reconstructionists do not have an optimistic view of humanity. They are strict Calvinists, believing above all else that people are totally depraved and will never progress without conversion. The progress toward the millennium reign of peace will not occur through social work, but rather through the divine work of the Holy Spirit on both individuals and institutions. Social and political progress in history depends upon divine, not human effort. Consequently, one way to explain North's obsession with the year 2000 is that he, like the premillennialists who look for signs of Christ's return, was looking for a sign of God's imminent "victory." Y2K was to be a sign that God was disrupting the social order to clear the ground for his theonomy.

Besides decoding the cumbersome categories of "postmillennial," "premillennial," and "amillennial," one must exegete the label "Christian Reconstructionism." This study will provide a brief sketch of Christian Reconstructionism's history and beliefs in order to set the stage for understanding North's views on the millennium and religious liberty.

A SHORT HISTORICAL SKETCH OF THE CHRISTIAN RECONSTRUCTION MOVEMENT

The most proper place to begin any history of Christian Reconstructionism (hereafter CR) is with the Westminster Seminary professor, Cornelius Van Til. Although he never condoned or affiliated with CR, he is in many ways the grandfather of the Reconstructionist project. Called the "demolition expert," Van Til systematically called into question the intellectual grounds of all aspects of modern secular society. In his books and lectures, he presented a rigorous apologetic for the Christian faith. The problem was that after he "detonated" the foundations of secularism, he did not leave "blueprints for the reconstruction of society."[13] Enter Rousas John Rushdoony, the father of the movement. While he appreciated the work of Van Til, he believed Christianity had to do more than simply dismantle secularism; it needed to offer a means to positively rebuild society according to biblical principles. Thus, in 1965, he started the Chalcedon Foundation[14] in Southern California that began publishing the monthly Chalcedon Report and hosting seminars and workshops. In 1973, the foundation began to gain momentum with the publication of Rushdoony's *Institutes of Biblical Law*. During the same year, Greg Bahnsen and Gary North joined the staff of Chalcedon. Rushdoony, Bahnsen, and North together formed the original triumvirate of the Reconstructionists.

All three share a Calvinistic Presbyterian background. All hold earned doctorate degrees: Rushdoony in educational philosophy, Bahnsen in philosophy, and North in history. All are prolific writers (over eighty books can be attributed to North and Rushdoony alone). All three are fiercely independent; they worked together until 1981 when North and Rushdoony clashed over a seemingly minor issue in one of North's articles. Although North is Rushdoony's son-in-law, the two men did not speak to each other for the final twenty years of Rushdoony's life. A permanent rift was generated within the movement between North and the Chalcedon group. The argument between the two camps became so vehement that in 1995 North and Chalcedon's Andrew Sandlin signed a "truce."[15] This is significant in our discussion of the Y2K crisis because the Chalcedon Foundation did not jump on the Y2K bandwagon like North but neither did it oppose it. Did they silently concur with North's analysis? Or, more likely, were they adhering to their agreement to avoid North altogether? Either way, any discussion of the millennial expectations of Christian Reconstructionists with regard to Y2K must be limited to North and others who openly advocate his position. As a consequence, this study will concentrate primarily on North, drawing upon other Reconstructionists as they either support or refute North.

At any rate, after the falling-out, North moved to Tyler, Texas and launched the Institute for Christian Economics, which publishes various monthly journals and books. North lived in Tyler until some months before the turn of the millennium when he relocated to a secluded location in Arkansas. Bahnsen moved to Orange County, California, where he pastored a small Orthodox Presbyterian church and served as dean of a teacher's college graduate school until his untimely death in 1999. His place among the leaders of the movement has been silently transferred to Gary DeMar, president of American Vision, an educational ministry out of Atlanta, Georgia. Although coming to the fore later than the others, DeMar has positioned himself as a spokesperson for Reconstructionism alongside North and Rushdoony by authoring such books as *The Debate over Christian Reconstruction* and coauthoring *Christian Reconstruction: What It Is, What It Isn't* with North. Meanwhile, Rushdoony continued to direct a twelve-member staff at the Chalcedon Foundation until his death in February 2001. Well before Rushdoony's death, most of the operational responsibilities had already been handed over to Andrew Sandlin, the foundation's executive vice president. Sandlin, author of *Christianity: Bulwark of Liberty*, continues to rise in stature among the second generation Reconstructionists.

Reconstructionism experienced its greatest flourish in the late 1980s. It became especially popular among Reformed and Orthodox Presbyterians, as well as others associated with the Presbyterian Church of America and, more broadly, Christian fundamentalism in general. Along with its popularity, major Christian publishers like Crossway and Thomas Nelson began to release Reconstructionist titles. Pat Robertson, Jerry Falwell, and Franky Schaeffer V read Reconstructionist books and endorsed the movement. Gary North estimated that between 25,000 and 40,000 names were on various Reconstructionist mailing lists during that time. It was not long until *Newsweek* had named the Chalcedon Foundation as the Religious Right "think tank." Articles about the CR began appearing in the *Christian Century, Christianity Today, Westminster Theological Journal,* and *First Things.*[16] Clearly, the movement was gaining recognition. But, as soon as it stepped into the spotlight, its popularity began to plateau and fade. And then, the Y2K crisis arrived.

WHAT IS CHRISTIAN RECONSTRUCTIONISM?

What do Reconstructionists believe? The big picture is rather complex for a number of reasons. First, a shroud of technical, "insider" jargon veils the heart of CR. Consider, for example, the boggled definition of Christian Reconstructionism given by Michael Gabbert:

> Christian Reconstructionism is a complex movement of neo-Puritan scholars and evangelical Calvinist theology. Drawing history and the Scriptures together, Reconstructionists attempt to combine a dominion-

oriented, postmillennial understanding of theonomy with various historical examples of anti-Erastian church-state structures. The goal of the
movement is to integrate every aspect of American life into a consistent
worldview based upon the abiding validity of the Old-Testament Law in
exhaustive detail.[17]

Could this definition be any more convoluted? One reason why CR has
been so often misunderstood is because it is hard to define, as exemplified by
Gabbert's good-natured attempt. Yet, CR does not help its own case when it
comes to intelligibility. The movement makes some very radical claims on issues
ranging from politics, economics, and sociology, to education, historiography,
and theology. Inevitably, these claims are exaggerated by detractors and misunderstood by analysts. As a result, the underlying seminal beliefs are neglected by
all. Academia has yet to correct the problem of misunderstanding; the majority of academic reviews and critiques of CR have capitalized on its eccentric and
sometimes shocking pronouncements.[18] In essence, scholars have repudiated
and discarded CR as an extreme fundamentalist fad.

Fortunately, Gary DeMar and Andrew Sandlin have helped resolve the confusion by outlining CR's major tenets. Each has independently composed lists
of non-negotiable Reconstructionist beliefs. We will combine the lists of both
DeMar and Sandlin and propose five key tenets of CR. Hopefully, these will
provide a framework for understanding the movement.

1. Calvinism.[19] DeMar differs with Sandlin on the first tenet. He suggests
"Regeneration" is the primary belief of CR, not Calvinism. Both in his 1988
and his 1991 definitions of CR, regeneration is first. However, Calvinism
remains the first tenet here because it qualifies the type of regeneration that
occurs. When Reconstructionists speak of regeneration, they are specifically
referring to a Calvinistic understanding of the event.[20] Calvinistic theology is a
non-negotiable component of Reconstructionism. Full adherence to the five
points of the TULIP[21] is expected of the Reconstructionist. Sandlin asserts the
true Reconstructionist "holds to historic, orthodox, Catholic Christianity and
the great Reformed confessions. He believes God, not man, is the center of the
universe and beyond; God, not man, controls whatever comes to pass; God, not
man, must be pleased and obeyed."[22] Calvinism's emphasis on correct dogma,
biblical law, God's rule, and Christianized government form an excellent theological foundation for the advancement of Reconstructionist ideology. Not only
is Calvinistic theology adhered to, even the failed historical instantiations of
Calvinism in Geneva and America become authoritative exemplars of a
Christian society.[23]

2. Biblical law. "The continuing validity and applicability of the whole law
of God, including, but not limited to, the Mosaic case laws."[24] This "law" is the
standard for individual, familial, ecclesiastical, economic, and governmental
conduct. It is alternatively known as "theonomy." Theonomy is the key term for
a form of government characterized by God's direct and personal rule over soci-

ety ("Reconstructionist" is often interchanged with "theonomist"). However, since the inerrancy debates of the 1980s, theonomy has come to mean more than just God's law; it means *biblical* law. Thus, Sandlin suggests that a more precise term is "biblionomy." He goes on to say:

> As a theological expression, it means the abiding authority of all the Bible's teachings, unless the Bible itself asserts that those teachings have been fulfilled or rescinded (for example, such distinctively Jewish practices as the national feasts and festivals, circumcision and the Passover). The law of the Old Testament as the authority for the believer and all of society has not been set aside.[25]

Bahnsen defended this idea in his 1985 seminal work, *By This Standard,* by saying that, "[W]e presume our obligation to obey any Old Testament commandment unless the New Testament indicates otherwise. We must assume continuity with the Old Testament."[26] Although many Christians would agree that a continuity exists between the Old and New Testaments, the continuity is normally defined as "spiritual" or religious, but not sociological or liturgical. Bahnsen, by contrast, believed that "the New Testament does not teach any radical change in God's law regarding the standards of *socio-political morality.*"[27] The Pentateuch should be studied and applied by legislators and jurors in the same manner that the U.S. Constitution is studied and applied.[28] This is affirmed by Sandlin's statement in the declaration that the Old Testament laws remain valid not only for individual believers, but for "all of society." Those who reject such an approach are labeled "antinomian" in the same way that those who reject the authority of the Constitution are labeled "anti-American."

CR's idealistic affirmation of continuity quickly encounters trouble. Modern civility and humanity have disavowed such practices as slavery and stoning, which are discussed in the Old and New Testament. But, loyal to their convictions, the Reconstructionists uphold all of the Law, including some of the unsavory dictates of Pentateuchal law such as capital punishment[29] and slavery statutes.[30]

3. Presuppositional apologetics. Presuppositionalism is an idea that comes directly from Van Til, who argued that religious faith should not be established or debunked on the basis of historical or scientific investigation. Rather, faith presupposes certain realities without proof. For instance, the Christian must presuppose God exists and that the Bible is true in order to come to faith in Christ because God's existence cannot be proved or disproved scientifically. Reconstructionists extend this idea to contend that every belief about reality, religious or not, is loaded with presuppositions. Modernity's confidence in impartiality and neutrality is a myth. Theonomists recognize that there is no such thing as an unbiased government, unbiased science, or unbiased education. Indeed, such institutions are biased—they are biased toward secularism. And on the other hand, theonomists admit that they are biased towards biblical law. So because North presupposes biblical law to be *the key* to Christianity

and the world, he can claim, "The battle of the mind is between the Christian reconstruction movement, which alone among Protestant groups takes serious-ly the law of God, and everyone else."[31]

In the Van Tillian defense of the faith, the objective is not to prove the empirical validity of Christianity's claims. Rather, the argument proceeds along these lines: "Yes, as a Christian I assume certain realities by faith, but so does the non-Christian. They simply presuppose different realities by a similar leap of faith." What is significant about this form of apologetics is that it never lets an intellectual opponent have the upper hand. It simply asserts the superiority of the Christian faith based on biblical revelation. Furthermore, it provides a rationale for stances that are uncompromising and even intolerant.

4. Decentralized social order. This point is probably CR's most pragmatic and strategic. CR espouses a "minimal state." Reconstructionists seek to reduce the power of the state and give power to the individual, the family, the church, and various local structures.[32] They see that democracy is an unattainable hoax. In fact, Rushdoony has called democracy a "heresy."[33] Democracy, rule by the people, is a fantasy that will never be obtained and furthermore, it is not a form of government legitimized by the Bible. The solution: "self-government under biblical law." This will be further elaborated under the heading below on "Religious Liberty."

5. Postmillennialism. As mentioned earlier, postmillennialism is the belief that Christ will return after the thousand-year period of peace described in Revelation 20 (symbolically understood). It provides key motivation for Reconstructionist hope. According to DeMar, "A victorious view of the future progress of the kingdom of God prior to the return of Christ is foundational for the building of a Christian civilization."[34] As mentioned earlier, a progres-sive view of history is central. Just seven months before the turn of the millen-nium, Gary North was emphatically insisting upon a linearly progressive under-standing of history in his bimonthly newsletter, *Biblical Economics Today*.[35] At any rate, Reconstructionists intend to prepare the way for the eventual thou-sand-year reign of peace. Their goal is to get people ready to reinstitute biblical law in civic life. During this millennial reign, government will not be by democracy but by theonomy.

Here enters the genius of Y2K. Not only did 1 January 2000 signal the inau-guration of a new millennium (at least in the popular mind), it also became the herald of potential worldwide disaster. A catastrophic collapse of life as we know it would actually prepare the world for a new world order—a millennial, theonomist world order. When the millennium begins, regenerated man (the masculine is used intentionally) will regain dominion over the earth, a domin-ion that was lost in Paradise. "Dominion" has become a key term for the belief that, during the millennium, Christians will be given authority over the entire world. It has become so important that Andrew Sandlin lists "Dominionism" as one of the five core beliefs of Reconstructionism.[36] Conveniently, in the mil-lennium reign, Christians will be charged with the duty of enforcing God's law on those who do not submit. "Those who refuse to submit publicly to the eternal sanctions of God by submitting to His Church's public marks of the covenant— baptism and holy communion—must be denied citizenship, just as they were in ancient Israel."[37]

RELIGIOUS LIBERTY: A QUESTIONABLE NOTION

So, what is to become of religious liberty? In the theonomist utopia, there will be no toleration for "pagan" religions. North asserts:

> [W]e must use the doctrine of religious liberty to gain independence for Christian schools until we train up a generation of people who know that there is no religious neutrality, no neutral law, no neutral education, and no neutral civil government. Then they will get busy in constructing a Bible-based social, political and religious order which finally denies the religious liberty of the enemies of God.[38]

According to this quotation, religious liberty is a useful tool to Christians in the present world order, yet it is ultimately to be denied to anyone who is not Christian once Christians are in power. Such a position is not unique to North. Even Rushdoony, who was a vocal advocate of political, religious, and ecclesiastical liberty, as demonstrated in his books, *The Nature of the American System* and *This Independent Republic*, believed that religious liberty was ultimately a fantasy. He saw that every law is nothing more than "enacted morality" extracted from some sort of religious assumptions, whether theistic or non-theistic. In other words, there are no religiously neutral moral principles and thus there are no religiously neutral laws. According to Rushdoony, America operates out of humanism—a very real and definite religion disguised as nonreligious, objective neutrality.[39] So, the question is not, "Will government be religious or non-religious?," but rather, "Which religion will the government follow?"[40] At this juncture one may wonder if the Reconstructionists are being paradoxical or are they inconsistent? They advocate the separation of church and state, yet long for the restoration of a "Christian America." They advocate the right to home-school, yet oppose prayer in school. They label democracy a heresy, yet champion political involvement and voting rights. They advocate religious liberty all the while denying the reality of the notion. Are they talking out of both sides of their mouths? Perhaps. Or maybe the situation is not as clear-cut as it appears.

True to their Reformed heritage, North, Rushdoony, and the other Reconstructionists do not understand "liberty" (political, religious, or otherwise) outside of a theological context. Authentic liberty is only found in a salvific encounter with Jesus Christ. Anyone outside of the Christian faith is in bondage. It is important to note that one of the most elemental presuppositions undergirding all Reconstructionist thought is the tripartite division of life: person, family, government. These are the three basic spheres of life. Each sphere has its own members, structure, rules, authority, and dominion. If Christians believe that God is lord over their person and their family, then why not their government? The Bible makes provision for each sphere of life and gives ultimate authority over all areas to God. Thus, if coming under the lordship of Christ on a personal level is not oppressive but rather liberating (as evangelical Christians claim), then similarly, government by rigorous theonomy is not oppressive but liberating. This is dramatized by the cover illustration on North's 1987 *Liberating Planet Earth: An Introduction to Biblical Blueprints.* Pictured on the cover is the earth encircled by chain links that are fastened together by a padlock with the inscription, "Adam Locks." Hovering above the keyhole of the lock is a silver key with an imprint of the cross. The message is clear: the problem with the world and its inhabitants is spiritual, not social, economic, political, or otherwise, and thus the solution is spiritual. North explains:

> Liberty and God's law: the two are inseparable. He who preaches against the law of God preaches against liberty. Anyone who says that we can build our lives, our families, our churches, or our civil governments on any foundation other than the law of God, and still have liberty, is a liar. He is a deceiver. He is laying the foundation of tyranny.[41]

When Reconstructionists participate in public debates about society, education, and politics, they formulate the issues and answers in a spiritual (more specifically "biblical") vocabulary. They give no consideration to accommodationist or politically correct jargon. If this consideration is lost, confusion about how to interpret CR quickly arises.

It is often assumed that Reconstructionists conspire to realize their millennial "dominion" through some version of the Holy Roman Empire or Constantinian Christianity (and certainly such an expectation would provide another rationale for CR's denial of pluralistic religious liberty). Yet, CR vigorously denies such suppositions. In a seminal article on "Covenantal Postmillennialism," Ray Sutton repudiates any topdown governmentally enforced religion (which he calls "Charlemagne's triumphalism"). He also rejects the rule of society by an institutional church (i.e. the Holy Roman Empire experiment). Sutton even foregoes the idea of a revivalistic postmillennialism (in this scenario there is no institutional expression of the millennium, but rather worldwide personal revivals). He refuses this option because the millennial reign must be institutional as well as personal. Sutton contends that any hope in a millennial reign of God over the nations must be peaceful, noncompulsory, initiated and guided by the Holy Spirit.[42] North fully agrees, realizing that none of his theonomistic and dominionistic designs will be put into practice without voluntary acceptance of biblical law, "when the Holy Spirit begins His visibly triumphant sweep of the nations." Such a worldwide conversion and spiritual sanctification makes it evident how North can assert, "self-government under God's revealed law is the starting point for liberty."[43] As was stated earlier, "theonomy" means rule by God's law, not by an aristocracy of priests or even elected leaders. North best characterizes his vision as a "decentralized, international, theocratic *republic*."[44] The guiding document of this republic would not be the Declaration of Independence or the Constitution, but the Bible.

CONCLUSION

So, what has become of Reconstructionism after 2000? The Chalcedon Foundation continues to distribute its monthly publications and maintains an active web page. It continues to be involved in politics, especially regarding home-schooling and public education issues. North continues to publish—he released two large economic commentaries during the course of 2000.[45] He boasts a steady stream of books (12,000 to 20,000) being downloaded per month from his website, www. freebooks.com. When asked about the future of Reconstructionism after Y2K, North declares, "The future of Reconstructionism is the same as future of the kingdom of God on earth: complete victory."[46]

Chapter 9

A Not So Charitable Choice

New Religious Movements and President Bush's Plan for Faith-Based Social Services

Derek H. Davis

Nearly three months after the initial winds of the election controversy began to blow and nine days after his inauguration as the forty-third president of the United States, President George W. Bush announced the creation of the White House Office of Faith-Based and Community Initiatives. This office, created by executive order and placed under the directorship of University of Pennsylvania political science professor John DiIulio, Jr., a professed Catholic and new Democrat, will work in conjunction with another new office, the Corporation for National Service, headed by former Jewish mayor of Indianapolis, Stephen Goldsmith, to coordinate partnerships between five departments of the federal government and religiously-based social service organizations. Departments involved include those of Justice, Health and Human Services, Housing and Urban Development, Labor, and Education. Such collaboration between the government and private charities will ostensibly level the playing field between government and faith-based charities and allow those charities to conduct their mission without stooping to a never-ending list of government regulations.

When he announced the creation of the new office, Bush pledged his support of a policy of nondiscrimination against any religion and referred to this collaboration initiative as one of the most important his administration will implement. "We will encourage faith-based and community programs without *changing their mission*. We will help *all* in their work to change hearts while keeping a commitment to pluralism."[1] Bush rightfully recognizes the limitations of government efforts to solve social ills; no secular agency that simply throws money at a problem can cure an illness that is the result of more serious internal problems than lack of resources. And exactly how some faith-based organizations will spend government resources is a subject of much controversy. Some churches and religious institutions that receive this money will undoubtedly zero in not on the outward needs of individuals that come to them for help, but on the inward, spiritual needs those individuals may or may not recognize. Herein lies a significant problem. Government then becomes an agent to transform the human soul. But under the church-state separation principle imbedded in the American way of life, crafting the human soul is assigned to the spheres of religion and civil society, not government. The American founding fathers, fully aware of centuries of abuse of persons whose religious sentiments did not line up with the officially proclaimed doctrines issued by powerful church-state partnerships, sought to assign the business of soulcraft primarily to the private sphere, free from the corrupting influence of government. Alexander Hamilton properly delineated the roles of church and state when he wrote in Federalist 69 contrasting president and king: "The one has no particle of spiritual jurisdiction; the other is the supreme head and governor of the national church. What answer shall we give to those who would persuade us that things so unlike resemble each other? The same answer that ought to be given to those who tell us that a government, the whole power of which would be in the hands of the elective and periodical servants of the people, is an aristocracy, a monarchy, and a despotism."[2]

It was a prerogative of divine right monarchs to assume headship over their national church and to dictate what was and was not acceptable in terms of doctrine, practice, and belief. Such spiritual despotism was exactly the reason the Puritans sailed for New England to establish their own city on a hill where neither king nor prince nor royally appointed bishop could dictate what they could or could not do in their practice of religion. The spirit of man is best left under the jurisdiction of communities of faith, not the government. And, interestingly enough, it is this same acknowledgement that Bush makes by proposing that the government support faith-based charities without mandating strict religious conformity from every service provider. Religion must be kept vital and free of government restraint, he says.

So, does President Bush recognize the limitations of government in transforming society? Well, perhaps to some extent. He proposes to prohibit government from proselytizing by requiring that government money not be used for such purposes but rather only to administer the secular aspects of a program. But there is no limitation, nor could there be constitutionally, on a faith group using its own funds to proselytize—and to do it in a way that coordinates with the administration of the government-funded social program. Thus under the Bush plan government remains, at least indirectly, an agent to transform the human soul. It is the province of the religious community, not government, to provide services to the poor and needy in such a way that, through training in faith and practice, their innermost being is transformed spiritually.

Confusing the roles of church and state leads to another problem with the Bush plan. It is the proper place of the religious community to be a prophetic voice that speaks out against government encroachment upon freedom and justice. If religious institutions are to receive government handouts, even simply to provide social services, how can they exercise their prophetic voices effectively without lessening some of the sting that often accompanies such criticism? Government may expect a quid pro quo—we gave you money, now you lend us your moral support. How can religious communities dodge the control that inevitably follows the receipt of government money? How can religious institutions maintain their independence, preserve their right to proselytize and indoctrinate, and carry out their social functions in the manner their canons or rules mandate if they are dependent on government assistance from a government that is constitutionally prohibited from establishing any or all religions and prohibited from infringing upon the free exercise of religion? Will strictly religiously-based social services become the norm, thereby alienating the poor and needy atheist who has nowhere to turn for social services? There is a provision in current charitable choice law that a secular service provider has to be offered as an alternative to the religious services, but what if the secular service is too far away to make it reasonable that someone not wanting to go to the religious organization could travel there? A few miles for one person may seem like twenty-five or thirty miles without an automobile or some sort of reliable and affordable transportation. Would an atheist-based social program be considered religious so as to receive funds under the new program? Or would it be considered a secular alternative?

A number of critics have emerged, and surprisingly, several are from the conservative evangelical camps originally expected to be the most enthusiastic about the Bush program. While these conservative critics are important to the debate over this issue and will be addressed in what follows, they are not the primary concern of this essay. What is discussed here are the responses of the religious minorities, especially the so-called new religious movements, to Bush's plan—are they for it, against it, undecided? And what are the reasons behind their positions? Also, what are the constitutional issues that arise out of this new program that may aid or hinder participation by religious minorities? Will it be viewed as an establishment of religion? Will it be recognized to encroach upon the rights of religious minorities who have no social services provided by their own religious organizations? What will be the ethical concerns raised when the government is asked to fund contradictory social services such as abortion counseling in one institution and adoption counseling in another? Is it really the goal of some of these new religious movements to change the hearts of men and direct them to do good and succeed in the world? Can there be order amidst this seeming chaos?

FAITH-BASED INITIATIVES—AN OVERVIEW

Before proceeding to the heart of the argument, it is first necessary to address the history and overall goals of Bush's plan for government and faith-based organization collaboration. Charitable choice, as a general concept of religious organizations receiving government funds, is not new. Beginning in the 1996 Welfare Reform Act, charitable choice was instituted to enable welfare clients to "choose" between secular providers and religiously based providers. Charitable choice has since been written into several pieces of federal legislation—for example, the 1997 Welfare-to-Work program, the Community Services Block Grant program of 1998, and the Substance Abuse and Mental Health Services Administration's drug treatment programs in 2000, all without much controversy. Several religious groups, of course, including Catholic Charities and Lutheran Social Services, have for many years received government funds to aid their secular social endeavors. These organizations accept government funding on the condition that they not discriminate on the basis of religion in their hiring or proselytize their clients. Such organizations operated effectively long before charitable choice sought to soften these rules, thereby making it possible for faith-based organizations to receive government contracts without forfeiting any of their religious character. It is important to grasp what charitable choice really does for the American government and for religious social services and also to understand why President Bush's plan has caught so much flack given the seven-year history of charitable choice that has transpired with little controversy.

The faith-based initiative, despite the president's strong push, has experienced difficulty in getting congressional approval. In July 2001 the House passed its version of the faith-based initiative, the Community Solutions Act of 2001, co-sponsored by J.C. Watts (R-OK) and Tony Hall (D-OH), which, among other things, provided tax incentives for charitable contributions by individuals and businesses and expanded the charitable choice provision of the 1996 Welfare Reform Act.

The faith-based initiative then stalled in the Senate. The Charity Aid, Recovery, and Empowerment Act of 2002 (the CARE Act), co-sponsored by Joseph Lieberman (D-CT) and Rick Santorum (R-PA), sought to amend the Internal Revenue Code to offer tax incentives to encourage charitable giving and provide financial support for nongovernmental community-based organizations. While the Senate bill did not contain the controversial expansion of the 1996 charitable choice provision included in the House version of the bill, CARE sparked debate over the kinds of church-state partnerships it would allow. Senators failed to reach a consensus on the CARE Act before Congress adjourned for the year.

In September 2002, the White House vowed to pursue its initiative through the federal agencies, regardless of Congress' concerns. At a 12 December 2002 conference in Philadelphia co-sponsored by the White House and five Cabinet departments, President Bush announced that he would implement, by executive order, key elements of his faith-based initiative, including some elements contained in the failed House and Senate bills.

The president's order effectively applies charitable choice principles through administrative regulation rather than legislation. Under the existing charitable choice provision, as well as the new executive order, social service providers are not allowed to discriminate against beneficiaries of services on the basis of faith, but they are allowed to discriminate in hiring and in selecting board members on the basis of religious faith. They are not allowed to use federal grant or contract dollars to fund any "inherently religious" activity, and they must separate "in time or location" services funded by direct governmental aid from "inherently religious activities." But religious organizations can compete for government funding to provide public services without having to abandon "their independence, autonomy, expression, or religious character." They also may display religious art, icons or scripture in their facilities, and they may retain religious terms in their organization name, their mission statements and other governing documents.

Bush also signed an executive order opening new Centers for Faith-Based and Community Initiatives at the Department of Agriculture and the Agency for International Development, and he directed the Federal Emergency Management Agency to allow religious nonprofit groups to qualify for aid after disasters like earthquakes and hurricanes in the same way that secular nonprofit groups can qualify.

Despite the president's controversial expansion of the faith-based initiative through executive orders, the initiative was revived in the subsequent session of Congress. On 9 April 2003, the Senate, in a 95-5 vote, passed a modified version of the CARE Act (S 476). To facilitate passage, cosponsors of the bill agreed to strike language from the bill that would have allowed faith-based groups to maintain their religious character while receiving federal funds for their social service programs. The House was likely to pass similar legislation.[3]

While the entire faith-based initiative is controversial and faces an uncertain future, President Bush has pledged to move forward, believing that it is an initiative that will greatly enhance services to America's worst off. He is already moving forward, in fact, as demonstrated by the executive orders he signed in 2002 that implement charitable choice and other features through administrative agencies. It is essential, then, to given further analysis to the initiative in order to ascertain its merits and demerits.

The charitable choice provisions address religious social service providers' participation in the system of providing a variety of services to the needy. Religious organizations are not required to dilute their faith in order to receive money, nor are the states able to discriminate against faith-based charities if they receive federal block grants. Several congressmen, including three top-ranking Republicans, and numerous other supporters including the Center for

Public Justice, The National Association of Evangelicals, and the Union of Orthodox Jewish Congregations, hail this not as an accommodation of religion disallowed under the Establishment Clause but rather an attempt to amend too many long years of discrimination against religion in the area of social service provision. These organizations had previously expressed concern over secular institutions receiving funds while religious institutions had been left out in the cold simply because they were religious. Said House Majority Whip Tom DeLay, "It's wrong for government to discriminate against organizations that can effectively provide services just because they are religious."[4] They recognize religion's rightful and responsible role in serving the human as well as the spiritual needs of the community and see charitable choice as a chance to reinvigorate certain services that have withered and died on the vine due to lack of sufficient funds. One has to ask, however, if some religious groups' hesitation to provide social services in the past was not due more to a theological position that disregarded the present world for the sake of the world to come than to a lack of sufficient funds. It may also be quite possible that some of these religious groups see dollar signs and think of ways they can promote their own agendas without thinking about how they can best serve the community here and now in a manner that does not discriminate against social service recipients. Nevertheless, Bush's executive order creating the White House Office of Faith-Based and Community Initiatives attempts to answer their concerns and leaves wide open the door to all religious groups, experienced and non-experienced, in providing social services: "The paramount goal is compassionate results, and private and charitable community groups, including religious ones, should have the fullest opportunity permitted by law to compete on a level playing field, so long as they achieve valid public purposes, such as curbing crime, conquering addiction, strengthening families and neighborhoods, and overcoming poverty."[5] Theoretically at least, this could mean that all religions are funded equally and without consideration of what they believe. The government would merely purchase the results offered by the religious-based social services, neither aiding nor inhibiting religion. Stephen Goldsmith noted, "The government is trying to furnish shelter, it's trying to furnish food." But he added, "For me, I don't think that Wiccans would meet the standard of kind of being humane providers of domestic violence shelters."[6]

President Bush's plan for charitable choice has received severe criticism since it was announced, but why should this be the case? The reasons are several, but two are most glaring. One is that his proposals would urge dramatic and immediate change in funneling federal money to charitable organizations. American democracy is such that the gradual phasing in of a new and innovative program is not nearly as painful as the institution of a new program in the shortest period of time possible. Several Republicans in Congress are even concerned that Bush is plunging too fast into introducing charitable choice in all parts of American aid to society's poverty-ridden and would prefer not to introduce or support a lump sum bill but rather a series of bills over time establishing a charitable choice framework. Another reason behind the backlash against Bush's program is its public prominence. When charitable choice was originally passed in 1996, it was an obscure part of a much larger welfare bill, not an effort of a prominent public policy agency within the executive branch. By highlighting his faith-based program and making it a centerpiece of his administration, Bush has inadvertently opened the floodgates of public scrutiny and criticism. When few knew about it, it was not a public concern, but the more there are who know, the more there are who will attempt to fight it.

Of all the concerns, the possibility of equal funding is that which most upsets some and assuages the fears of others, and it is likely that the harshest criticism of faith-based government initiatives will stem from the methods by which funds are distributed to the various charities that are eligible. Bush himself has claimed that funds will go to those who provide the best services with the highest success rates. All groups, regardless of religiosity, are equally eligible for federal money, but of course not all shall receive. Thus it is an equal opportunity initiative, and not an equality-in-reality that Bush's proposal creates. If there were true equality of funding, then the large First Church downtown would receive exactly the same provisions as the tiny rural Hindu Temple. That alone is not proportionally fair. Another way would be to give to all charities funding proportionate to the size of their parent religious organizations. This is problematic because membership totals for religious organizations are kept differently by different denominations and organizations, and seeing as how there is only a limited supply of money to go around (Bush has proposed spending $8 billion in the first year, none of it "new" money, but all of it coming at the expense of existing programs), when that is divided amongst all organizations proportionally, there is hardly any benefit to receiving federal funds at all. Another problem would stem from the relative number of parties aided by the particular charity. Suppose a Buddhist charity in a large urban China Town is the most prominent in the area, but the total Buddhist population is a mere fraction of the whole. It would seem that the charity would be the victim of discrimination and would be disproportionately under-funded despite its size and services to the community. But it would not seem right, either for the large Buddhist charity and the much smaller Methodist charity to receive equal funding. In terms of gain, the Methodist charity would benefit more substantially than the Buddhist charity simply because of its smaller size. It could afford to spend more money on each person it helps and thereby offer better services to a more select community.

Detractors from charitable choice are from all parts of the spectrum. One would expect to find such groups as the American Civil Liberties Union, the Americans United for the Separation of Church and State, the Baptist Joint Committee, and the Coalition Against Religious Discrimination to be against charitable choice on constitutional grounds. Providing federal funds to religious charities, generally speaking, is an impermissible act under the Supreme Court's traditional interpretation of the Establishment Clause of the First Amendment.

But their concern is also for the long-term health of religion in America after federal funding is made available. One compelling argument they make is that once religious organizations receive federal funding, dependence upon these funds will be the result and will eventually become a chronic illness of the system as it is in Europe and other parts of the world where church-state separation is less observed. When the charities receive government funds, they are ecstatic and believe they are then capable of expanding their social outreaches. The trouble with money is that it eventually is exhausted and more must be attained before further work can be conducted. Since money was given once to a religious institution by a state agency, it is highly possible that this state agency will be generous enough to write another check when the original money is exhausted. Once this happens, a cycle of receipt of government money by religious organizations, spending it, and then returning for more money becomes inevitable. This cycle further erodes the private citizen's perceived responsibility to fund these same religious organizations because he sees the government standing in for him and using his tax dollars in the process. Private funding eventually ceases or becomes negligible, and the religious organization is fully dependent upon the state money for survival. When this has occurred, the religious institutions are effectively subordinated to the state, lose their autonomy, and are compromised in their religious mission. The church becomes an arm of the state akin to any other bureaucratic agency, disrespected and reviled by the average citizen.

Another area of concern is that of discrimination in hiring and firing on the basis of religion. Is it right for any organization, regardless of its proclaimed mission, if it receives federal funds, to discriminate against otherwise qualified applicants on the basis of religion or sexual orientation? Senator Patrick Leahy (D-VT) has expressed concern that "religion [may be] used as a pretext to discriminate against homosexuals," and that "by allowing discrimination on the basis of religion, we may open the door to other forms of discrimination, including race."[7] Such fears are not unfounded. If a group such as the Ku Klux Klan could be considered a religious organization, then it would be eligible under Bush's plan for funds and would not have to compromise its tenets of racism and anti-Semitism. Bush claims that such groups as this that preach hate would not receive funds, but then observers ask whether this is not in reality a discrimination against religion, even if it is offensive to the general public. For some faith communities, it would violate their core orthodoxy to be forced to consider homosexuals or members of certain races for employment. Would they not then cease to be a church if they violated these tenets simply to receive government funds? Can the government require churches to abandon the very foundational beliefs that constitute them as churches?

Another category of opponents to charitable choice, surprisingly, comes from the very ranks that would most likely spawn its proponents—evangelical Christians. Jerry Falwell and Pat Robertson have both gone on record to voice opposition to Bush's expanded charitable choice plan because they fear money going to religious groups with whom they fundamentally disagree. Such aberrant organizations would include the Church of Scientology, Wiccans, the Unification Church, the Hare Krishna, and the like. Said Robertson:

> I mean, the Moonies have been proscribed, if I can use that, for brainwashing techniques, sleep deprivation and all the rest of it that goes along with their usual proselytizing. The Hare Krishnas much the same thing. And it seems appalling to me that we're going to go for somebody like that, or the Church of Scientology, which was involved in an incredible campaign against the IRS. I mean, they were accused of all sorts of underhanded tactics.[8]

Robertson would promote, however, a system that, instead of direct cash payments, offered tax credits to persons and corporations that donated money to religious groups. He also advocates a government registry of participating religious organizations that track the participating groups and ensure that they segregate the funds they receive specifically for social services and not for religious indoctrination or proselytization. That appears neutral on the surface, but how would Robertson react to the government's telling him that he could use certain funds only in a specified manner and could not conduct social services with religious proselytization as a key component?

It is this group of opponents and its respective targets that are the subjects of this essay. What will follow is a study of how these and other new religious movements and religious minorities perceive the charitable choice proposals of the Bush administration and how they plan to use or not use the money offered to them. What are their reasons for accepting or rejecting these funds? Is it primarily theological, moral or ethical, or is it humanitarian or a fear of public backlash? The answers may prove surprising to some.

NEW RELIGIOUS MOVEMENTS AND CHARITABLE CHOICE

As previously noted, President Bush's plan theoretically opens the door for all religions offering social services to the community to participate equally in sharing federal funding. White House officials have been sending mixed messages to the public when asked whether fringe religious groups would be eligible to apply for federal aid for their social services. If America is to remain committed to a principle of freedom, whereby religion is a sacred right as much as a sacred rite, how far can and should the government go to ostensibly evenhandedly aid the multiplicity of religious sects in their quest to provide spiritual as well as social guidance to their constituencies and to the broader public? President Bush has several times emphasized that he is only concerned with the results the programs produce. Goldsmith seems to believe there are limitations. DiIulio, before he resigned his office in September 2001, appeared to advocate a performance model that may end up channeling money to groups that people do not like.

Are new religious movements clamoring to receive government recognition and aid, or are they content to remain where they are in the overall spectrum of religious diversity? By all indications, the community of new religious movements is as divided on the issue as the general public. Some, such as the Unification Church, are eager to feed at the government trough. Others, like the Church of Jesus Christ of Latter-day Saints, are issuing a staunch NO to government funds. The following shall address some of the major pros and cons as seen through the eyes of these new religious movements. It is not at all intended to be a rating or thorough examination of the theologies of each of these movements, nor can it be a complete examination of new religious movements and their opinions on the matter from every angle due to the very difficulty of defining a "new religious movement."

It is good to begin with the largest proponent of Bush's faith-based initiatives from the new religious movement spectrum—the Unification Church run by the Rev. Sun Myung Moon. Moon's official church was disbanded several years ago and replaced by the Family Federation for World Peace and Unification to lessen its unpalatable image in the eyes of conservative Christians. Few if any conservative Christians would openly and willingly channel funds to such a group that, among other controversial theological doctrines, hails its leader and his wife as the "True Parents," or the second messiah sent to complete the failed mission of Jesus Christ. Some critics have charged Moon with heresy or outright fraud. Nevertheless, several such religious conservatives as Jerry Falwell and top officials in Pat Robertson's Christian Coalition have joined Moon-sponsored efforts to promote family values and to create Christian unity against a hostile secular front. Moon appeals to the Christian Right often through the use of cash donations to certain organizations. Falwell's Christian Heritage Foundation, for example, received $3.5 million from a Moon group to offset some of the debt incurred by Liberty University. At another time, a Moon group gave gold wristwatches worth several thousands of dollars apiece to ministers who attended "We Will Stand" events that were part of a 50-state tour to promote family values and Bush's faith-based initiatives program.

Moon has also enlisted the support of several members of the African-American clergy as he has emphasized the renewal of the urban communities and the need for racial unity. The Rev. Donald Robinson of the office of Washington, D.C. Mayor Anthony Williams stated, "I don't see a conflict. I just see this as an opportunity for the city to align itself with like-minded people. We want the renewal and restoration of families, the renewal and revival of community. We want a sense of racial harmony."[9] If that is what they want, what is wrong with letting them have it? Moon has interests that run deeper than the family values, sexual abstinence, and Christian unity he appears to espouse.

By promoting Bush's plan for faith-based initiatives, Moon hopes to ingrati-
ate himself to the leaders of the Republican Party. Moon could then easily win
government funds for his teenage abstinence program. But that is not the whole
of it by any means. Moon's theology teaches the unification of all religions
under a Moon-headed theocratic state. It seems preposterous to most
Americans to think that these naive goals could ever be realized, but that is not
the concern of those who advocate separation of church and state. Why should
the government and its supporting taxpayers channel money to an organization
that is bent on taking over the world? It is a religious organization without a
doubt. It has a theology, a charismatic leader, and organized structures. Under
Bush's plan, it would only have to produce results with its social services to
receive funds and would not have to alter its fundamental theology or its efforts
at proselytizing. But is it morally acceptable for a government to fund an organization that advocates its demise? That would be the equivalent of the government shooting itself in the foot. Many patriotic Americans would not want
this sort of organization to use their tax dollars for pernicious ends. The doctrine of equality of all religions, given the plurality of sects and denominations
in America, therefore demands that none receive government funds for any
work that could remotely be connected to winning converts to their cause.

A far less radical take on charitable choice is that of the Sikhs. Concerns
from the Sikh community include the possibility of government funds alienating religious minorities from mainstream acceptance since this could have a dis-
proportionate impact upon Sikhism in the United States. For this reason, dialogue has been encouraged, but the community has been reluctant to make a
commitment. According to the executive director of the Sikh Mediawatch and
Resource Task Force (SMART), a Sikh advocacy organization, "We are not saying yes or no to this proposal by the Bush Administration, but we would like
to hear more about how government funds could help social service programs
in this country and we would like to participate in a dialogue that allows public funds to go towards non-proselytizing religious organizations."[10] Non-proselytizing provisions seem to be the key to Sikh acceptance of faith-based initiatives. But how can a faith-based charity that is truly *faith*-based be anything but
an effort to proselytize those that come to it for help? If the charitable services
are divorced from the parent religious organization, then can that charity be
said to be faith-based at all? Would it not then be simply another secular organization, only having a religious namesake instead of one from the government?
This seems to be the concern of several who oppose the Bush initiative.
Religion will have to be watered down in order to meet government funding
standards. And with that, all parties lose out.

Other new religious movements have not been as sympathetic to the Bush
program. Several such detractors come from the Neo-Pagan, Wicca, and earth
religions traditions. In February 2001, a coalition of representatives from these
diverse traditions sent a letter to Bush addressing their concerns about the

Office of Faith-Based and Community Initiatives. Their concerns were twofold—fear of discrimination and fear of inequality. These fears require extended explanation.

According to the letter, for the government to fund faith-based organizations while at the same time withholding funding from secular alternatives is contrary to the principle of separation of church and state. (Remember, Bush has not allocated any new money for the faith-based initiatives he is proposing; all money will simply be redirected to faith-based charities rather than secular ones in one massive campaign of wealth redistribution). Federal funding of faith-based initiatives may inevitably lead to supplementing or fully paying the salaries of those "who may support and spread intolerance or violence based on religious, racial or ethnic supremacist ideals. They would be able to discriminate in hiring and firing persons with views not in sympathy with their own."[11] For them, it is not the government's place to promote or support individuals whose ideologies lend themselves to discrimination and exclusion. One difficulty with that, however, is that the definition of discriminatory and exclusionary is not as agreed upon as one would imagine it to be. Some, if not all, religions are discriminatory or exclusionary by their very nature. A religion that teaches one doctrine obviously discriminates against other doctrines that do not conform. And it will inevitably exclude someone from its rites and sacraments if that individual is not yet initiated into its fellowship. The definition of religion itself, therefore, would preclude faith-based organizations from receiving government funds. That may be what the earth/nature religions are driving at when they emphasize their concern that secular organizations will be forced to shut down when money begins flowing to faith-based groups.

Their concern with inequality is also high atop the list of problems with the faith-based initiatives. They assert that already some government officials have made derogatory and discriminatory comments about Wicca and other pagan religions. These officials have suggested that Wicca may be an inferior or substandard religion when put alongside more conventional religions. Of course, this "inferiority" would preclude them from receiving government funds. Because of their qualification for IRS tax exemption, state incorporation, and their recognition in the U.S. Army Handbook for Chaplains, Wiccans believe they deserve the respect of everyone else in the government as well. And in all due respect to the government officials' prerogative to decide who shall and shall not receive federal funding, the Wiccans have a valid argument. It is not likely that the IRS or the Army will back away from their stances, so why not press for further government recognition if the means are available? The next to last paragraph of the letter sums up the Wiccans and all neo-Pagan organizations' desires: "This country and its resources are for everyone regardless of race, religion, sex or age. We ask that our tax dollars be given to initiatives, programs and organizations that do not discriminate."[12]

It would seem the Wiccans have a legitimate claim against government officials in charge of the faith-based initiatives. When asked at a Congressional hearing in April 2001 whether Wiccans would be eligible for federal funding under Bush's plan, John DiIulio responded that he could not understand why anyone in Congress would focus on Wiccans as a point of concern. Said DiIulio: "It just baffled me."[13] DiIulio sidestepped the question and never clearly stated whether the Wiccan organizations would qualify for funding or not.

Some groups have been the targets of religious fundamentalists such as Jerry Falwell and Pat Robertson. Inevitably, the Church of Scientology is dragged into the debate as a religion that many fundamentalists are against providing funds for due to its unorthodox beliefs and practices. But surprisingly, not all of the animosity toward Scientology comes from the far right. In a survey conducted in the early months of the Bush administration, only 26 percent of the general public supported giving money to the Church of Scientology if it wanted to participate in the federal programs.[14] Scientologists themselves have been somewhat vague about whether they are willing and wanting to receive federal funds. To illustrate, it is good to cite a lengthy passage from the Vice President of the Church of Scientology International, Janet Weiland:

> Government funding of social betterment activities is nothing new. Religious charities, such as Catholic Charities, Lutheran Services of America and the YMCA collect billions of dollars in federal money for their charitable programs. The organizations that sponsor these charitable activities happen to be affiliated with major religious movements. Up to now, this has not been controversial. When the programs are chosen based on the merits and effective results, then there are no reasons for complaint. We support very effective drug rehabilitation and literacy programs that have always enjoyed excellent relations with the communities they serve, and they are open to people of all religions. These programs have freed more than 250,000 people from the ravages of drug addiction and have helped thousands more learn to read.
>
> The religious leaders of this country should not be climbing over the backs of their brethren in a mad scramble for government coins. Clergy of all faiths need to work together to solve the problems of escalating drug use, crime and illiteracy and the crashing moral values in this country. That is our traditional role in the community as religious institutions and it is a role we are uniquely designed to fulfill.[15]

On the one hand, they seem to be willing to accept government funds; on the other, they seem to say "no thank you" to the president's proposal. A February 20 *New York Times* article cited officials of the Church of Scientology as hoping to benefit from Bush's funding proposals, and already, Church of Scientology's drug rehabilitation program, Narconon, has in some instances received government funds for its services, even without the Bush program in place.[16] These programs, however, are devoid of religiosity and operate in much the same manner as Catholic Charities and Lutheran Social Services, divorced from the parent religious organization in all but name. The last lines of Weiland's statement above indicate the church's position on charitable choice that will fund religious charities without regard to their degree of religiosity:

"Clergy of all faiths need to work together to solve the problems of escalating drug use, crime and illiteracy and the crashing moral values in this country. That is our traditional role in the community as religious institutions and it is a role that we are *uniquely* designed to fulfill." In other words, leave the religious social work and missions to the religious organizations, supported by their parishioners' generosity, not the government's handouts. Government-funded religious social services are simply secular bureaucracy in religious garb. It cannot let the religious community operate independently; and only in its independence is that community effective in transforming society. Furthermore, offering funds to seemingly desperate religious charities can only create animosity in an age when cooperation among religious leaders is needed more than ever. Many major wars in the history of the West were the results of religious competition. The beauty of America is its diversity and the harmony such diversity fosters. In the words of James Madison, "Whilst all authority in [the United States] will be derived from and dependent on the society, the society itself will be broken into so many parts, interests and classes of citizens, that the rights of individuals, or of the minority, will be in little danger from the interested combinations of the majority."[17] To keep the peace, government cannot offer to fund some religions and potentially discriminate against others. The Church of Scientology's answer to Bush's plan is apparently NO.

Another perennial target of religious critics is the Nation of Islam, the leader of which is the notorious Louis Farrakhan. This controversial organization has in the past received government funding, including money to fund Nation of Islam security guards at public housing projects in several major U.S. cities. The program was eventually terminated after two Republican congressional figures began making inquiries. However, the security guard programs had served to reduce crime and drug deals in their projects despite its effort to proselytize and distribute copies of its newspaper, *Final Call*, which many critics charge is laden with anti-Semitism and racism. While Bush had earlier publicly stated that the Nation of Islam would be ineligible for funding because it preached hate, this security guard program is an example of a successful faith-based program. If, as DiIulio maintained during his tenure, the federal money will go to those faith-based efforts that have the highest rates of success, then the Nation of Islam, at least in this instance, would undoubtedly qualify. However, despite its past cooperation with the federal government, Louis Farrakhan stated in February that he is no longer interested in receiving government money. "Bush is not foolish. He wants to win you, preacher."[18] According to Farrakhan, Bush's entire plan is an effort to coddle the nation's black clergy and to win favor from them in return—just another way to keep the black man enslaved to the whims of the white majority.

Another group, the Mormons, is more widely accepted in the American mainstream and is well known for its pro-family, pro-life agendas. Surprisingly, the Church of Jesus Christ of Latter-day Saints has rejected the Bush plan for faith-based charities. But this rejection does not stem from any particular ideology. Rather, the church has the resources to sustain itself and would rather not be tied down by government regulations. "We're neutral. That's not saying we think it's wrong for every organization, but we just don't need it," spokesman Dale Bills said.[19] The LDS has from the beginning prided itself on self-sufficiency. And in its social services, the church requires that all its recipients repay the charity in some way as they become self-reliant. By taking government money, the church could not insist upon this essential element to helping people become better citizens.

Mormon, Wiccan, Scientology, and Nation of Islam's rejection of federal money is a breath of fresh air to many, if not most in the American public. And undoubtedly, the efforts of Sun Myung Moon to gain credibility and funds is appalling to many. According to a March poll, the American public by a 2-1 margin rejected the idea of government funds going to the Nation of Islam, to Scientology, and to the Hare Krishnas.[20] If these controversial groups are not interested in receiving government money and the more generally accepted religious organizations are, what is the difficulty with Bush's proposals? Would not the requirements of religious neutrality have been met? The answers are not easily discerned, and the difficulties abound by the dozens.

CONCLUSION

President Bush's creation of the Office of Faith-based and Community Initiatives unnecessarily invokes a host of church-state issues of fundamental importance. Congress could still steer clear of First Amendment problems if it limits the scope of potentially participating organizations to private organizations, including religiously affiliated organizations that have an organizational charter or bylaws establishing their secular function. Houses of worship and other religious groups, including the array of religious minorities across America, could then participate in the new social service programs, performing their contractual responsibilities with the state in a secular setting and without proselytization. This arrangement would be in keeping with Supreme Court precedent and would protect both church and state from encroachment by the other.

Many members of Congress seem convinced that meeting the needs of the nation's poor and needy can only be achieved by enlisting the aid of faith-based institutions. But why does this also require an infusion of government money, with all of the attendant problems, both practical and constitutional? If it is a lack of financial resources that hinders faith-based institutions from a full participation in social programs, Congress would do better to offer economic incentives (e.g., tax credits and multiple write-offs) to corporate America for donations that would enable faith-based institutions to administer needed social programs. The possibilities here are endless, but the notion of corporations adopting and providing the financial means for charities, churches, synagogues, and other faith-based organizations to administer social programs, in effect creating a new strain of partnerships across America to solve social problems that government cannot and should not be expected to solve, is an attractive prospect.

But apart from these possibilities, and even in the new world created by charitable choice, houses of worship and other religious organizations can still exercise the same option that was open to them even before the charitable choice provisions became law: assist the poor and needy on their own terms, with their own financial resources, in an expressly religious environment, and with complete freedom to proselytize and teach their own religious beliefs. America's tradition of religious liberty could never be more faithfully or effectively exercised.

Chapter 10

Fighting for Free Exercise from the Trenches

A Case Study of Religious Freedom Issues Faced by Wiccans Practicing in the United States

Catharine Cookson

Now that the three hundredth anniversary of the Salem witch trials (1692-1992) has passed, it seems appropriate to re-examine the Wiccan experience of religious freedom. While the heretical beliefs of strange Others is no longer good cause to burn them, how much progress has really been made toward religious freedom for groups whose religious beliefs are considered anathema by Christians? The results, as various Wiccan sources show, are mixed.

Wiccans report that the biggest challenges to their religious freedom are directly traceable to (1) misperceptions and (2) intolerance. Misperceptions due to false rumors and ignorance are easily cleared up with educational efforts. Wiccans are not Satanists, nor do Wiccans worship devils or demons.[1] They do not mutilate or sacrifice babies or animals or people, nor do they seek to do evil or promote evil. In fact, the Wiccan ethic is precisely the opposite. Wicca is a life-affirming, positive system of spiritual beliefs and ritual practices. As noted by J. Gordon Melton,

> most modern witches are followers of a nature-oriented, polytheistic faith. . . . Witches and Neo-Pagans worship the great Mother Goddess, usually seen in her triple aspect as maiden, Mother, and crone, thus representing the basic stages of life. Beside her is the Horned God (Pan), her consort, and together they represent the male and female principle basic to life. . . .
> Ethically, Witches value freedom and harmlessness. . . . They also believe that the effects of magic will be returned threefold upon the per-

son working it, a belief that severely limits the pronouncing of curses. A basic love of nature and natural things pervades the Pagan community and leads many to espouse ecology, natural foods, and love of animals. . . . [2]

Wiccan religious rituals occur within a sacred circle, which normally includes an altar area. As noted above, Wiccan rituals are nature-oriented, and ideally these rituals are performed in an outdoor setting. Wicca's religious practices are coordinated with cycles of nature, and the themes of the major holy days are likely to correspond to the nature of the season. As Gordon Melton has explained:

> Witchcraft is organized in small autonomous groups called "covens" (variously, "groves," "nests," and "circles"). . . . They meet semi-monthly at the new and full moons for regular meetings called "esbats." There are eight major solar festivals, "sabbats," beginning with Samhain or Halloween (October 31) and continuing with Yule (December 21), Oimelc or Candlemas (February 2), Spring Equinox (March 21), Beltane (April 30), Summer Solstice (June 21), Lammas (August 1), and Fall Equinox (September 21). Sabbats are frequently occasions for several covens to come together. . . . It should also be noted that there are many solitary witches who practice apart from a coven though they may join in major festivals.[3]

The outdoor setting and ritual nature of much of Wiccan worship, as well as an overlap of some holy days and sacred symbols (such as the pentagram) with that of Satanism, have contributed to the misidentification of Wicca with Satanism. Some anti-cult experts have added to the misperceptions by failing to adequately distinguish between Wiccans and Satanic groups in their lectures and materials warning against Satanic ritual abuse.

For example, one group of materials distributed in Virginia contained warnings to be alert for "Satanic Symbols." Included among these symbols were those deemed spiritual and used as sacred by Wiccans. The materials failed to alert readers that the symbols illustrated on the sheet were not necessarily Satanic.[4]

A checklist included with these materials, titled "Signs and Symptoms of Ritualistic Abuse in Children," warns of numerous "danger signs" of Satanic abuse among children, including the following:

> 3. Problems associated with the supernatural, rituals, occult symbols, religion:
>   C. Child is preoccupied with wands, sticks, swords [all, it is to be noted are also tarot symbols, as well as items which may be used in ritual worship by Wiccans], spirits, magic potions, [herbal remedies? beverages used in ritual?] . . . supernatural powers, . . . and asks many or unusual questions about them. Child . . . attempts magic, . . . calls on spirits, prays to the devil [danger, here, of confusing the pagan "horned God" with the Christian devil].

D. Child sings odd, ritualistic songs or chants. . . .

E. Child does odd, ritualistic dances which may involve a circle or other symbols. . . .

F. Child is preoccupied with occult symbols such as the circle, pentagram, number 6, horn sign. . . .

I. Child states that (s)he or someone else prayed to the devil [open to interpretation here, again: many Christians would see any pagan deity as a "devil"], threw curses, made potions, performed ritualized songs or dances, called upon spirits, did magic. Child states that (s)he or someone else wore ghost, devil, dracula, witch, etc., costumes, used ceremonial wands or swords. . . .[5]

These materials also included behavioral "warning signs" which are quite ambiguous. For example, one information sheet advises that further symptoms characterizing Satanic ritual abuse include:

1. Low self-esteem. . . .
2. Child is fearful, clingy, regresses to "baby" behavior. Separation anxiety.
3. Child is angry, aggressive, acts out.
4. Child acts wild, uncontrolled, hyperactive.
5. Child is accident prone. . . .
6. Child is negativistic, resistant to authority. Child mistrusts adults.
7. Child is overcompliant with authority, overly pleasing with adults.
9. Child is withdrawn, does not play. . . .
12. Child's speech is regressed and babyish. . . .
17. Child pulls down pants, pulls up dress, takes off clothes inappropriately. . . .[6]

It would be hard to find a child who has not exhibited many if not most of these characteristics at one time or another. Furthermore, these materials, while taking great pains in the beginning to note that one should not overreact or be quick to judge a situation, also emphasize that Satanist families may indeed appear to be "normal":

> If a school refers a child for treatment, cult parents (or friends of the parents) may be sophisticated consumers of the mental health system and may encumber evaluative efforts while playing the role of concerned parents. . . . Generational cult children will at times present like healthy well adjusted children. This is possible due to dissociative abilities and makes an abusive history seem doubtful to judges and others who might interview the children. . . . It is important to understand that children born into orthodox satanism . . . will most likely have developed dissociative splits prior to age 6, and will not be evidencing such obvious symptoms of cult abuse.[7]

Certainly, it is necessary to combat ritual torture, killing, and other abusive practices. Nevertheless, anti-Satanic materials which are seriously misleading as applied to Wiccanism promote fear and could lead to harassment and even legal action against Wiccans by those in authority such as teachers, police, social workers, and prosecutors. Indeed, Wiccan parents are perennially fearful that their children may innocently relate stories of holy day celebrations or ritual practices to misunderstanding persons who, out of fear, report the parents to school authorities, social workers, or the police, or even take matters into their own hands.[8] One Wiccan narrative from Indiana told how a person had over-heard a private religious discussion between a Wiccan husband and a wife. The person "condemned them as devil worshippers" and told people throughout the small town that they were "Satanists."[9] Another openly-Wiccan parent wrote that after Lifetime Cable Channel aired a fictional anti-witchcraft piece titled "To Save A Child," eight Jehovah's Witnesses came to her door, went through her trash, and "grabbed neighbors to tell them that 'Pagans' lived in this house."[10] One can see how a minor situation might escalate, and thus under-stand the paranoia of Wiccan parents who fear they may find themselves unable to convince those in authority that they are harmless.

Concerted educational and public relations efforts by Wiccans themselves have helped to establish trust, overcome misperceptions and correct misinfor-mation. Wiccans have been working hard at building good community rela-tionships and disseminating information about their religion which clearly dis-tinguishes it from Satanic groups. Wiccan educational efforts have most suc-cessfully focused upon governmental agencies and agents such as police, judges, prison officials, the military, etc., not only to effect fairness in institutional poli-cies, but also to help insure that the discretionary power of these public officials is exercised knowledgeably and without prejudice.

Some educational success stories include a full acceptance of Wiccan chap-lains by the military, and a fair and accurate portrayal of Wiccan groups in the Military Chaplains Handbook.[11] Wiccans in 1985 finally were permitted to reg-ister as clergy with the City of New York in order to be eligible to perform legal weddings.[12] Much progress has also been made by Wiccans working with and within prison systems, such as the Wisconsin state system, to gain greater free-dom of worship for Wiccans.[13] Another narrative told of success in a child cus-tody action in which a Wiccan mother was being challenged as unfit due to her beliefs. The Wiccan's attorney anticipated the issue, and early in the proceed-ings had a Wiccan priestess submit testimony concerning the nature of the reli-gion and its beliefs and practices. The religious issue was defused, and the Wiccan ultimately was awarded custody.[14]

Educational success stories have also frequently included the establishment of cordial relationships with local police departments. In contrast to the nor-mative Christian experience of worship in denominational churches, Wiccans report that it is not uncommon for circles which hold group rituals outdoors to have experienced at least one interruption of their religious services or festivals by police. The police were usually acting upon a complaint of Satanic activity, human sacrifice, and the like, and thus were understandably nervous. At one midwestern coven's outdoor ritual, police surrounded the group and, shining flashlights *into* the fire, exclaimed that it was no ordinary fire.[15] Wiccans reportedly understand the misperceptions and fears of outsiders, and in these situations usually have acted calmly and politely, and have used the opportunity to educate the local police authorities to their religious customs and the ethical nature of their practice. To calm police fears, one group even issued an open invitation to the police to come onto their private land at their discretion and see for themselves what was going on.[16] The police, in many if not most of these situations, have responded positively and good relations have been established.[17]

Some opposition and harassment, however, is due not to mere misinformation but to deep-seated worldviews, both scientific and theological. A rational, scientific worldview can deem Wiccans as irrational and superstitious and therefore potentially dangerous. And, as already noted, anti-cult experts based in helping professions such as psychology are conducting active anti-Satanism campaigns and actively seeking out victims of Satanism, and at times their nets are cast far too widely.

Intolerance driven by theological worldviews is characterized by a personal, religious worldview that believes in the power of Satan *and* believes that Wiccans are a part of that evil. Such intolerance is usually the root of person-to-person, emotional (but not violent) actions and reactions against Wiccans which occur on the job, in the neighborhood, at school, and in all other routine settings. More feared by Wiccans is the theologically-driven political and social activism that deems Wiccans to be a threat to God, Christianity, and/or American society. Such activists believe they are justified in mounting organized or group efforts against Wiccans, which tends to lead to vandalism and other overt actions against Wiccan persons and property. It must be noted that religiously-based intolerance and harassment of Wiccans is not satisfactorily described as belonging to "fundamentalist" Christians, or even "conservative" Christians. Instead of a denominational or ideological type of descriptive label, it would perhaps be more accurate to posit nothing more than a certain type of religious worldview. The belief in the devil as an active force for evil cuts across most Protestant denominations (Unitarian-Universalists are the one exception which comes to mind) and is even found among Catholics. When that belief is coupled with a belief that Wiccans (either consciously or unwittingly) are in league with such evil forces, the result can be a deep-seated intolerance, irrespective of denominational affiliation. Because of the complexities of modern American Christianity, it is therefore inaccurate to designate any one denomination as the source of active intolerance against Wiccans.[18]

With this caveat in mind, it is possible to explore the reasonings and reactions of those with an active religious belief in the power of witchcraft as an evil. In her work among one group of Pentecostals in southern Indiana, for example, folklorist Elaine Lawless noted

> a traditional, even Puritan view, which syncretized notions of witches and
> devils with the Holy Ghost and a personalized Christ figure. Everything
> that happened in Beulah's [Beulah is one of the Pentecostal women inter-

> viewed by Lawless] world had something to do with God's will or with
> Satan's wily intervention in her life. . . . She recalled her mother telling her
> and her sisters how girls would become witches—that they would pray
> and pray to the devil until they were completely controlled by him. . . .
> Beulah figured people wanted to become witches because they can cause
> things to happen, because they feel powerful.
>   Belief in . . . witches . . . is possible because of a strong belief in Satan
> as a living reality, a daily, constant threat to health and well-being. . . . For
> them [the Pentecostal women of Southern Indiana whom Lawless stud-
> ied], the supernormal, the supernatural and the normal worlds cross
> often.[19]

Beulah told Lawless that "The bible talks about witchery. They've got a contract
with the devil, you know."[20] Beulah indicated that her father was the one who
told her about witches: "[He] wanted us to be afraid so that we would go to
church and only trust in Jesus not to pray to the devil ever. He never told us
any fairy stories. He would never tell anything untrue; he's only told us true stories."[21]

It is hard for even the best public relations campaign to compete with such
a deep-seated worldview of witches as direct agents of the devil. One Wiccan,
for example, related how Wiccans were regarded as "wolves in sheep's clothing"
by the Campus Crusade For Christ. The group, on a Big Ten campus, had
sponsored a speaker on Satanism, and local Wiccans attended it in order to correct any potential misinformation which might be given out concerning Wicca.
At that meeting the Wiccans made ecumenical overtures to Campus Crusade to
work together to combat Satanic abuse, because such Satanists were desecrating
not only Christian sacred symbols and beliefs but those of Wicca as well. The
guest speaker for the Crusade, however, rebuffed the offer, indicating that there
was nothing the two groups could do together because Christians could not
trust Wiccans—Satan might be working through them.[22]

Moreover, public misperceptions and misgivings are often fueled by organized national political action groups which have targeted Wicca and the Neo-
Pagan spiritual movement as a threat to Christian America and American values. The American Library Association indicated that activist Christian Right
groups have led in efforts to remove books on the occult and witchcraft from
school and public libraries.[23] Concomitantly, some Christian publishing houses
have been publishing books focused on "Paganism" (a term used interchange-
ably with "New-Agers") as a source of modern evils and a threat to the nation's
well-being.

For example, one book[24] traces "Paganism"/"the New Age movement" back
to its alleged origins in the ancient Babylonian and Canaanite cultures. The
Babylonians and Canaanites, the book points out, were mortal biblical enemies
of God and the Israelites. The Book of Isaiah is then quoted as follows:

> The *offspring of the wicked* will never be mentioned again. *Prepare a place
> to slaughter his sons* for the sins of their forefathers; they are not to rise to

inherit the land and cover the earth with their cities.
Isaiah 14:20, 21, *spoken of Babylon, but applicable to all cultures which are the "sons"of Babylon*[25]

The mention of slaughtering the sons (i.e., the cultural descendants) of the Babylonians (i. e., the "New Agers") is enough to give most Wiccans pause, particularly when the Book of Exodus also states, "You shall not permit a sorceress to live."[26]

In DeParrie and Pride's *The Ancient Empires*, religious tolerance is not a virtue but a serious sin against God. Indeed, the book "points out how odd it is that total religious tolerance (as practiced in Babylon and many other ancient empires) always went hand-in-hand with human torture and sacrifice."[27] After direct comparisons are drawn between the ancient Israelites/today's conservative Christians, and the Canaanites/today's Pagan New Agers, God's warnings to the Israelites are then repeated:

> Obey what I command you today. Behold, I will drive out before you the . . . Canaanites. . . . Be careful not to make a treaty with those who live in the land where you are going, or they will be a snare among you. *Break down their altars, smash their sacred stones and cut down their Asherah poles.* . . . Be careful not to make a treaty with those who live in the land.[28]

The lesson drawn in *The Ancient Empires* from this biblical episode was that the failure to eliminate the Canaanites from the Promised Land was a compromise that went against the will of God. Such a compromise eventually, but directly, led to the demise of the Israelites as a nation. The unmistakable message is that if good Christian Americans tolerate pagans and compromise with them, God will bring down the United States just as he punished and destroyed Israel.[29]

Christ's proclamation in the Gospel of Luke, "He who is not with me is against me . . . ,"[30] is also used by activists to prove that religious toleration of non-Christian religions (i.e., Wicca) is not a viable option for Christians. Indeed, religious toleration is described as a "pagan" rule, and

> *Christians do not have to play the game according to the pagans' rules.* The rule that all religions, even Satan worship, must be given equal treatment under the law is not in the Bible. The rule that we must not hurt the fragile self-esteem of non-believers by pointing out their evil practices and ungodly beliefs is not in the Bible. The rule that we must obey Supreme Court decisions that forbid our children to pray in school is not in the Bible.[31]

Readers are then given a history lesson which is aimed at constitutionally validating active religious intolerance:

> "Oh," some will protest, "surely the 'freedom of religion' mentioned in the Bill of Rights means the founders intended to create a free bazaar of religions, where everything from Satanism to Ba'hai gets equal protection." Not a chance.

> We would like to suggest that what the Founding Fathers meant by "freedom of religion" was "freedom of Biblical religion," e.g., Christianity and its associated sects. They were worried that one of these sects might become an established state religion, but not at all opposed to generally promoting Christianity.[32]

These attitudes towards non-Christians in general, and against religious tolerance in particular, are not limited to such publications but have become "common coinage" in defense of activists' harassments and protests against Wiccans: In newspaper accounts and personal narratives of incidences of Wiccan harassment, Christian ministers from various parts of the country have been reported as justifying their promotion of active intolerance of Wiccans by using the very arguments reflected above, particularly the denial of constitutional protection for non-Christians and an active promotion of intolerance of those who do not worship the Christian God.[33]

The following narratives and analysis of the Wiccan experience of religious freedom must be read and considered in light of the above setting. Wiccans have made great strides in gaining religious freedoms taken for granted by other religious groups. But, as indicated in Wiccan narratives, harms and harassments still are occurring. For analytical purposes, this essay has divided the more common reports into three types: the use of the law as a weapon of religious harassment, abuse of power by government agents, and private personal attacks on Wiccans.

THE USE OF LAW AS A WEAPON
OF RELIGIOUS HARASSMENT

This section explores several areas of law that reportedly have been used as weapons against Wiccans: child custody law, zoning law, distorted Establishment Clause challenges to Wiccan attempts to correct public misperceptions, and, finally, the unsuccessful attempt in the United States Congress in 1985 to prohibit Wiccan religious groups from claiming tax exempt status and the benefits which accompany such status.

Several narratives related that the Wiccan religion is used as a trump card to turn courts against Wiccan parents in order to cut off or limit property settlement, to gain total custody of the children, or to cut off visitation rights.[34] One narrative by a Wiccan mother, for example, noted the difficulties she had in simply retaining a lawyer to represent her. Several of the lawyers she contacted to handle the divorce refused her case out of a fear of paganism, or from a fear that her being a "Witch" would prove "too controversial." Her husband, who had a history of wife and child abuse, was awarded custody of the child because the judge "did not approve of her lifestyle." The judge considered it child abuse to take the child to Wiccan ceremonies, rituals, or celebrations of pagan holi-days. The court went so far as to order that there be no mention of Wicca or Wiccan-related subjects in the child's presence, and the child was to have no further contact with the members of the mother's religious group or their chil-dren (who had been the child's playmates). Indeed, the Wiccan's first lawyer had advised her coven to stop practicing their religion until her divorce case was over.[35]

Even when the outcome of such a challenge is successful, the victory may be Pyrrhic. One Wiccan from Maryland related that she had filed for divorce from her husband (whom she described as abusive), and sought child custody. To "equalize" the situation, her husband accused her of being a devil worshipper. When her husband eventually lost the custody fight, she alleged that he sought assistance from an activist group who kidnapped the children and took them out of state on what the Wiccan mother described as a "fundamentalist under-ground" which "rescues" children awarded to pagan parents.[36]

Zoning is another area of law which Wiccans report is being used against Wiccan religious groups and believers. As noted, Wiccan religious ritual ideal-ly occurs out-of-doors, in a natural setting which is considered as sacred space. But religious categories in zoning laws are usually written with respect to "churches," and these sacred circles are not normative Christian church build-ings. This very argument was advanced in a fight against one Wiccan group's application for a church variance for a large acreage area zoned for farmland. In fact, the county zoning administrator himself defined the term "church" for zoning purposes as a gathering of Christians, and called the Wiccan group "anti-church" at the initial public zoning hearing. Few Wiccan groups have the resources for protracted legal battles, and as a practical matter, this Wiccan group wished to resolve the matter amicably and not by legal force. Despite the Wiccan group's efforts at compromise, the approval process for their zoning variance was dragged out for many years, primarily due to stiff and unyielding opposition from some churches in the area.[37] Indeed, at one opposition rally at a local Christian church, an ABC *20/20* television show documentary on Satanism was shown, and many locals left the church convinced that the Wiccan group advocated, if not practiced, torture, abuse, and ritual animal or even human sacrifice. Notably, in the midst of this highly-publicized and pro-tracted zoning process, the county changed its zoning law in order to ensure that no Wiccan or other similar religious group could purchase and use land for sacred purposes: it enacted a carefully worded, neutral-on-its-face ban of all church/religious variances for property zoned for farming.[38] After finally threat-ening a lawsuit (now with backing from the local ACLU), the Wiccan Circle eventually was given a "church" conditional use permit. The new zoning regu-lation did not affect their application since it had been in the zoning process before the change took effect. On the positive side, all two hundred acres were allowed zoning as a church. Included in the conditional use permit, however, were restrictions severely limiting the number of persons (an average of thirty-five adults) who could attend religious services on the two hundred-plus acre property.[39] Can one imagine the outcry that would be heard if a Christian church, with a capacity of two hundred for fire regulation purposes, were to be limited to thirty-five persons per Sunday?

Another problem is the selective enforcement of zoning and building codes. In Wisconsin, a local highway commission told a Wiccan proprietor of a Wiccan/New Age shop that she had a nonconforming sign, and had to move it back a competitively-disadvantageous thirty-three feet from the road. Other business signs in the area, although not in conformance with this requirement, were not similarly required to be moved.[40]

Profoundly disturbing to Wiccans are Christian activists' efforts to limit or even deny Wiccans' civil rights. As one Wiccan has put it, "mainstream religions have more right to first amendment rights than we do."[41] Ironically, at a time when the activists of the Religious Right have stepped up efforts to put Christian prayer back into public schools and events, and have won the right to place Christmas nativity displays next to Santas on the lawns of public property, they have also successfully blocked Wiccans from giving purely informational speech on Wicca in public forums.

In New Mexico, a local Wiccan was invited to speak to a high school class on the differences between Wicca and Satanism. She did this without incident for a few semesters, until she was interviewed for the school newspaper by a student who had heard her lecture. Parents read the article and became irate that a witch had been allowed inside their school. A state-wide Christian television channel took up the cause. Announcers on the channel equated Wicca with Satanism, and indicated that "satanic witchcraft in the schools was responsible for teenage murders, suicides, and drug addiction." The male co-host stated, "God has given us the right to bind these witches." The Wiccan was never invited back to speak at the school.[42]

At a Halloween festival co-sponsored by a private group and a New Jersey coastal resort city, a Wiccan had been invited to give a purely educational (*not* evangelical) talk about Wiccanism for the stated purpose of correcting popular misconceptions about the religion. The talk was to be in a limited access, enclosed upper room of the municipal auditorium/convention center on the boardwalk. A person would have to deliberately choose to be exposed to the talk, for the public could not overhear it while simply walking by on the boardwalk.

Some ministers found out about the Wiccan's scheduled appearance. One week before the festival, the Wiccan was denounced from a few local church pulpits for "bringing Satan" to the city. Threats of disruptions of the festival were made, and thus under pressure from these ministers, the mayor canceled the Wiccan's speaking engagement. A local Methodist minister was quoted by the Associated Press wire service as stating, "This issue is not about freedom of expression or freedom of speech. . . . I object to him speaking in a public forum where the presence of children is allowed. [The minister] said he is tolerant of other religions, but that witchcraft falls into Satanic worship because it does not acknowledge the existence of God."[43] The local Baptist minister was quoted in a newspaper article as stating, "A good witch is an oxymoron."[44]

In San Jose, California, the public library had hired a Wiccan, Z Budapest, to give a public informational/educational lecture aimed at dispelling misinformation about modern witchcraft. One city council member protested because "it's a matter of promoting witchcraft, which is of no benefit to the community."[45] Rev. Scott Hagen, a protest organizer, stated that the Wiccans' appearance amounted to "state financial support for a religion—therefore unfair, illegal, and a change in the rules under which other churches operate."[46]

The United States Supreme Court, however, has not prohibited speech directed at purely educational efforts concerning various religions in public schools. The speech it limited under the Establishment Clause was preaching: evangelizing efforts, devotional worship, the "teaching *of*" religion. What the Wiccans in the above instances were asked to do was simply convey information *about* their religion in order to dispel misunderstanding and promote the civic good of religious tolerance. Indeed, the distinction between teaching "about" religion versus the teaching "of" religion lies at the very core of Establishment Clause limits on speech. It was devotional worship and proselytizing in the public schools, or directly or indirectly with public support/funding, which had been banned under the Establishment Clause. In contrast, teaching theology, not with the intent of encouraging students to personally inculcate the beliefs, but as an *academic enterprise*, is teaching "about" religion. The Supreme Court found "teaching about" religion to be a constitutionally acceptable form of teaching in the public sector:

> The holding of the Court today plainly does not foreclose teaching *about* [Justice Brennan's emphasis] the Holy Scriptures or about the differences between religious sects in classes in literature or history. Indeed, whether or not the Bible is involved, it would be impossible to teach meaningfully many subjects in the social sciences or the humanities without some mention of religion.[47]

Speaking in a non-coerced, optional, public forum to educate "about," to clear up misperceptions about a religious group, is not qualitatively different from either teaching "religious studies" in a state college or maintaining a reference collection on various religions and religious groups in public libraries. Certainly, the latter two activities are quite routine. The fact that the religion is anathema to some does not qualify it for censure from an educational forum or for book banning from a public library: "The state has no legitimate interest in protecting any or all religions from views distasteful to them."[48] To be sure, the contrast between proselytizing and educating is quite stark in most situations.

Lastly, as noted above, Wiccan narratives commonly report police questioning and investigation of their outdoor religious rituals has occurred at one time or another. Wiccan groups have indicated that tax registration indicating the group is a religious, non-profit organization quickly eased tensions and give credence to their explanations. Thus, Wiccans perceived it to be a serious threat when, in 1985, Senator Jesse Helms and Representative Robert Walker[49] sought to remove "witchcraft" from tax-exempt religious status through what became known among Wiccans as the "Helms Amendment." The text of Senator Helms's proposed legislation was as follows:

> No funds appropriated under this Act shall be used to grant, maintain, or allow tax exemptions to any cult, organization, or other group that has as a purpose, or that has any interest in, the promoting of satanism or witchcraft: *Provided,* That for purposes of this section, "satanism" is defined as the worship of Satan or the powers of evil and "witchcraft" is defined as the use of powers derived from evil spirits, the use of sorcery, or the use of supernatural powers with malicious intent.[50]

Such a move would have been costly to the small Wiccan organizations as well as their members, since the covens would have lost bulk mailing privileges and contributions from religious adherents would no longer have been tax exempt. But, as noted above, the amendment also posed a far more serious threat: a review by the IRS and a grant of tax-exempt status serves as unofficial notice to all other governmental agencies that non-dominant religious groups such as Wicca are to be accorded "the benefit of the doubt" as credible religions. In essence, the practical effect of the Helms Amendment would have been to deny religious legitimacy to the Wiccan religion.

In support of his amendment, Senator Helms introduced into the record the entire transcript of a report on Satanism done by the ABC television series, *20/20.*[51] Representative of the tone and content of the show was ABC correspondent Hugh Downs's introduction of the segment: "Perverse, hideous acts that defy belief. Suicides, murders, and the ritualistic slaughter of children and animals. Yet so far police have been helpless."[52] Downs cautioned the viewers that the segment contained graphic footage and might scare younger children. The program offered no warning, however, that Wiccan witchcraft was *not* to be confused with the Satanism depicted in the show.

Helms made it quite clear in his colloquy that Wiccan groups fell under the rubric of "use of powers derived from evil spirits, the use of sorcery, or the use of supernatural powers with malicious intent." He introduced a letter from then-Secretary of the Treasury James Baker into the record, which was written in response to Helms's inquiry about the tax-exempt status of groups "promoting witchcraft." Baker had indicated that "under the [IRS] standards [for determining religious exemptions]" such exempt status had been granted to groups "that espouse a system of beliefs, rituals, and practices, derived in part from pre-Christian Celtic and Welsh traditions, which they label as 'witchcraft.' We have no evidence that any of the organizations have either engaged in or promoted any illegal activity."[53] Senator Helms's response was to condemn the IRS's judgment:

Mr. President, despite the reasoning of the Secretary [Baker], I simply cannot believe that Congress ever intended for section 501(c)(3) of the Internal Revenue Code to be used to promote witchcraft or other cult-related activities through the granting of tax-exempt status. To whatever extent such activities occur in this country, they certainly should not be subsidized—directly or indirectly—by the U.S. taxpayers.

After all, Mr. President, we allow tax-exempt status for *bona fide religious organizations because we believe they help promote the common good. Cults and witchcraft do not; in fact they lead to violent and unlawful behavior.*[54]

Thus, the Wiccan gods and goddesses were, by Helms's definition, "evil spirits" and Wiccan worship and ritual was, by definition, "sorcery" done with "malicious intent."

Helms's amendment was passed by voice vote in the Senate,[55] and went into Joint Conference. The Wiccan community, a scattered group, became united and galvanized by the passage of the amendment. Indeed, the Wiccan community ultimately benefitted by the legislative threat in that it served as a "wake-up call." Wiccan communications and grassroots letter-writing networks became organized for the first time. After heated lobbying efforts from both opponents and proponents, the Committee ultimately dropped the amendment for what the Wiccans deemed a rather noncommittal reason: the Committee rejected the Helms Amendment because, according to one Wiccan source who was closely involved in the matter, it deemed it "legislation not appropriate to the Bill to which it was attached."[56] Wiccans, however, believed that they deserved a rejection on the merits and on the record.

ABUSE OF POWER BY GOVERNMENT AGENTS

Government employees, supported by taxpayers, theoretically and ideally are "servants" of *all* the people, and not just of those who agree with their political and religious beliefs. Ideally, government employees hold their jobs in trust for the good of the populace as a whole. Former Surgeon General C. Everett Koop is a living example of this ethic. What he explains in the following quote, while directed at his field of public health, is applicable in the abstract to all civil servants:

It's very difficult to explain to someone the awe . . . that goes with the responsibilities of this office. You can never divorce yourself from your religious beliefs, from your ethical or moral beliefs, but when you are in the position of being, let's say, what most people consider to be the primary health officer of a country of 240,000,000 people, and they are all your charges—whether you like what the way they behave, whether you like their politics, whether you like what they do with their lives or not—you have to have an understanding that when you speak, you not only speak for their benefit, but you are preserving forever, if you can, the integrity of the office you hold.[57]

Some public servants, however, have been unwilling or unable to act on behalf of all the public but instead have acted on their particular religious beliefs to the detriment of their fellow (non-Christian, Wiccan) citizens. Such active and personal harassment of a person based upon their religious beliefs is unacceptable under any circumstances, but when conducted by a taxpayer-supported government employee the matter becomes even more deplorable, for it violates the public trust and calls into question the fairness and integrity of the government itself.

According to Wiccan reports, the most common arena for such harassment is the government workplace. Wiccans working in law enforcement, at state universities, and as social workers have related incidences of fear and job harassment.[58] There is a common theme that emerges from the various narratives. Job performance is satisfactory, if not commendable, until the employee's religious beliefs become known to an intolerant employee or supervisor. From that point on, whispering campaigns ensue and lies and rumors are spread about the employee, until those in power over the employee come to believe that the Wiccan employee should not be promoted, or should even be fired. As is evident from difficulties in pursuing claims of sexual harassment or racial prejudice on the job, claims of religious harassment are difficult to prove. One Wiccan job discrimination case actually reached federal court. In the Southern District of Mississippi, the U.S. District Court ruled in favor of Jaime Dodge, holding that a private, Christian social welfare agency which accepted government funds for its program to assist battered women could not fire a Wiccan case coordinator in that program solely because she was a Wiccan.[59]

And despite the *institutional* progress made by the military toward Wiccan religious freedom, the extent to which such freedom is experienced is, as in the area of job discrimination, very much dependent on the conscience and goodwill of immediate officers. For example, shortly before her husband was deployed in Operation Desert Storm, one military wife was told by her husband's squadron chaplain that she would not be getting any help with problems while he was gone because she was a Satanist and did not deserve any help. This writer noted that the military listens more to military outsiders "on these issues" than to the military people themselves.[60] Another Wiccan wrote that his sergeant had confiscated his altar and called him a devil worshipper.[61]

Wiccan prisoners in many states report[62] that they are denied Wiccan reading materials, or that such materials must be first approved by "Christian reverends," and no donations are permitted to Wiccan groups. One Wiccan prisoner complained that "Moslems get a pork-free diet" and yet she is not similarly accorded a vegetarian diet in keeping with her Wiccan-based practice of twenty years. Furthermore, she is denied use of her altar cloths and Wiccan bible, while Christian prisoners "have their Bibles and crosses and Bible studies."[63] Another Wiccan prisoner reported that while in theory the federal bureau of prisons recognizes Wicca as a legitimate religion, in reality the restrictions imposed make it impossible to practice the religion: no loaning of books or materials, no Wiccan books in the chapel, cannot use the chapel for ritual worship, no robes, no essences, no oils, no alter clothes or tools, no tarot cards. They are allowed to practice only within the confines of their cells.[64]

School atmosphere and teacher conduct are also reported as sources of harassment of Wiccan children. One Wiccan reported that her son was discriminated against at school for being pagan and wearing pagan symbols.[65] Another Wiccan reported that her daughter had been converted to Christianity when a Baptist group had been permitted to "recruit" at the local public junior high school. Since that time, her daughter has been alienated from every other family member, "as have several of those who were her fellow students."[66] A Wiccan high school student reported that she and her Wiccan friends are kicked out of class for reading witchcraft books while the student in front of her who is reading the Bible is left alone. She continues, "Some of the teachers have took it upon themselves to preach to us. My english teacher . . . even went so far as to call my religion evil. . . . Alot [sic] of kids in this school want to do something about it [religious discrimination coupled with preaching] but are afraid of the consequences [sic]."[67]

Some Wiccans who opposed the Helms Amendment did not feel safe in writing even their own elected representatives to voice their opposition to the measure. One letter from North Carolina, Senator Helms's own state, is telling: "As you will note from my return address and postmark, I am in NO [emphasis in original] position to write my representative nor to my state senator. Burning crosses, I've heard, do nothing for one's landscaping."[68] A Wiccan from South Carolina wrote that she would give prayer assistance to help defeat the Helms Amendment, but that she was afraid to do anything publicly about it, "as you can see by the area I live in."[69]

But Wiccans have not only been given a signal from some of their elected representatives that they are not to be tolerated or given equal protection under the laws. For, while it is true that Wiccans have had great success in correcting and preventing acts of harassment by police and prosecutors, there have been instances where the police and/or prosecutors have not been willing to pursue with much vigor those who have committed religious hate crimes against Wiccans. Two narratives are quite revealing of this problem.

One such example of prosecutorial laxity concerned the crimes of trespass and assault committed against Wiccans in (of all places) Salem, Massachusetts by Christian fundamentalist activists. On or about 7 June 1992, a local Christian minister sponsored a "concert" which turned into a staged anti-witchcraft rally. A former rock singer-turned-anti-witchcraft-activist from Upland California Messiah Ministries sang four songs and then primarily focused his energies on the necessity of ridding Salem of witches. The organizers had invited witches to attend, and they became worried that the crowds would get worked up to the point that they would attack them. Thereafter, it is alleged that the anti-Wiccan activist and a film crew (both with alleged connections to Trinity Broadcasting Network located in Ontario, California) entered a local Wiccan/New Age shop and are alleged to have made abusive remarks about the Wiccan religion and intimidated and threatened the store manager (all while on film). Although they were asked to leave, the film crew continued to photograph the store and harass and photograph the persons inside the store. When the police arrived, the crew continued to film even as the police forced them to leave.

The activist and his television crew then left the store, went down the street, and were reported to have accosted a mother who was pushing her infant in a carriage with her 7-year-old daughter beside her. This woman was allegedly recognized as a witch, and the contingent of approximately fifteen people surrounded her. The woman reported that she was trapped and became frightened for her safety and the safety of her children. She was confronted by the activist and was reportedly harassed by him while their cameras filmed the entire encounter. The Wiccan was asked if they could pray for her, and she said yes, if she could in turn pray for them. Without any warning that they would be touching her, two of the activists apparently pulled the terrified[70] woman's hands from her daughter's, breaking her contact with her children, and held them up in the air to "witness" with her in "prayer."

Despite these allegations of direct assaults, battery, personal threats and harassments, and despite full cooperation from the local police department, the local prosecutor's office refused to prosecute. It was left to the Massachusetts attorney general to take action in the case; the Civil Rights Division issued a letter of warning against the anti-Wiccan activist based upon a violation of a Massachusetts law which prohibits harassment directed against persons for their religious beliefs.

The local police captain has received hate mail from those who have seen the broadcasts on the Trinity Broadcasting Network and think he is the devil because his police officers investigated and aided the victims of the (alleged) harassment and assault. Salem police Captain Paul Murphy noted that he is "just doing his job" upholding the law and protecting people from illegal assault and harassment, and that he in fact is not Wiccan but a Roman Catholic. Hate mail has also been sent to the city manager's office, with blame directed at the city for allowing witchcraft to flourish in Salem.[71] In particular, activists have condemned the erection of a public monument honoring religious freedom, as a celebration of witchcraft.

Another incident in Georgia in September 1985[72] involved destruction of a Wiccan coven's sacred outdoor worship area that was located on private land. The group responsible had actually notified a television film crew of what they were about to do, and the Wiccans were shocked as their local television stations showed actual footage of vandals desecrating and demolishing their altar and worship area while the police stood by and watched. Indeed, the police had also had advance warning of the vandalism and did little about the desecration other than to instruct the Wiccan group to stay away from their property for their own safety until the vandals were gone!

Later, as members of the Wiccan group ritually closed down the sacred site, they were threatened with gun shots, and then suffered verbal abuse from approximately twenty men in seven or eight pick-ups/jeeps/four-wheelers. These men then drove their vehicles directly at the Wiccans, who came within inches of being run over. Despite the fact that the Wiccans had license plate numbers of the trucks, photographs of the incident, and a tape recording of the entire episode, prosecution lagged. The Wiccan group persistently pursued their complaints with the prosecutor's office to get charges brought, but justice was not forthcoming. The district attorney assigned to the case showed up at court without a case file and knew nothing about it, so the Wiccans' personal attorney (who was there for "moral support") prosecuted the case on their behalf. Despite the plethora of evidence (witnesses, clear audio tape, and photographs) supporting a simple assault charge, the prosecutors had refused to charge it. Criminal trespass was therefore the only charge at issue. When the judge called the case, he sent the court reporter out of the room, and thus none of the Wiccan testimony ever made it into a record. The vandals were all *acquitted* because although the property had been posted with "No Trespassing" signs, *and* a legal notice had been run in the newspaper indicating that the property was posted, notice had not also been posted with the local courthouse. Hence, no trespass had occurred.[73]

PRIVATE ATTACKS ON WICCANS

Wiccans report evictions from rented homes, rented land, professional offices, and retail stores, motivated by religious hatred and fear.[74] They also report job firings and job harassment and discrimination.[75] Another common report is the vandalism of sacred lands and altars, vandalism of their homes, and verbal threats and harassment waged against Wiccans themselves.[76] After one member of a Wiccan group in Oregon began publishing a newsletter, its sacred circle was desecrated. The publisher discontinued the newsletter noting that the publication was not worth the risk to his coven.[77] Wiccans report being personally assaulted for simply wearing a sacred pentagram around their necks in public, or because they are otherwise known to be witches.[78] Wiccan covens have been fired upon with guns during services.[79] It appears to be a consensus among Wiccans that these incidents are on the rise.[80] Yet, too often Wiccans and covens cannot vindicate their rights because they simply do not have the resources it takes to hire a lawyer and go through a protracted litigation and appeals process.

CONCLUSION

This essay has not focused on abstract, narrow, constitutional arguments concerning religious freedom. Rather, it has considered the Wiccan experience of religious freedom in the United States in the broadest, most commonly understood sense of the phrase, i.e., the freedom to worship according to the dictates of one's own conscience within reasonable limits of the law. Those who object to the information presented simply because they do not feel that some of the incidents rise to the level of a technical constitutional violation, have missed the point. Wiccans represent a litmus test for the state of religious freedom and tolerance in America: they are non-Christian outsiders whose normative practices are within the bounds of the law. It is quite clear that any religious discrimination and hatred directed at them arises purely from disagreements with their theology and a misunderstanding of their practices, and not because they are normatively lawless or disruptive to the peace and good order of society.

Great progress has been made toward eliminating religious prejudice against Wiccans through education. But greater progress is needed before Wiccans enjoy the same measure of religious freedoms that Christians take for granted: the freedom to worship in peace without fear of disturbance and even violence from outsiders; the freedom to have a permanent place in which to conduct religious services; the freedom to wear and thus honor the sacred symbols of their religious belief without being bodily assaulted or put in fear of bodily harm; the freedom to correct misinformation and simply educate others about their religion in order to prevent harassment and promote tolerance; the freedom to raise their children according to their faith and religious practices without fear of losing custody of them, or having to defend their fitness as parents to teachers, social workers, police, or judges merely because of their religious affiliation; the freedom to live wherever they can afford to; and the freedom to work without fear of harassment and of being judged not by their abilities but by their religious beliefs.

What assistance can the government and the law give to assure a fuller and thus more equal experience of religious freedom for Wiccans? First, the concept of a government job as a position held in trust for all of the people is an ethic which should govern all civil servants and elected representatives, from the local to the national level. These positions cannot be seen as platforms from which to carry out personal theological vendettas against fellow citizens. Second, informational courses in schools and lectures in libraries that survey religions in America in a fair manner, and do not seek to advance or inculcate any particular religion, could serve to dispel misunderstanding about "outsider" groups. Third, a firm stand by public leaders and officials in favor of the seemingly forgotten civic virtue of religious tolerance would set an important example and give notice that American society will not tolerate religious harassment. Swift and strict prosecution of any and all crimes committed out of religious hatred would also send a message that intolerance and religious harassment are not permissible activities.

Finally, for every inroad made in the courts by the Christian Right favoring greater "free exercise" or "free expression" rights at the expense of former Establishment Clause principles, the court issuing such an opinion should make it quite plain that *all* religious groups have these same rights. For example: since the practice of having ministers and chaplains for legislative bodies has been approved, Wiccan priestesses are as equally qualified as Christian ministers in the eyes of the law to offer prayers at the start of a legislative day. If Christian student groups can meet at school for prayer and worship purposes, then it should be made clear that student-run Wiccan worship groups have the same freedom to use public facilities. Pagan Yule symbols should be placed along side of nativity scenes and Santa Clauses on public properties. And, should Christians ultimately win the right to pray in public schools, certainly prayers should similarly be offered to the Wiccan gods and goddesses.

The principle of equal liberty at stake here is foundational to the American system of justice. As explained by John Rawls:

> Suppose those who do not believe in toleration, and who would not tolerate others had they the power, wish to protest their lesser liberty by appealing to the sense of justice of the majority which holds the principle of equal liberty. While those who accept this principle should, as we have seen, tolerate the intolerant as far as the safety of free institutions permits, they are likely to resent being reminded of this duty by the intolerant who would, if positions were switched, establish their own dominion. The majority is bound to feel that their allegiance to equal liberty is being exploited by others for unjust ends. *This situation illustrates once again the fact that a common sense of justice is a great collective asset which requires the cooperation of many to maintain.* The intolerant can be viewed as free-riders, as persons who seek the advantages of just institutions while not doing their share to uphold them.[81]

Similarly, on the issue of Wiccan religious freedom, a democratic society must refuse to accept religious intolerance which goes beyond speech in a pulpit but becomes active harassment of those who are guilty of nothing more than holding religious beliefs which some Christians deem to be anathema.

Chapter 11

The Persecution of West Virginia Jehovah's Witnesses and the Expansion of Legal Protection for Religious Liberty

Chuck Smith

INTRODUCTION:
JEHOVAH'S WITNESSES AND RELIGIOUS LIBERTY

Few Americans are aware of the valuable contribution Jehovah's Witnesses have made to our nation's laws. A mention of them brings to mind the picture of persistent, sometime annoying, teams of door-to-door preachers whose aggressive proselytizing campaigns have made them a symbol of the troublesome irritants of daily life. Legal scholars, however, have long acknowledged Jehovah's Witnesses as champions in the constitutional battle to protect religious liberty.[1] A 1942 examination of the sect's contributions to protection for the free exercise of religion contended:

> Seldom, if ever, in the past, has one individual or group been able to shape the course, over a period of time, of any phase of our vast body of constitutional law. But it can happen, and has happened here. The group is the Jehovah's Witnesses.[2]

During the 1940s, legally significant Jehovah's Witnesses litigation arose in almost every state. Justice Harlan Fiske Stone noted the importance of this legislation. "I think the Jehovah's Witnesses ought to have an endowment in view

155

of the aid they give in solving legal problems of civil liberty," he quipped in a letter.[3]

Scholars have seldom noted that the legal influence of Jehovah's Witnesses was not limited to constitutional law; the sect's efforts also led to the expansion of legal protection for free exercise of religion in other areas of law. Four cases that arose in West Virginia are particularly worth examining because they significantly expanded legal protection for religious liberty, each in a different area of law. In the first case, an early example of "new judicial federalism," the Hancock County Circuit Court used the West Virginia Constitution to increase protection for the free exercise of religion beyond the safeguards provided by the U.S. Constitution. The second instance, the infamous Richwood castor oil case, expanded the protection of religious liberty through judicial interpretation of the Civil Right Act. The third action concerned the firing of seven glassworkers in Clarksburg; it brought about an unprecedented use of administrative law to protect the free exercise of religion. The final case, a 1943 landmark U. S. Supreme Court decision that expanded the constitutional safeguards for free exercise of religion and freedom of speech, was also a bellwether case that reflected the U.S. Supreme Court's move toward more expansive protection of First Amendment rights.

The Jehovah's Witnesses' aggressive, unconventional style of evangelism resulted in many confrontations in communities across the United States. Sociologist M. James Penton reported, "Between 1933 and 1951 there were 18,866 arrests of American Witnesses and about 1500 cases of mob violence against them."[4] To cope with these problems, the sect established its own legal department and sustained a determined campaign of litigation to assert the right to freely exercise its beliefs.[5] By 1950, Jehovah's Witnesses had won 150 suits in state supreme courts and more than thirty precedent-setting decisions in the U.S. Supreme Court.[6] These cases contributed significantly to broadening the protection of the free speech and religious liberties guaranteed by the First and Fourteenth Amendments and by various provisions of state constitutions.

Animosity toward the Jehovah's Witnesses resulted, in large part, from the militant methods they employed in promulgating their beliefs. The sect began its aggressive campaign of door-to-door proselytizing in the late 1920s. Convinced that any concessions to the convenience of the public were an affront to Jehovah, the Witnesses accepted none of the constraints usually imposed by time, place, or propriety. A contemporary observer frankly summarized a widely held perception of members of the sect:

> Witnesses assume an exceedingly aggressive, intolerant, and even boorish
> attitude toward a prospective convert, apparently assuming that, since he
> is himself the repository of all religious wisdom, the other must be a dolt
> if he does not immediately see the light.[7]

Throughout the 1930s, the dogmatic, uncompromising message of the Witnesses was matched by an escalation of the contentious manner in which it was spread.[8] At times hundreds of Jehovah's Witnesses would descend on a small town going from door to door insisting aggressively that their message be heard.[9] They also began parading down main streets and picketing in front of Catholic Churches on Sunday morning with signs that proclaimed such things as, "Religion is a Snare and a Racket."[10]

The sect was also scorned because of its contemptuous attitude toward secular authority and the widely held perception that Witnesses were unpatriotic. Their extensive disassociation of themselves from the government was particularly manifested in their refusal to salute the flag. Witnesses maintained that to salute would be to ascribe salvation to the government represented by the flag. They contended, therefore, that the flag salute was forbidden by the scriptural command against making and bowing down to graven images.[11] A seminal study of the nature of patriotism argues that Jehovah's Witnesses are among those people of faith "who take their religion most seriously and cannot, therefore, be patriotic."[12] This imputed lack of patriotism was the catalyst for most of the attacks on Witnesses, violence that escalated in 1939 and 1940.[13] These attacks coincided with the outbreak of World War II and a U.S. Supreme Court decision that held public schools could expel students who refused to salute the flag.[14] War-fever and heightened patriotism intensified hostility toward the Witnesses. Many people suspected them of being "fifth columnists" who sympathized with Nazi Germany and of undermining the potential American war effort.[15] In the early 1940s, state and local officials enacted new policies—or used existing laws—to regulate or suppress the sect's proselytizing activities.[16] During this period, hundreds of actions against Jehovah's Witnesses occurred in rural and small town America;[17] a number took place in West Virginia.[18] Most of these confrontations revolved around the refusal of Jehovah's Witnesses to participate in flag salute ceremonies. A 1991 incident in Hancock County contained the standard elements of a typical conflict involving the Jehovah's Witnesses. The legal action taken to resolve it, however, was unusual.

USING THE STATE CONSTITUTION
TO SAFEGUARD RELIGIOUS PRACTICE

High school senior Joseph Clementino resolutely petitioned the Hancock County Board of Education to allow him to graduate with his class—the Weir High School class of 1941. Over the previous two months, he and at least twenty-five other Jehovah's Witnesses students in West Virginia's northernmost county had been expelled from school because they refused to salute the flag.

The board was unimpressed by Clementino's sincerity or tenacity, and it turned a deaf ear to the teenager's request to be readmitted along with his nine-year-old brother, Albert.[19] Clementino did not graduate with his class, but that was not the only cost of his adherance to religious convictions. The following year, his father and four other fathers of expelled children were indicted for violating the state's draconian truancy law.[20]

Throughout America, children of Jehovah's Witnesses were being expelled from schools because they refused to take part in flag-salute ceremonies. Three years earlier, in 1938, Jehovah's Witnesses families in Pennsylvania requested a federal court to issue an injunction prohibiting the Minersville School District from expelling children who refused to salute the flag. They claimed that the expulsions violated the U.S. Constitution's First Amendment provision protecting the free exercise of religion. After the Jehovah's Witnesses won in the Federal District Court and at the U.S. Court of Appeals, the school district asked for a review by the U.S. Supreme Court. In *Minersville School District v. Gobitis*, the Court ruled that schools did not violate the Free Exercise Clause of the First Amendment when they expelled students who refused to salute the flag.[21] Eighteen months after the *Gobitis* ruling, the West Virginia State Board of Education adopted a resolution that required students salute the flag and provided "that refusal to salute the Flag [sic] be regarded as an act of insubordination and refusal shall be dealt with accordingly."[22]

In Hancock County, after students were expelled for refusing to salute the flag, the county's prosecuting attorney punished them further by obtaining misdemeanor truancy indictments against five fathers of expelled children.[23] Circuit Judge J. Harold Brennan consolidated the indictments into one case,[24] which could have easily been an open-and-shut matter. The *Gobitis* decision, after all, held that such expulsions did not violate the Constitution; moreover, the State Board of Education made student participation in flag-salute ceremonies a requirement for attending school. Finally, the previous year, the West Virginia Legislature responded to students' refusal to salute the flag by amending the school law. The new provisions required that students who were expelled for not complying with school regulations must comply with those requirements before readmission and that they were unlawfully absent until the requirements were met.[25] A strict application of the letter of the law would require a sure and speedy conviction.

Judge Brennan, however, was clearly uneasy with the question posed by this case and explained "that he could not take upon himself 'the right to hold a religious view unreasonable.'"[26] He enunciated a broad understanding of what constitutes religious liberty,

> The moment that any court takes to itself the right to hold a religious view unreasonable, that moment the American courts begin to deny the right of religious freedom. The very purpose of our guarantees of freedom of religion is that unpopular minorities may hold views unreasonable in the opinion of the majorities.[27]

Judge Brennan recognized, though, that his construction of the meaning of the free exercise of religion was broader than that of the U.S. Supreme Court's decision in *Gobitis*. Therefore, he decided this case based on the provisions for religious liberty in the West Virginia Constitution. Today, a state court occasionally rules that its state's constitution provides more extensive protection of basic rights than the United States Constitution,[28] but in the 1940s such rulings were quite rare. Nevertheless, Judge Brennan held that expulsion of the school children in Hancock County violated the religious liberty provisions of the state's constitution.

The West Virginia Constitution provides that "no man shall be compelled to frequent or support any religious worship, place of ministry whatsoever; nor shall any man be forced, restrained, molested or burthened, in his body or goods, or otherwise suffer, on account of his religious opinions or beliefs. . . ."[29] Citing this provision, Judge Brennan held that it would be difficult to maintain that a "court has the right to fine or imprison a man because he will not force his child to do a positive act wholly inconsistent with the religious beliefs of them both."[30] Judge Brennan relied on the West Virginia's Constitution to safeguard religious liberties that were not protected by the Bill of Rights. His decision is particularly noteworthy because it was the first of four decisions in which state courts used their state constitutions to protect the religious freedom of school children who refused to salute the flag.[31] Unfortunately other public officials in West Virginia were not as concerned about religious liberty as Judge Brennan; two years earlier a Nicholas County deputy sheriff was a ringleader in one of the most bizarre of all the attacks on Jehovah's Witnesses.

THE CASTOR OIL INCIDENT:
STATUTORY PROTECTION OF RELIGIOUS LIBERTY

Deputy Sheriff Martin Catlette watched approvingly as fellow members of the American Legion forced four Jehovah's Witnesses to drink large doses of castor oil. Earlier that bright Saturday morning in June 1940 in Richwood, West Virginia, Catlette detained the Jehovah's Witnesses in the mayor's office at the town hall. The previous day, two of the young missionaries were in Richwood engaged in house-to-house canvassing. A West Virginia State Police officer interrupted their work, questioned them and seized a petition they were circulating. Several members of the American Legion, including Deputy Catlette, confronted the Witnesses, demanded that the two men leave town, and ordered them to stay away.[32]

The next day, 29 June 1940, the two missionaries, accompanied by seven others of their faith, returned to recover their petition. Three of them went to the town hall with a letter entreating the mayor to provide them with police protection as they continued to canvass the bustling little mountain town. When they reached the mayor's office, Deputy Catlette confronted the Witnesses and detained them. He then telephoned members of the American Legion and said, "We have three of the sons of bitches and we want you to round up the rest."[33] Soon, a Legionnaire brought the other six Witnesses into the office, which shortly thereafter fairly bristled with indignant members of American Legion Post 97. One of the veterans was a doctor; he prepared the debilitating doses of castor oil.[34] This event was among the most outrageous of the numerous of brutal assaults on Jehovah's Witnesses that swept America during June 1940.[35] The criminal prosecution that followed the attack, however, conferred it with historical significance and the appellate decision in this case upheld an interpretation of the federal civil rights statute that expanded protection for religious liberty.[36]

The confrontation with Jehovah's Witnesses in Richwood began when Charles Jones and C. A. Cecil came to Richwood to work as door-to-door preachers of the sect's apocalyptic message. The two native-born West Virginians came from Mount Lookout, a little community at the opposite end of Nicholas County.[37] They rented sleeping quarters in a Richwood rooming house and began distributing their sectarian literature. The men also sought signatures on a petition, which objected to the State of Ohio's cancellation of a contract, which allowed the Jehovah's Witnesses to use the Ohio State Fair Grounds for their national convention.[38] Even though the doorbell-ringing Jehovah's Witnesses hailed from nearby Mount Lookout, residents of Richwood quickly pegged them as outsiders. Among the townspeople, speculation burgeoned concerning the objective of these members of the nonconformist sect.

The house-to-house canvassing by these men raised suspicion among members of the American Legion. A veterans' organization founded in 1919, the Legion fostered patriotism and especially promoted the American flag as the preeminent icon of Americanism. It lobbied for statutes to protect the flag and urged state lawmakers to require public schools to conduct the flag salute daily. The Richwood post, like local Legion posts around the nation, actively promoted respect for the flag and salute ceremonies in the schools. Throughout America, members of the Legion frequently participated in persecutions of Jehovah's Witnesses.[39] In Richwood, Legionnaires instigated the police investigation of the door-to-door preachers.

On Friday, 28 June, Jones and Cecil were summoned to the State Police headquarters in Richwood. There, Officer Bernard McLaughlin questioned them about their work, and members of the American Legion also interrogated them. Three of the Legionnaires, Lee Reese, Louis Baber, and Deputy Sheriff Catlette, accused the Jehovah's Witnesses of being spies and Fifth Columnists and ordered them to leave town within four hours. Late in the afternoon, Jones and Cecil made their way back to Mount Lookout.[40]

After the Witnesses departed, members of the American Legion went to the home of Mrs. Maggie Stark, where the Witnesses rented sleeping accommodations. Mrs. Stark allowed a search of the house, which did not locate any additional Witnesses. That evening, the Legionnaires expanded their extralegal investigation. They contacted the attorney general of Ohio and were reportedly told that the communist beliefs of the Jehovah's Witnesses led to the denial of the Ohio State Fair Ground for their national convention. The Legion inquisitors examined the literature distributed by the Witnesses, which confirmed that members of the sect would not swear allegiance to the Constitution or salute the American flag.[41] The Legionnaires also discerned something sinister about a petition addressed to the governor of Ohio being circulated by Jehovah's Witnesses in West Virginia. Furthermore, they discovered a map, drawn by the Witnesses, showing the area of Richwood they had canvassed.[42] To these self-proclaimed patriots, these maps provided clear evidence that the Witnesses were spies.[43]

The following morning, Jones and Cecil returned to Richwood accompanied by seven other Witnesses from Mt. Lookout: Walter Stull, 31; Arthur Stull, 30; Howard Stull, 20; Carlton Stull, 27; John Leedy, 39; Harding Legg, 21; and Robert Shawver, 18.[44] The nine men, traveling in two cars, arrived at the Richwood Town Hall at about 10:30 a.m.; they intended to demand their confiscated petitions. Cecil, Jones, and Carlton Stull left the others in the cars and went to the mayor's office; there Deputy Sheriff Martin Catlette confronted them. He converted the office into a makeshift jail and detained the Witnesses. He asked Richwood Chief of Police Bert Stewart to watch the office door to ensure that the Witnesses did not escape. Deputy Catlette spent about ten minutes telephoning members of the American Legion informing them that the Jehovah's Witnesses had returned. Within an hour the news spread through Richwood and hundreds of people converged on the town hall.[45]

One of the first to arrive was Legionnaire Louis Baber. He went to the cars in front of the town hall and told the Witnesses that they were needed inside and escorted them to the mayor's office. Men from Post 97 and the nine Witnesses now filled the office to capacity. Catlette took control of the situation. He removed his deputy sheriff's badge and proclaimed, "What is done from here on will not be done in the name of the law."[46] Among the Legionnaires was a physician, who brought a stomach pump and a large container of castor oil. Fifty-six years later, Harding Legg recounted,

> I remember the doctor well. . . . He had a rubber hose, which looked to be at least a quarter of an inch. And he said, "If you don't drink it, we will force it down." Now who in the world would not drink it? Would you stand up there and let them punch it down your throat, a rubber hose? We didn't have no alternative.[47]

C. A. Cecil initially resisted; they forced him to drink sixteen ounces of castor oil. Carlton Stull, Walter Stull, and Harding Legg each drank four ounces.[48] The Legionnaires compelled the sectarians to drink the castor oil, a strong laxative, to cause their humiliation and degradation.

After the Jehovah's Witnesses had choked down the castor oil, the Legionnaires tied the Witnesses by the left wrists three or four feet apart along a rope. Their captors led the nine men out of the town hall and through a jeering mob of more than fifteen hundred people. They marched down the street to the Richwood Post Office. There, the captives refused to salute the flag, thereby confirming the mob's suspicion that Jehovah's Witnesses were indeed Fifth Columnists. The Legionnaires led the men, "tethered like cattle," to the Stark house. The Witnesses carried their belongings from the house with their right arms. Then, they walked back to Main Street and marched west to the town limits. The townspeople advised them never to return[49] and that if they returned, they would be "confronted with buckshot."[50]

Area newspapers provided only limited coverage of the event.[51] Nevertheless, news of the attack spread slowly throughout south central West Virginia. Soon after the attack, the United States Attorney for the southern district of West Virginia learned of its nature and of the participation of the two police officers. He passed that information on to the Federal Bureau of Investigation to investigate. Over the next two years, however, the prosecution of the attackers fell victim to foot-dragging and indecision by the local U.S. Attorney, the F.B.I., and high officials in the Department of Justice.[52] In Washington, the case attracted the attention of the Civil Rights Section of the Department of Justice. In February 1939, Attorney General Frank Murphy had established the Civil Rights Section to study and combat, by criminal prosecution, if need be, the violations of citizens' constitutional and statutory civil rights. Hundreds of attacks against Jehovah's Witnesses were reported to the Civil Rights Section; government lawyers chose the Richwood attack and several other serious assaults on Witnesses to present to grand juries; but none of the juries returned indictments. Consequently, the Civil Rights Section proceeded with a different tack in the Richwood case. This new strategy led to the only civil rights conviction in the United States arising out of an attack on Jehovah's Witnesses.[53]

The U.S. attorney in Charleston, Lemuel Via, was reluctant to proceed with the prosecution. Via's hesitancy was the product of both the nature of civil rights litigation and the characteristics of the office of U.S. Attorney. Victims of civil rights violations are usually part of an unpopular, or even despised, segment of the community. The members of both grand juries and trial juries are apt to share the prejudices of the accused and be reluctant to decide against them.[54] Furthermore, every U.S. District Court is located within the boundaries of a single state. Each state's U.S. senators exercise considerable influence over the appointment of U.S. district judges and U.S. attorneys, thereby "ensuring a strong local coloration in district court personnel and decisions."[55]

U.S. Attorney Via requested that a criminal division lawyer be sent from Washington to help with the prosecution. He argued that the presence of such an attorney "would remove the question of local prejudices and faction from the picture and would have a very fine effect on the jury."[56] He also maintained that the presence of a lawyer from Washington "would be an open avowal to the grand jury and the petit jury that this case was being prosecuted by the Department of Justice, rather than the United States Attorney."[57] Like all U.S. attorneys, Via had local loyalties; he did not want to alienate police officers because his success as a prosecutor depended to some degree on their goodwill and cooperation. Moreover, as the Richwood attack demonstrated, Jehovah's Witnesses were quite unpopular among the general public. Therefore he approached the prosecution of Catlette and Stewart cautiously. He hoped that the presence of a lawyer from Washington would indicate the decision to prosecute was not wholly his.

In the spring of 1942, Raoul Berger, a lawyer from the Justice Department's criminal division, traveled to West Virginia to assist the U.S. attorney in presenting the case against Catlette and Stewart to the grand jury. The grand jury proved to be hostile to the Jehovah's Witnesses and refused to return an indictment. Berger recorded the grand jurors' unfriendly attitudes in a memorandum for the case file,

> Unfortunately, the jury was patently unfriendly to the "Witnesses" from the outset, as their queries showed. The witnesses were repeatedly questioned about the particulars of their religion, their refusal to bear arms, their invasion of Richwood in search of "trouble." We were asked if one who refuses to defend his country has constitutional rights, etc. etc.[58]

The participation of the lawyer from the Department of Justice evidently did not, as U.S. Attorney Via predicted, cause the grand jurors to overcome local prejudices.

The Civil Rights Section attorneys in Washington maintained their resolve to pursue a prosecution. They wanted a conviction in at least one case involving attacks on Jehovah's Witnesses. Therefore, Assistant Attorney General Wendell Berge directed the U.S. Attorney in West Virginia to proceed with the prosecution by filing for an indictment by information—a prosecutor's formal statement of the evidence against the accused person.[59] The Fifth Amendment requires that an indictment for "capital and otherwise infamous" federal crimes must be issued by a grand jury. The U.S. Supreme Court has construed an infamous crime to be one for which a person may be sentenced to a penitentiary for more than one year.[60] Misdemeanors are crimes for which the punishment is imprisonment for less than a year. Federal Courts may issue indictments for misdemeanors based on information. The information filed by the U. S. Attorney accused Catlette and Stewart of a misdemeanor—depriving the Jehovah's Witnesses of their civil rights under color of state law, a violation of Title 18, Section 52 of the *United States Code* (1925). A crime committed under color of law is one perpetrated by public officials while using the authority of their office.[61]

The color of law statute originated in the Civil Rights Act of 1866.[62] It received little use, however, having been applied in only two reported federal district court cases.[63] The statute's usefulness in protecting civil rights was, therefore, largely untested. Furthermore, the phrase "color of law" was not clearly defined. It was clear that it applied to public officials, who, while they perform a duty imposed on them by statute, violate the civil rights of others.[64] Did it also apply, as in the Richwood case, to officials, who are not performing a statutory duty, but who interfere in the civil rights of others in a way that violates the laws prescribing the officials' powers and duties? In pursuing the prosecution of the Richwood case, the Civil Rights Section argued for acceptance of the second application of the statute.

District Judge Ben Moore presided over the trial on 2-3 June 1942 in the United States District Court in Charleston. Eight of the Jehovah's Witnesses who were attacked in Richwood testified at the trial. They explained why they came to Richwood and recounted what happened to them at the hands of Catlette, Stewart, and the mob.[65] The U. S. Attorney argued that both Catlette and Stewart, as officers of the law, were required to maintain the peace and protect the Witnesses in the exercise of the rights and privileges secured or protected by the Constitution and laws of the United States. Their failure to do this, he contended, violated the color of law provision of the civil rights statute. Catlette's defense was that he did not act under color of law, and that the government failed to show any statute of West Virginia under which he acted. Furthermore, Catlette claimed that because he removed his deputy sheriff's badge, he did not act as a law officer. During his testimony Catlette revealed that, while the Jehovah's Witnesses were being paraded through the streets, he took a man into custody. The judge asked him if he was acting as a deputy sheriff or a private citizen. Catlette replied he acted as a private citizen, but conceded he never before taken someone into custody as a private citizen. In his testimony, Catlette emphasized that the Jehovah's Witnesses refused to salute the flag.[66]

The government charged that Richwood Police Chief Bert Stewart aided and abetted Catlette. Stewart denied a connection with the attack and claimed that he did not know of it until it had almost ended. In response, the Witnesses testified that, on the morning of the attack when they arrived at the town hall, they gave Stewart a letter requesting police protection. They claimed further that, when they were held in the mayor's office, Stewart acted as a doorkeeper.[67] On 3 June, the jury returned a guilty verdict against both Catlette and Stewart.[68] Nine days later, Moore passed judgment in the case. He fined Catlette $1,000.00 and sentenced him to one year imprisonment at the Federal Prison Camp at Mill Run, West Virginia. He fined Stewart $250.00.[69]

Catlette appealed his conviction and the Fourth Circuit of the U.S. Court of Appeals heard oral argument on the case in Baltimore, Maryland on 13 November 1942. The court affirmed the findings of Judge Moore. The most significant issue in the appeal was Catlette's argument that U.S. attorney's information failed to show that Catlette was acting within the scope of his authority during the attack on the Witnesses.[70] During arguments the Court asked the government's attorneys to file a memorandum of law with references to the

statutory and common law duties of sheriffs in West Virginia.[71] This memorandum established that West Virginia common law requires a sheriff to preserve the peace, and more specifically to protect prospective victims from
assault or illegal restraint in the officer's presence. Moreover, the state statutes
authorize deputy sheriffs to discharge the duties of the sheriff.[72] The Court
ruled an official's failure to perform a duty to protect people in the exercise of
their civil rights was a violation of the color of law provision. Catlette had violated the statute because he failed to perform his duty to protect the Jehovah's
Witnesses in their activities.

Ruling against Catlette, the court rejected the contention that "an officer can
divorce himself from his official capacity merely by removing his badge of office
before embarking on a course of illegal conduct."[73] The court held,

> We must condemn this insidious suggestion that an officer may thus light-
> ly shuffle off his official role. To accept such a legalistic dualism would gut
> the constitutional safeguards and render law enforcement a shameful
> mockery.[74]

It also addressed the significance of the attack on the Jehovah's Witnesses in
Richwood and the importance of protecting the civil liberties of all citizens,

> We are here concerned only with protecting the rights of these victims, no
> matter how locally unpalatable the victims may be as a result of their seem-
> ing fanaticism. These rights include those of free speech, freedom of reli-
> gion, immunity from illegal restraint, and equal protection.[75]

The judges of the U.S. Court of Appeals shared Judge Moore's abhorrence
of this blatant disregard for the constitutional guarantee protecting the free
exercise of religion.

This case resulted in several significant legal developments.[76] It was the
Department of Justice's newly-established Civil Rights Section first prosecution—and one of the few ever undertaken—that used the color of law section
of the civil rights statute to enforce the protection of religious liberty. The case
also broadened the application of color of law provision. This ruling of the
Court of Appeals embraced the understanding that the color of law statute
applied to those instances when a public official acted in violation of the laws
prescribing his powers and duties. Three years later, in its decision in *Screws v.
United States,* the U.S. Supreme Court accepted this construction of the
statute.[77] This case also resulted in the only successful federal prosecution of
persons involved in the numerous brutal assaults on Jehovah's Witnesses.
Moreover, it demonstrated the difficulty of procuring a grand jury indictment
for attacks on unpopular minorities. Finally, it was the first civil rights prosecution in which the Civil Rights Section proceeded with an indictment by
information after a grand jury failed to indict.

CLARKSBURG FIRINGS:
ADMINISTRATIVE PROTECTION OF RELIGIOUS FREEDOM

The day after the jury found Catlette and Stewart guilty, George C. Schmidt, a Charleston, W. Virginia attorney retained by the Window Glass Cutters League of America, wrote to the union's national president. He was concerned regarding the implications of the Catlette trial for the union. In December 1941, seven Jehovah's Witnesses had been fired from a window glass plant in Clarksburg. The lawyer had heard that the fired workers might be planning to sue members of the union who had provoked their dismissal. Schmidt contended that the outcome in the *Catlette* prosecution indicated the possibility of plaintiff success should the fired workers proceed with a lawsuit. The union, he argued, should regard the firing as a serious matter.[78] The dismissal of the Clarksburg glasscutters was the third incident involving West Virginia Jehovah's Witnesses that expanded legal protection for religious liberties. The workers' efforts to regain their jobs resulted in an unprecedented use of administrative law to enforce the civil rights of victims in cases of religious discrimination.

The voice of President Franklin D. Roosevelt crackled from the radio in the warehouse washroom, "Yesterday, December 7, 1941—a date which will live in infamy—the United States of America was suddenly and deliberately attacked by the naval and air forces of the Empire of Japan."[79] About eighty workers at the Pittsburgh Plate Glass Company's Works No. 12 in Clarksburg, West Virginia listened intently to the six-minute speech in which the president asked the Congress to declare war on Japan. They felt anger as they heard the description of Japanese attacks on Pearl Harbor, Guam, the Philippine Islands, Wake Island, and Midway Island. They were sad as the president solemnly related, "that very many American lives have been lost."[80] At conclusion of the speech, the "Star Spangled Banner" reverberated from the radio. As the men stood and removed their caps, they were annoyed that Clyde Seders neither stood nor removed his cap.[81] For Seders, a Jehovah's Witness, such deference was contrary to his religious belief. For the other men present, Seders's behavior was unpatriotic, if not outright complicity with the enemy.

Within an hour, word of Seders's nonconformity had spread throughout the plant warehouse and the workers in the shipping department refused to work with him.[82] When plant superintendent Howard Halbach approached him, Seders explained that his religion compelled his behavior. Halbach told him that if he did not change his attitude he must either quit or be fired. Seders quit his job at the end of the day.[83] Seder's behavior drew the attention of the workers to other Jehovah's Witnesses employed by the plant. The incident upset most of the glass workers, many of whom were veterans of World War I and members of the American Legion.[84] They chose a fellow veteran and Legionnaire, Clarence James, to confront the Jehovah's Witnesses and test their patriotism. Accompanied by about one hundred men, James asked three Jehovah's Witnesses if they would salute the flag and defend the country. The men answered that they would not.[85]

The Jehovah's Witnesses' stance on the flag salute clearly conflicted with the sense of patriotism burgeoning among the people of Clarksburg and contributed to the growing animosity toward the sect. In July 1940, several Jehovah's Witnesses in Clarksburg had been removed from the relief roles because they refused to salute the flag.[86] A year later, tensions had heightened between the Jehovah's Witnesses and the other citizens of this industrial town of 30,500 in the center of the state. On 5 August 1941, the local school board had unanimously adopted the policy that "children failing to pledge allegiance to the Flag [sic] will not be admitted to school this fall."[87] Soon after the term began, school officials expelled several Jehovah's Witnesses children and the sect opened West Virginia's first "Kingdom School" in Clarksburg's Northview neighborhood.[88] On 16 December, the regular meeting of the Norwood Local of the Window Glass Cutters League of America considered a motion to notify the plant management "that we refuse to work with any person male or female who refuses to salute the flag of the United States of America."[89] After much discussion the members voted to table the proposal.[90] The American Legion in the Clarksburg area was conspicuous in promoting respect for the flag. On 18 December, an editorial in *The Clarksburg Exponent* praised the Legion for placing flags in every schoolroom in the county and promoting the Pledge of Allegiance.[91] On 17 December, the day before the editorial appeared, the American Legion had sponsored a flag raising and salute ceremony at the glass plant, and the company urged employees to attend. Six Jehovah's Witnesses, in an effort to avoided confrontation, stayed away from the ceremony;[92] union leaders and the company management noted their absence.[93] The next day, one of the six men, Paul Schmidt, was fired because his failure to attend the flag ceremony irritated members of Local No. 2 of the Glass, Ceramic, and Silica Sand Workers of America.[94] Over the next few days, five more Jehovah's Witnesses were fired or resigned under pressure because other workers refused to work with them.[95] The last of them, Paul Schmidt's son, Bernard, was fired on 24 December.[96]

The matter of the firing of the Jehovah's Witnesses would have ended with the last worker's dismissal, had it not been for the persistent, yearlong effort of Paul Schmidt to regain their jobs. Schmidt had worked many years as a glass-cutter[97] and had been employed at the Pittsburgh Plate Glass plant for more than twelve years.[98] To provide for his family and gain reinstatement to his job, Schmidt pursued several courses of action.[99] But his eventual success grew from the complaint he filed with the President's Committee on Fair Employment Practice.

The action taken by the Committee on Fair Employment Practice made this case significant. Most legal studies that investigate religious freedom examine civil liberties and protection from government interference with religion provided by the United States Constitution and the constitutions of the various states. The Clarksburg firings, though, concerned civil rights protection from religious discrimination by private employers. The 1940s predated the extensive government protection of people's civil rights that followed the enactment of the Civil Rights Act of 1964. Yet, during World War II, a small executive office served as an equal opportunity agency to protect the employment rights of minority groups. President Franklin Roosevelt's Executive Order 8802 had created that agency, the Committee on Fair Employment Practice. The committee was to promote full employment in defense industries and the government by ending discrimination "because of race, creed, color, or national origin."[100] From its creation in June 1941, until its termination in June 1946, the committee reviewed nearly 12,000 complaints of discrimination and resolved approximately 4,800 of them.[101] About 80 percent of the complaints were based on claims of racial discrimination; African Americans filed most of them. Nearly 14 percent of the alleged discrimination was based on national origin, chiefly against Mexican Americans; close to 6 percent of the cases were claims of religious discrimination, made primarily by Jews.[102] The committee's limited authority emanated from the president and was delineated in four executive orders.[103] Its specified powers were to investigate complaints and issue non-binding directives. In its fight against discrimination, the committee relied heavily on bluff and negotiation. Its behind-the-scenes bargaining and mediation in the firing of the Clarksburg Jehovah's Witnesses demonstrated how extensively it depended on such tactics.

Paul Schmidt's grievance reached the Committee on Fair Employment Practice by an indirect route. His initial step, on 16 January 1942, was to send Eleanor Roosevelt a complaint about the firings. He asked her to bring the matter to the attention of the president. Mrs. Roosevelt referred his letter to the committee,[104] but it was almost two months before Schmidt heard from the committee. On 7 March, the committee notified Schmidt that it had received information about the firings from Mrs. Roosevelt and asked for details about the situation.[105] He filed a formal complaint with the committee on 10 March.[106] Within a short time the committee began its investigation. Daniel Donovan, a committee field investigator, arrived in Clarksburg on 24 April and spent several days examining the situation and interviewing company managers, union officials, plant workers, and the fired workers.[107] He reported that his investigation "appears to confirm Mr. Schmidt's allegations."[108] Donovan concluded that the Jehovah's Witnesses lost their jobs because of their religious beliefs. He also determined that the Pittsburgh Plate Glass managers fired or forced the Witnesses to quit because a large number of the workers in the warehouse refused to work with them or handle glass cut by them. Furthermore, although this was not an official union action, officials of the union's locals did little or nothing to prevent the slowdown. In his meeting with more than one hundred warehouse workers who were members of the Glass, Ceramic, and Silica Sand Workers, Donovan found that generally the workers held that it was their responsibility as good citizens to compel the Jehovah's Witnesses to show respect for the flag.[109]

Soon after Donovan's investigation, the committee determined that the seven Jehovah's Witnesses had been discharged in violation of Executive Order 8802, and it began to encourage union officials to have the union workers accept the rehiring of the Witnesses. The workers at the plant were represented by two labor unions. The glasscutters were members of a craft union, the Window Glass Cutters League of America, which was affiliated with American Federation of Labor. The Glass, Ceramic, and Silica Sand Workers of America, an affiliate of the Congress of Industrial Organizations, represented most of the workers in the plant. The presidents of both the A.F.L. and C.I.O. were members of the Committee on Fair Employment Practice. The committee asked the presidents of the A.F.L. and the C.I.O. to contact the national presidents of their union affiliates and ask them to intercede with the union locals to bring the affair to an end. By 20 May, this softening strategy had begun, and Frank Fenton, the director of organization for the A.F.L., wrote J. E. Mayeur, president of the Glass Cutters League, to encourage him to ameliorate the situation in his union.[110]

This intercession with the unions seems to have produced no result; neither the files of the committee, the American Civil Liberties Union, nor the Glass Cutters League indicate any development in the case between May and mid-August. By August, the fired worker's unemployment benefits were depleted. Paul Schmidt, without a way to support his family, found the situation to be "extremely terrifying."[111] He went to look for work in New York City, and then he went on to Washington, D.C. in order to present the committee "one last appeal for justice."[112] At the committee's headquarters, Schmidt found the Clarksburg case file buried under a stack of files about a foot deep.[113] But his visit had a positive effect; within a week, the committee increased its demands for a resolution of the case. On 19 August, the committee's executive secretary, Lawrence W. Cramer, sent letters to the presidents of the Glass Cutters League,[114] the Glass, Ceramic, and Silica Sand Workers,[115] and to the superintendent of Pittsburgh Plate Glass Company's Clarksburg plant.[116] He formally notified the unions and the company that the committee found that the workers had been discharged solely because they were Jehovah's Witnesses, and that this clear violation of national policy must be rectified. He requested that the president of the American Federation of Labor encourage action by the Glass Cutters League.[117]

On 26 August, Harry D. Nixon, secretary-treasurer of the Glass Cutters League, wrote to Stanley R. Meredith, head of the union's local at the Clarksburg plant, and asked him to address the matter. In his reply, Meredith did not take a strong position; he blamed the company management for the firing and claimed that he attempted to forestall that action. He suggested that the committee "should request that the company correct its action by wrongfully discharging these men."[118] Nixon delayed sending information from Meredith's reply to the committee because the union president, J. E. Mayeur was away from the office. On 9 September, Frank Fenton of the A.F.L. again sent a letter to Mayeur, asking him to mediate the Clarksburg conflict.[119] On 14 September, Mayeur sent Fenton a copy of Meredith's September 1 letter;[120] but this letter did not satisfy the committee. After the committee made further investigation, Cramer wrote Mayeur on 16 October. He rejected Meredith's explanation of firing of the Witnesses, but noted that Meredith was in favor of rehiring the Witnesses.[121] That same day Cramer notified the Clarksburg plant superintendent that the union favored rehiring the Jehovah's Witnesses, and requested that they be reemployed immediately.[122]

When the company did nothing to reinstate the workers, the committee grew impatient. It discussed the matter on 9 November,[123] and on 24 November it drafted a notification to the company.[124] This letter was by far the most forceful directive given by the committee in this matter. It directed the immediate reinstatement of the Jehovah's Witnesses to the positions they held at the time of their dismissal, with full seniority based on employment since their initial hiring. It further required the company to notify the unions of the reemployment and that the unions would be expected to exercise control over the behavior of their members.[125] In order to increase the effect of its directive, the committee issued a news release for publication the following Sunday, 29 November 1942.[126] This statement called the directive "an unprecedented action," and reiterated the points made in its notice to Pittsburgh Plate Glass Company. It also revealed that the committee had notified the unions to "exercise the necessary controls over their members."[127] The news release resulted in national coverage of the story.[128]

Both the company and the unions resisted the committee's directive. When the Pittsburgh Plate Glass Company received notice of the directive, it asked the committee for a reconsideration of the matter.[129] After William M. Saas, president of Local No. 2, Glass, Ceramic, and Silica Sand Workers, was notified, he met with two large groups of his union members and explained the order to them. He then informed the management that his workers would not accept the fired worker back in the plant.[130] The heads of the locals of both unions in the Clarksburg plant, Saas and Stanley R. Meredith, chief preceptor of the Norwood Local, Window Glass Cutters League, went to Washington to object to the committee's directive. They met informally with the committee the afternoon of 4 December[131] and argued that the committee had reached a decision without hearing their views on the rehiring.[132] At its 7 December meeting, the committee agreed that it would provide the company and the unions the opportunity to present their arguments at its meeting on 21 December.[133] It allotted the company, the unions, and the Jehovah's Witnesses one-half hour each to present their views.[134] The committee was, nevertheless, beginning to weaken resistance to the reinstatement of the fired workers. Three days before the hearing, J. E. Mayeur, national president of the Glass Cutters League advised the committee that his union "has, and has had, no objections to the continuance of Paul G. Schmidt and Bernard L. Schmidt in the employment of the Pittsburgh Plate Glass Company."[135] He stated further that the union's policies provide its members protection against discrimination, and that all members of the union must comply with that policy.[136]

The committee's hearing on the Clarksburg case, on 21 December, one of only thirty public hearings held during the committee's five-year existence,[137] lasted all day.[138] The union members did not present formal arguments. They were, rather, witnesses on behalf of the company position, supporting it in affidavits appended to the company's brief.[139] The company's main argument was that rehiring the Jehovah's Witnesses would cause the plant's seven hundred workers to organize a walkout, thereby imperiling wartime production.[140] But in its brief and in the hearing, the company presented several other arguments. It maintained that its actions against the Jehovah's Witnesses, based upon their refusal to participate in patriotic exercises, were not discrimination based on creed and that the fired workers were impeding the war effort at the plant.[141] The company further argued that the reinstatement of the fired workers would, in fact, be contrary to the express purpose for which the committee was created: to ensure an adequate workforce for wartime production.[142]

Each of the eleven men who testified for the company, emphasized two points: that most of the workers would walk out if the Jehovah's Witnesses returned to work and that the Jehovah's Witnesses were unpatriotic.[143] The testimony of Paul Schmidt closed the hearing. He was confident of a favorable outcome. He had prepared testimony for the hearing that would demonstrate that he was fired because of his beliefs, rather than because he could not get along with other workers, a claim he called "an absurd charge."[144] He said that he did not attend the flag ceremony at the plant because he had been warned there could be violent attacks on him and the other Witnesses. He stayed away to avoid a confrontation.[145] He also maintained that he would not have saluted the flag had he attended the ceremony.[146] Schmidt explained his attitude toward America at the time of the bombing of Pearl Harbor by claiming,

> As far as my attitude toward the country, at that time, I believe, it was the attitude of a true patriot, of a man that loves his country, of a man who has gazed upon the National Emblem and has said to himself: "This is my own, my native land."[147]

Pittsburgh Plate Glass Company's attorney, Leland Hazard, asked Schmidt to justify various beliefs of Jehovah's Witnesses. The chairman did not allow such questions. The committee's function, he said, was not to determine if a particular religious belief is excluded from the protection of Executive Order 8802.[148]

Throughout the hearing, the company and the men representing the workers were uncompromising in their view that the reemployment of the Jehovah's Witnesses would precipitate a walkout at the plant. Newspaper coverage of the hearing emphasized that the workers would not accept the return of the fired men.[149] An American Civil Liberties Union issued a press release, meanwhile, claiming the walkout "nonsense" and encouraged the committee to stand by its order.[150]

For the committee, the hearing confirmed its earlier findings. It continued to press for the reinstatement of the Jehovah's Witnesses, though it postponed issuing another order. Instead, the committee began negotiations with the company and the unions to ensure that there would be no resistance at the plant when the Witnesses returned to their jobs. By early March, the committee had drafted the substance of its summary, findings and directions.[151] Over the next two weeks, the committee and the company's attorney reached agreement on the wording of the final order.[152] The national and local officers of both unions were also informed and asked to take action to prevent union members from interfering with the company's compliance with the order.[153] William Saas, the president of the local chapter of the Glass, Ceramic, and Silica Sand Workers negotiated for some changes in the wording of the final directive. He also continued to predict a walkout when the Witnesses returned to work.[154] At its meeting on 15 March, the committee considered changes recommended by the company's counsel and adopted the final wording of its findings.[155]

Monday, 27 March, was set as the date for the workers' return. The company drafted a notice explaining the behavior it expected of the plant employees and sent it to union officials for their response.[156] To ensure a peaceful transition, the committee requested the company to hold a special meeting for employees the day before the Jehovah's Witnesses were to return to work.[157] About 350 employees attended the meeting in the Masonic Temple Auditorium to hear representatives of the committee, the company, and the unions, explain the directive. W. G. Koupal, the plant superintendent, announced that the fired workers were returning "with the understanding that there is to be mutual respect by all parties concerned of the religious and patriotic convictions of the other (sic.)."[158] The following morning the company posted a notice throughout the plant[159] that required that workers respect the convictions of the Jehovah's Witnesses concerning the flag salute and that the Witnesses refrain from preaching or "witnessing" while on company property. It ended with the requirement that "all employees, (sic) including Jehovah's Witnesses, will refrain from any words or conduct on this Company's premises which might impair mutual tolerance concerning their respective beliefs and convictions."[160]

Paul Schmidt and his son, Bernard, returned to work without incident; the other five Witnesses had secured other employment.[161] Before he returned to Washington, Ernest Trimble, the committee's representative, talked with Paul Schmidt, who was eager to return to his old job. He told Trimble he would warn other Jehovah's Witnesses to avoid religious discussion on the job and that he would purchase war bonds.[162] When he returned to work, Schmidt reported that the company officials treated him well, but most of the workers would not speak to him. He was keenly aware of the tense situation and treated the other workers with consideration. He also requested the Jehovah's Witnesses in

Clarksburg to refrain from boasting about the victory.[163] Bernard Schmidt only spent three weeks back in his job. His draft board ordered him to report to a conscientious objectors camp in Hane, Pennsylvania on 21 April. Paul Schmidt worked as a glasscutter at the plant until the mid-1950s when he retired.[164]

The directive to reinstate the fired Jehovah's Witnesses was an unparalleled use of civil rights policy to protect religious freedom.[165] The committee described the directive as an "unprecedented action."[166] The case is notable because it accentuated the principle that the civil rights and civil liberties of an unpopular minority cannot be contingent on the popular will of the community. In the United States, decisions concerning matters of conscience and religious belief have been placed outside of the political will of the majority. The Clarksburg firings and the nationwide wave of persecution against Jehovah's Witnesses demonstrate that, in a democracy, popular religions and political views are not those in need of protection; they are seldom the focus of persecution. Religions that are apt to need protection are those that the majority may perceive as obnoxious, weird, mysterious, peculiar, and nontraditional. Certainly, such religions will possibly raise the ire of the majority, particularly in insulated, relatively homogenous communities. The committee emphasized that, legally, the rights of the Clarksburg Jehovah's Witnesses to their jobs did not depend on their fellow worker's acceptance of their nonconformist, religious practices.

The Clarksburg case was also significant because it provided an excellent illustration of the Committee on Fair Employment Practice's evolution into an effective civil rights protection agency. Executive Order 2088 established a legal cause of action against employment discrimination by private businesses. For the first time since 1883, when the U.S. Supreme Court struck down statutes that provided similar protections,[167] persons had a federal course of action against private employers who discriminated based on creed, race or national origin. The committee resolved more than 4,800 employment discrimination complaints.[168] This record produced grassroots support for anti-discrimination actions by the government. As early as 1943, black civil rights leaders called for the committee to be established as a permanent agency. Calls for a permanent committee were written into the 1944 presidential platforms of the Republican, Socialist, and Communist Parties. When Harry Truman became president, he spoke of the need for a permanent agency to monitor fair employment; however, bills to make the committee into a fixed statutory agency failed in Congress.[169] The Clarksburg case was a high-profile illustration of the need for government protection from discrimination in employment.

Finally, the case is significant because it demonstrates a government agency's effective use of persuasion to exercise political power. Political scientists generally identify three major means governments use in exercising power: (1) command authority—making rules that are binding on the whole community and, if need be, can be enforced by coercion; (2) economic incentives—financial benefits provided to people in exchange for compliance with government directives; and (3) persuasion—logical and reasoned arguments and/or persistent appeals from the government for conformity with public policy.[170] The committee's legal authority was limited to making recommendations to resolve discrimination complaints. It could also make use of economic incentives by recommending the withdrawal of uncooperative companies' defense contracts, but throughout its existence, the committee never made use of this authority. To settle the Clarksburg dispute in a persuasive manner, the committee had to overcome obstacles greater than in most of its other discrimination cases. It had to change the thinking not only of a private employer, but also of seven hundred union workers. In other cases the committee relied on appeals to patriotism and the need for maintaining full wartime production as the rationale for employers to abandon discriminatory practices. In the Clarksburg case, however, patriotism and the war effort were arguments that the Pittsburgh Plate Glass Company had used to defend its firing of the Jehovah's Witnesses. Thus the committee's remaining argument was to challenge the basic unfairness of religious discrimination: that minorities should not be required to conform to religious values of the majority. To do this the committee spent months conferring with the company and union leaders. Clearly the company and unions thought they were reaching compromise positions with the committee. But when the workers finally returned to work, it was under the same requirements outlined in the committee's original directive. In this case, the committee's persistent insistence that religious discrimination is basically unfair, allowed it to preserve the civil rights of a politically unpopular religious minority. The case was a rare and unprecedented use of administrative law to protect religious liberty.

EXPANDING PROTECTION OF RELIGIOUS LIBERTY USING THE BILL OF RIGHTS

During the Committee on Fair Employment Practice hearing on the Clarksburg firings, an interesting exchange took place between the committee's counsel and Leland Hazard, the company's attorney. Hazard pointed out that the U.S. Supreme Court had held in *Minersville School District v. Gobitis*[171] that it was reasonable for states to require the children of Jehovah's Witnesses to salute the flag at school and expel those who refused. The refusal of the glass workers to salute the flag and their dismissal was, he argued, a similar situation. Ernest Trimble, the committee's lawyer, replied by citing a case that "came up from Charleston, West Virginia of all places."[172] He was referring to *Barnette v. West Virginia State Board of Education*.[173] In that decision, the U.S. District Court of the Southern District of West Virginia did not follow the precedent established by the U.S. Supreme Court in *Gobitis*. The *Barnette* case eventually resulted in a landmark U.S. Supreme Court decision protecting religious liberty.

The earliest clash with school officials over opposition to saluting the flag concerned a Mennonite whose foster daughter was expelled in 1918 for refusing to salute the flag in a West Liberty, Ohio school.[174] Over the next fifteen years several other religious groups clashed with school officials over mandatory flag ceremonies.[175] The Jehovah's Witnesses entered the flag-salute controversy relatively late. They did so not because of a theological position developed by the sect's theological leaders but, instead, in response to the actions of a young boy.[176] In 1933, Adolph Hitler banned the Jehovah's Witnesses movement in Nazi Germany; the Witnesses openly defied the ban and refused to give the Nazi salute. By 1945, approximately ten thousand members of the sect were confined in concentration camps. At the 1935 American national convention of Jehovah's Witnesses, the head of the sect, Joseph F. Rutherford, launched an ardent attack on the Nazi persecution of the sect. He warned that, by placing his agents in positions of worldly authority, the devil deceives people as to the source of salvation. "A striking example of this," Rutherford argued, is the exaltation of one Hitler in Germany. He issues the command that all persons shall 'Heil Hitler,' which in the English language means 'Salvation is by Hitler.'"[177] That this same line of reasoning could apply to the American flag salute did not occur to the sect's leaders. It did, however, to a zealous young Jehovah's Witness. In the fall of 1935, Lynn, Massachusetts third-grader Carleton B. Nicholls, Jr. saw a similarity between the flag salute and the Nazi salute and refused to salute the flag.[178] His father, who supported him, was arrested on 30 September during an argument with school officials about the flag salute. On 6 October, Rutherford supported Nicholls's action in a radio address on the issue. He said that the boy ". . . has made a wise choice, declaring himself for Jehovah God and his kingdom. . . . All who act wisely will do the same thing."[179] The Jehovah's Witnesses developed their argument that saluting the flag was an act of religious homage that disobeys the biblical injunction against making or serving graven images.[180] Thus began the major point of contention between many Americans and the Jehovah's Witnesses.

Soon, an ever-increasing number of Jehovah's Witnesses children, around the nation, began refusing to participate in flag salute ceremonies. In response, school officials expelled hundreds of children from school.[181] The sect responded to the expulsions in two ways: pursuing major legal challenges to the constitutionality of the laws that imposed compulsory participation in the flag salute; and where possible, establishing "Kingdom Schools," which met compulsory education laws and allowed greater instruction in the faith.[182]

By 1940, flag-salute cases brought by Jehovah's Witnesses resulted in decisions made by the highest courts in six states.[183] Three of these decisions were reviewed by the U.S. Supreme Court ruling per curiam that the cases posed no substantial federal question.[184] These rulings effectively left in place the state court decisions that compulsory flag-salute ceremonies did not violate the First Amendment provision protecting the free exercise of religion. In 1939, the Court issued a one-sentence per curiam decision affirming the judgment of the

U.S. District Court in Massachusetts.[185] This judgment was much more important than the earlier per curiams; it revealed that the Court agreed that mandatory flag-salute requirements did not violate the First Amendment protections of speech or religious practice. Across America, school officials were expelling hundreds of Jehovah's Witnesses children for refusing to salute the flag. Most of these expulsions took place in Pennsylvania, and it was from the little town of Minersville, Pennsylvania that a flag-salute case arose that finally received full hearing before the U.S. Supreme Court.[186]

In early October 1935, seventh grader Lillian Gobitis and her fifth grader brother, William, stopped saluting the flag in the ceremonies at their Minersville school. The superintendent of schools, Charles E. Roudabush, attempted, unsuccessfully, to convince the children's father, Walter Gobitis, that the children should participate. On 26 October, a sixth grader, Edmund Wasliewski, began to refuse to salute. That same day, Pennsylvania's Attorney General Charles A. Margiotti, issued an advisory opinion upholding the authority of the Cannonsburg, Pennsylvania school board to issue binding mandatory requirements for flag salute ceremonies.[187] This reinforced Roudabush's determination to have the children participate in the flag-salute ceremonies. On 6 November, the Minersville School Board met to determine what response should be made in the flag-salute dispute. After it heard the parents of the Gobitis and Wasliewski children explain the religious scruples that prevented them from saluting the flag, the board unanimously adopted a resolution requiring all students to participate in a daily flag-salute exercise. After the vote, Superintendent Roudabush stood and expelled Lillian and William Gobitis and Edmund Wasliewski for insubordination.

Walter Gobitis wanted to challenge the constitutionality of his children's expulsion, but was stymied because the Jehovah's Witnesses national legal office already had many willing plaintiffs. Not until eighteen months later, on 3 May 1937, did Olin R. Moyle, the sect's national legal counsel, file the case in the U.S. District Court for the Eastern District of Pennsylvania. The ACLU took an interest in the suit and provided some assistance to Moyle. The following week, the Minersville School Board voted unanimously to fight the suit. The case was argued in Philadelphia on 15 February 1938 and four months later District Judge Albert B. Maris found that the board's requirement that the children salute the flag was an unconstitutional violation of their free exercise of religious beliefs.[188] Within two weeks, the school board unanimously agreed to appeal the decision. Oral arguments in the appeal were made before the Third Circuit of the U.S. Court of Appeals on 9 November 1938. One year later, the three-judge court unanimously affirmed the District Court decision.[189]

On 8 January 1940, the school board authorized its attorney to file a petition for a writ of certiorari with the U.S. Supreme Court, which the Court granted on 4 March 1940.[190] The Court heard oral arguments on 25 April. Joseph Rutherford, the domineering president of the Jehovah's Witnesses, himself a lawyer, took over the defense, assisted by the new head of the sect's legal office, Hayden Covington.[191] The ACLU and the Committee on the Bill of Rights of the American Bar Association filed amicus curiae briefs.[192]

The Court's decision was nearly unanimous; only Justice Harlan F. Stone dissented. Writing for the Court, Justice Felix Frankfurter relied primarily on the "secular regulation" rule, which weighs the secular purpose of a concededly non-religious government regulation against the religious practice it makes illegal or otherwise burdens the exercise of religion. He identified the Pennsylvania flag-salute requirement as an intrinsically secular policy enacted to encourage patriotism among school children. Weighing the circumstances in this case he argued that the social need for conformity with the requirement was greater than the individual liberty claims of the Jehovah's Witnesses. He emphasized that

> Conscientious scruples have not, in the course of the long struggle for religious toleration, relieved the individual from obedience to a general law not aimed at the promotion or restriction of religious belief.[193]

In *Gobitis*, the U.S. District Court and U.S. Court of Appeals had not been swayed by the U.S. Supreme Court's decision in *Johnson v. Deerfield*[194] and earlier per curiam opinions concerning the flag-salute. The Court expected that Frankfurter's extended treatment of the matter would lay the issue to rest.

The Court's ruling, however, contributed to an escalation of confrontations between Jehovah's Witnesses and their adversaries. Throughout the nation in the months following the *Gobitis* decision, there were hundreds of attacks on Jehovah's Witnesses. John Haynes Holmes, chairman of the American Civil Liberties Union claimed, "It is no accident that this long and violent succession of outrages against the Witnesses in recent weeks was coincident with the unfortunate decision of the Supreme Court refusing to interfere with the action of school authorities in demanding the salute."[195] The strength of the link between the violence and the Court's opinion is dramatically illustrated by a sheriff's explanation of why a mob chased seven Witnesses from a small Southern town. He explained, "They're traitors—the Supreme Court says so. Ain't you heard?"[196] That sheriff's explanation of the *Gobitis* ruling was clearly without sound basis, but it was the understanding claimed by many self-appointed defenders of Americanism as justification to attack or discriminate against Jehovah's Witnesses. The reporter who interviewed the sheriff concluded that, "North and South, East and West, the Court decision has served to kindle mob violence against Jehovah's Witnesses."[197]

After the *Gobitis* ruling, refusal to participate in flag-salute ceremonies resulted in the expulsion of Jehovah's Witnesses children in at least thirty-one states.[198] This increase in the enforcement of compulsory flag-salute regulations, however, was accompanied by substantial, unfavorable criticism of the Court's decision. Of the forty-two political science and law journal articles commenting on *Gobitis*, more than three-fourths of them were critical of the decision, less than 10 percent supported it, and 15 percent took no position. The editorial comments in the popular press were no less critical; 171 of the larger news-papers throughout the country disapproved of the decision.[199]

A more significant response to *Gobitis* were the rulings of several state courts that compulsory flag-salute ceremonies violated their state constitutions. In addition to the earliest of these, the Hancock County Circuit Court decision discussed above, a Minnesota trial court also relied on its state constitution to restrain enforcement of flag-salute regulations.[200] Even more dramatic were the opinions of the supreme courts in Kansas and Washington. Both courts expressed hostility for *Gobitis* and relied on the religious liberty provisions of their state constitutions to strike down the flag-salute regulations.[201]

The *Barnette* decision of the Federal District Court of Southern West Virginia presented the most notable judicial defiance of the *Gobitis* precedent. Appellate procedure requires that lower federal courts conform their rulings to those of the U.S. Supreme Court. Nevertheless, the Federal District Court in West Virginia openly discounted the *Gobitis* precedent and found that the state's compulsory flag-salute requirements violated First-Amendment protection of the free exercise of religion. The facts in *Barnette* resembled those in the hundreds of other flag-salute confrontations that occurred across the country. When the Jehovah's Witnesses' national legal office determined that it was again time to bring the flag-salute issue before the high court, West Virginia present-ed the most attractive forum for litigation due to the fact that challenges to the constitutionality of statewide regulation could be brought before a special three-judge Federal District Court, from which appeal could be taken directly to the Supreme Court. The sect's legal office chose three parents, Walter Barnette, Lucy McClure, and Paul Stull, who lived near Charleston to bring the a class action suit on behalf of themselves and all others similarly situated. Charleston lawyer Horace S. Meldahl filed the complaint on 19 August 1942.[202]

On 27 August, District Judge Ben Moore convened the statutory three-judge court. District Judge Harry E. Watkins and U.S. Court of Appeals Judge John J. Parker joined him on the panel.[203] Hayden Covington, national legal counsel of the Jehovah's Witnesses, represented the parents; West Virginia Assistant Attorney General Ira J. Partlow represented the State Board of Education. At the initial hearing on Tuesday, 14 September, it was soon appar-ent that Judge Parker disliked the regulation. He urged the board of education to amend its regulation to excuse students who, on conscientious grounds, refused to salute. In order to provide the board the opportunity to consider his suggestion, he recessed the hearing until the following day.[204] The next day, the board voted to reject a compromise position.[205] Later that day when the hear-ing resumed, Judge Parker maintained that it was "unfortunate that a case of this kind should be in court," and rejected the state's reliance on *Gobitis*.[206] The court denied the state's motion to dismiss the suit and gave the defendants two weeks to file an answer.[207] Before an answer was submitted, the lawyers for both sides agreed to submit the case for a decision based on the pleadings and briefs already filed.[208] On 6 October 1942, the unanimous three-judge court enjoined the West Virginia school system "from requiring the children of the plaintiffs, or any other children having religious scruples against such action, to salute the flag."[209] Based on cues it perceived coming from the high court itself, the District Court took the unusual step of ruling contrary to a precedent of the U.S. Supreme Court.

The judges on the District Court were aware of changes in both membership and attitude on the Supreme Court. In 1940, Justice Stone had cast the only dissenting vote in the Supreme Court's *Gobitis* decision to uphold compulsory flag-salute laws. After that decision, membership changed on the Court. In 1941, Chief Justice Charles Evans Hughes and Justice James McReynolds left the Court. President Roosevelt moved Justice Stone to the Chief Justice's chair, and filled the positions left vacant by McReynolds and Stone with James F. Byrnes and Robert Jackson. More significantly, some of the remaining justices modified their positions relative to constraints on religious liberty. In 1942, in *Jones v. Opelika*,[210] the Court upheld a law requiring a license to sell religious literature door to door. Justices Stone, Hugo Black, William Douglas, and Frank Murphy voted in the minority. Black, Douglas, and Murphy, who had supported the *Gobitis* decision, joined in a special dissenting opinion in *Jones* that was written to expressly declare that *Gobitis* was "wrongly decided."[211] These developments encouraged the three-judge Federal District Court in West Virginia to discount the precedent established by *Gobitis*. Writing for the unanimous court, Judge Parker argued:

> The developments with respect to the Gobitis case, however, are such that we do not feel that it is incumbent upon us to accept it as binding authority. . . We would be recreant to our duty as judges, if through blind following of a decision, which the Supreme Court itself has thus impaired as an authority, we should deny protection to rights which we regard as among the most sacred of those protected by constitutional guaranties.[212]

At the end of the 1941-42 term, Justice Byrnes resigned and President Roosevelt appointed Wiley Rutledge to the empty seat. On 3 May 1943, Justices Stone, Black, Douglas, Murphy, and Rutledge voted in *Murdock v. Pennsylvania*[213] to reverse a decision it made only nine months earlier in *Opelika*.[214] *Murdock* struck down city ordinances that required obtaining a license and paying a tax for members of religious organizations going from house to house and selling the printed propaganda of their sect. The Court ruled that even though such requirements were general and non-discriminatory, they still infringed on the liberties of free press, free speech, and free exercise of religion. That this decision came so quickly after the *Opelika* decision indicates how quickly a radical change of view came about on the Court. After its *Murdock* decision, the Court seemed poised to reverse *Gobitis* as well.

The West Virginia State Board of Education voted to appeal the *Barnette* decision to the Supreme Court. The state's principal argument was *Barnette* raised no substantial federal question because *Gobitis* settled the constitutional questions raised by the flag-salute expulsions. The state's brief quoted extensively from Justice Frankfurter's *Gobitis* opinion. Given the clear indications that at least five justices were ready to lay aside the *Gobitis* precedent, there was little else the state's lawyers could do. The American Legion's *amicus curiae* brief filed in support of the state's appeal did little more than duplicate the West Virginia argument.[215]

Covington answered the state's appeal in a brief that was a mixture of Jehovah's Witnesses Bible teachings and constitutional arguments. He included a fiery attack on the Court's *Gobitis* opinion, especially rejecting Frankfurter's deference to legislative policymaking authority. Such deference, he argued, allowed the legislature to define its own powers. He emphasized the nationwide persecution of Jehovah's Witnesses that followed *Gobitis* and concluded with a long list of law journal and newspaper articles that criticized the decision.[216] The American Bar Association's Committee on the Bill of Rights and the ACLU filed *amicus curiae* briefs that argued *Gobitis* was bad law and should be overruled.[217]

On Flag Day, 14 June 1943, the U. S. Supreme Court announced its decision in *West Virginia State Board of Education v. Barnette*.[218] In a six-to-three vote,[219] the Court overturned its *Minersville School District v. Gobitis* decision and thereby effectively terminated the legal controversy over compulsory flag salute ceremonies in American schools. The *Barnette* decision also indirectly repudiated the many violent attacks on Jehovah's Witnesses that followed *Gobitis*. Moreover, in this case Justices Black, Douglas, Murphy, and Rutledge formed the voting bloc that served as the Court's liberal core throughout the 1940s. Likewise, the *Barnette* and *Murdock* decisions reflected the New Deal Court's move toward broader construction of the Free Exercise Clause. In *Barnette*, Justice Jackson enunciated what has become a guiding principle in protecting individual liberties: "If there is any star in the constitutional constellation, it is that no official, high or petty, can prescribe what shall be orthodox in politics, nationalism, religion, or other matters of opinion or force citizens to confess by word or act their faith therein."[220]

CONCLUSION: THE UNIQUE LEGAL AND POLITICAL CONTRIBUTIONS OF THESE CASES

Meaningful developments in law resulted from hundreds of cases across America that grew out the Jehovah's Witnesses practicing their faith in ways that offended or inconvenienced others. The four West Virginia cases discussed above were particularly significant because legal protection for the free exercise of religion was expanded in each case using a different kind of law. The legal response to the expulsion of children who refused to salute the flag from

Hancock County schools resulted in an early example of "new judicial federalism." In that case, the Circuit Court used the Constitution of West Virginia to expand protection of religious practice beyond that protected by the United States Constitution and the federal courts. The criminal prosecutions that followed the castor oil incident in Richwood resulted in developments in judicial interpretation that expanded application of the federal civil rights statutes' color-of-law provisions. It was also the only successful federal criminal prosecution in the hundreds of violent attacks on Jehovah's Witnesses during the early 1940s. The legal action that followed the firing of the Jehovah's Witnesses glassworkers in Clarksburg was especially significant because it is most likely the finest example of the infrequent use of administrative law to protect religious liberty. It also provided an excellent example: the value of government use of persuasion to enforce public policy. Additionally, this high-profile case resolved by the Committee on Fair Employment Practice demonstrated the need for a permanent, statutory federal agency to protect the civil rights of minority groups. The best known of the four cases, *West Virginia State Board of Education v. Barnette,* is a landmark case in defining the Bill of Rights' protections for free exercise of religion and freedom of speech. It was also in this bellwether case that a strong liberal bloc coalesced; that bloc influenced the Court's decision-making over the next seven years. Therefore, it was a harbinger of the Court's movement toward a position of strong, unwavering rulings protecting individual liberties.

Notes

Chapter 1

1. The stories of Roger Williams and Anne Hutchinson can be found in most standard histories of American religion. See, for example, Martin E. Marty, *Pilgrims in Their Own Land: 500 Years of Religion in America* (New York: Penguin, 1985 [1984]), 75-82; Mark A. Noll, *A History of Christianity in the United States and Canada* (Grand Rapids, Mich.: Eerdmans, 1992), 58-62.

2. Sydney E. Ahlstrom, *A Religious History of the American People* (New Haven, Conn.: Yale University Press, 1972), 176-81.

3. The most extensive survey of Hutterite life and history is John A. Hostetler, *Hutterite Society* (Baltimore, Md.: Johns Hopkins University Press, 1974).

4. Stephen J. Stein, *The Shaker Experience in America* (New Haven, Conn.: Yale University Press, 1992), 5-16.

5. See Elizabeth A. De Wolfe, "'So Much They have Got For Their Folly': Shaker Apostates and the Tale of Woe," *Communal Societies* 18 (1993): 21-35.

6. Stein, *Shaker Experience in America,* 217-18.

7. For an overview history of the Harmony Society, see Karl J. R. Arndt, "George Rapp's Harmony Society," in *America's Communal Utopias,* ed. Donald E. Pitzer (Chapel Hill, N.C.: University of North Carolina Press, 1997), 57-87.

8. Fawn M. Brodie, *No Man Knows My History: The Life of Joseph Smith the Mormon Prophet* (New York: Knopf, 1946), 119.

9.   For a comprehensive history of Colorado City, see Martha Sonntag Bradley, *Kidnapped from That Land: The Government Raids on the Short Creek Polygamists* (Salt Lake City, Utah: University of Utah Press, 1993).

10.   Complex marriage is explained and analyzed in some detail in Lawrence Foster, *Religion and Sexuality: Three American Communal Experiments of the Nineteenth Century* (New York: Oxford University Press, 1981), 72-122. The complex events that led to the dissolution of the community are explored by Constance Noyes Robertson, *Oneida Community: The Breakup,* 1876-1881 (Syracuse, N.Y.: Syracuse University Press, 1972).

11.   John T. Noonan, Jr., *The Lustre of Our Country: The American Experience of Religious Freedom* (Berkeley, Calif.: University of California Press, 1998), 243.

12.   For a work that equates early Pentecostalism with pathology, see Alexander Mackie, *The Gift of Tongues: A Study in Pathological Aspects of Christianity* (New York: George H. Doran Company, 1921).

13.   For a survey of the history and life of the movement, see David E. Van Zandt, *Living in the Children of God* (Princeton, N.J.: Princeton University Press, 1991); see also James D. Chancellor, *Life in the Family: An Oral History of the Children of God* (Syracuse, N.Y.: Syracuse University Press, 2000).

14.   An independent book-length history of The Way has yet to be published. For a book published by the movement itself that contains some useful information, see Elena S. Whiteside, *The Way: Living in Love* (New Knoxville, Ohio: American Christian Press, 1972).

15.   The standard work on the Unification Church (which contains much material on the controversies it has endured) is David G. Bromley and Anson D. Shupe, Jr., *Moonies in America: Cult, Church, and Crusade* (Beverly Hills, Calif.: Sage Publications, 1979). For a more recent work see George D. Chryssides, *The Advent of Sun Myung Moon: The Origins, Beliefs and Practices of the Unification Church* (New York: St. Martin's, 1991).

16.   See Russell Paden, "The Boston Church of Christ," in *America's Alternative Religions,* ed. Timothy Miller (Albany, N.Y.: State University of New York Press, 1995), 133-40.

Chapter 2

1.   The jury awarded Jason Scott $875,000 in compensatory damages and punitive damages in the amount of $1,000,000 against CAN, $2,500,000 against deprogrammer Rick Ross, and $250,000 each against Ross's two accomplices.

2.   Philip Jenkins, *Mystics and Messiahs: Cults and New Religions in American History* (New York: Oxford University Press, 2000).

3.   Ibid., 5.

4.   See, for several excellent examples of scholarship on these trends: David Brion Davis, "Some Themes of Counter-Subversion: An Analysis of Anti-Masonic, Anti-Catholic, and Anti-Mormon Literature," in *The Mississippi Valley Historical Society* 47 (September 1960): 205-24; Thomas F. Gossett, *Race: The History of An Idea in America* (New York: Schocken Books, 1971).

5. See, e.g., Anson Shupe and David G. Bromley, "Introduction," in Anson Shupe and David G. Bromley, eds., *Anti-cult Movements in Cross Cultural Perspective* (New York: Garland, 1994), vii.

6. Anson D. Shupe, Jr. and David G. Bromley, *The New Vigilantes: Deprogrammers, Anti-cultists and the New Religions* (Beverly Hills, Calif.: Sage, 1980).

7. The symbiotic relationship between AFF and CAN is not dealt with in this report. See Anson Shupe and Susan E. Darnell, *Agents of Discord*, forthcoming.

8. See Anson Shupe, Kendrick Moxon, and Susan E. Darnell, "CAN, We Hardly Knew Ye: Sex, Drugs, Deprogrammers' Kickbacks, and Corporate Crime in the (old) Cult Awareness Network," paper presented at the annual meeting of the Society for the Scientific Study of Religion, Houston, Texas, 21 October 2000.

9. See, e.g., Sworn (notarized) Declaration of Eugene M. Ingram, licensed private investigator, Ingram Investigations, 30 October 1992, Los Angeles, California; Sworn (notarized) Statement of Dr. Lowell D. Streiker, 14 May 1992, San Mateo County, California; Sworn (notarized) Declaration of Mark Blocksom, 17 July 1992 (Blocksom allegedly later sought to refute his own declaration when confronted by a reporter from 60 Minutes as having signed the declaration to obtain future work.); "CAN Deprogrammers hit with Arrests," *The Bakersfield News Observer*, 12 February 1992; and Deposition of Marty Butz in *Cynthia Kisser vs. The Chicago Crusader et al.*, 26 October 1994. County of Cook, Illinois, Case No. 92 L 08593. Streiker in particular observed: "As a counselor of families disturbed by so-called cults and an opponent of forcible deprogrammings, I could estimate that 80 percent of all deprogrammings that have been reported to me were set up by CAN national headquarters, or its chapters."

10. Nora Hamerman, "Don Moore: Headed for the CAN," *The New Federalist* 8 (25 April 1994): 12.

11. Declaration of Jonathan Lee Nordquist, 26 August 1991, City of Los Angeles, Calif., 17-18.

12. (Notarized) Declaration of John M. Sweeney, Jr. on deprogramming and the Citizens Freedom Foundation, Maricopa County, Arizona, 17 March 1992.

13. Deposition of Cynthia Kisser in *Jonathan Nordquist vs. Larry Zilliox et al.*, 24 June 1992. No. 92 L1447, County of Cook, Illinois.

14. See deposition of Marty Butz in n. 9.

15. Letter of Rick Ross (Phoenix, Arizona) to Priscilla Coates (Glendale, California), 30 July 1985.

16. Deposition of Cynthia Kisser in *The Emery Wilson Corporation d/b/a Sterling Management Systems Plaintiff vs. Cult Awareness Network et al. Defendant*, Case No. BC 043028, 3 March 1994, Crystal Cove, Ill.

17. Letter of CAN president Ronald M. Loomis (on CAN letterhead) to ALL CAN Affiliates and ALL CAN Newsletter Subscribers, 26 June 1987, from Ithaca, N.Y., 4.

18. Preliminary Program for the October 1987 annual CAN Conference in Portland, Oregon.

19. Sweeney, n. 12.

20. Letter from John M. Sweeney, national director CFF-IS, from Redondo Beach, California, 18 February 1981.

21. See IRS Publication 557, Ch. 3 sec. 1 (3) and IRS Express Powers that

Cause Failure of Organizational Test [7.8.2] 3.3.4 (02-231999): C., D.

22.   *Cynthia Kisser v. The Coalition for Religious Freedom, et al.*, Motion by Defendants Church of Scientology International, "STAND," Bagley and Jentzsch to Dismiss, Or in the Alternative for Evidentiary Preclusion Order, Case No. 92C4508, 19 April 1995, United States District Court, Northern District of Illinois.

23.   FBI Special Agent Daniel Murphy, Affidavit to United States Federal Court, Eastern District of Pennsylvania, Exhibit A. "Application of the United States of America for an Order Authorizing the Interception of Wire Communications," 19 July 1997.

24.   Transcript of FBI Tape #2, T3: DMReel 6. 7/15/92; Edited by bmb, 30.

25.   Transcript of FBI Tape #2, T3: DMReel 16. 8/02-3,92; Edited by bmb, 2, 6.

26.   Transcript of FBI Tape #2, T3: DMReel 11. 7/21/92; Edited by ssw, 10.

27.   Ibid.

28.   *Kisser v. The Coalition for Religious Freedom.*

29.   Franklin H. Littell, "Cult Awareness Network Preys on Parents' Anxieties," *Jewish Times* 17, no. 33 (1992): 37.

30.   Correspondence in the (old) CAN boxes reveal a number of anxious letters from former CAN contributors who had sent their contributions by check or credit card numbers requesting to have the bankruptcy court trustee purge their names from CAN files before the latter were auctioned. (The trustee did not.) Likewise, there were several last minute bids and counter-bids by Cynthia Kisser, AFF's Herbert J. Rosedae, and others to purchase the records. The letters clearly reveal a range of emotion: from fear to desperation.

Chapter 3

1.   This chapter has grown out of more than three decades of observation of the Church of Scientology that began in 1964 in Chicago. Since 1985, when I moved to California, I have had many opportunities to visit Sea Org facilities in Hollywood, California, talk informally with Sea Org members, and gather literature on the Church and the Sea Org, all of which has been deposited in the American Religions Collection at the Davidson Library at the University of California—Santa Barbara. That collection now houses the large collection of material published by and about the Church of Scientology accumulated during the last three decades. This particular chapter has grown directly out of the book originally published in the series edited by Massimo Introvigne of the Center for the Study of New Religions, in Turin, Italy, and originally published in Italian in 1998. An English version was recently published as *The Church of Scientology* (Salt Lake City, Utah: Signature Books, 2000). This study also included structured interviews with members of the Sea Org and more than a dozen participants in the Rehabilitation Projects Force in Copenhagen, Los Angeles, and Clearwater, Florida, during the Summer and Fall of 2000. I was assisted in this study by two small grants from the J. M. Dawson Institute of Church-State Studies located at Baylor University, and the Society for the Study of Metaphysical Religion.

2. After this chapter was originally written at the beginning of 2001, I was able to visit the Sea Organization facilities at St. Hill in England following the annual meeting of the Center for Studies on New Religions in April 2001. This chapter has been slightly revised as a result of interviews made during that visit and some changes that occurred in the Church of Scientology in the first half of 2001.

3. There is an interesting body of recent literature written by Westerners who encountered the rigors of monastic life in various Eastern locations. See, for example, Anna Grimshaw, *Servants of the Buddha: Winter in a Himalayan Convent* (Cleveland, Ohio: Pilgrim Press, 1994).

4. E. Clifford Nelson, ed., *The Lutherans of North America* (Philadelphia, Pa.: Fortress Press, 1975), 197-98, 299-300; Frederick E. Weiser, *Love's Response* (Philadelphia, Pa.: Board of Publication, United Lutheran Church in America, 1962).

5. Lucy Rider Meyer, *Deaconesses: Biblical, Early Church, European, American* (Chicago, Ill.: The Message Publishing Company, 1889).

6. Newman Cryer, "Laboratory for Tomorrow's Church," *Together* 10, no. 3 (March 1966).

7. Robert Ellwood, *One Way* (Englewood Cliffs, N.J.: Prentice-Hall, 1973).

8. For accounts of such communities, see, for example, Donald E. Pitzer, ed., *America's Communal Experiments* (Chapel Hill, N.C.: University of North Carolina, 1997); Yaacov Oved, *Two Hundred Years of American Communes* (New Brunswick, N.J.: Transaction, 1993).

9. Cf. Mark Holloway, *Heavens on Earth: Utopian Communities in America, 1680-1880* (London: Turnstile Press, 1951).

10. The Holy Order of MANS was founded in the 1960s by Earl W. Blighton. See Phillip Lucas, *The Odyssey of a New Religion* (Indianapolis, Ind.: Indiana University Press, 1995).

11. See J. Gordon Melton, "The Theosophical Communities and their Ideal of Universal Brotherhood," in Pitzer, *America's Communal Experiments*, 396-418.

12. George Burke, *An Eagle's Flight: Autobiography of a Gnostic Orthodox Christian* (Geneva, Nebr.: Saint George Press, 1994).

13. "The Way Corps: Leadership Training for Proven Disciples," *The Way Magazine*, November-December 1992, 27-28.

14. Cf. Joseph E. Ross, *Krotona of Old Hollywood, 1866-1913* (Montecito, Calif.: El Montecito Oaks Press, 1989). Members of the Esoteric section may or may not live in a theosophical community, but do make a special commitment to belief in and practice of Theosophy and receive special training. Many also work for the Society and/or hold high positions in its organizational structure.

15. Given its size and importance, the literature about the Sea Org published by the church is quite small, the primary item being a recruitment piece, *Many Are Called and Few Are Chosen* (Los Angeles, Calif.: Church of Scientology International, 1999), and a brief description in *What Is Scientology?* (Los Angeles, Calif.: Bridge Publications, 1998). Some of the history may be found in a set of lectures Hubbard gave in 1969 concerning the Sea Org.

16. Any study of the Church of Scientology encounters a number of methodological problems, not the least of which are the (1) complex

organizational structure and (2) the massive literature (including an increasing amount of audio-visuals) in which the church's beliefs, practices, policies, and organizational procedures are spelled out in great detail. Added to that is a variety of important documents written by former members and critics filed as briefs or depositions in court cases, and a slowly growing number of more objective scholarly studies. At every step of the way, one must make critical decisions about relevant materials. Unlike many New Religions about which there is almost no written material, Scientology has led to the production of a veritable mountain.

17.   For the person unfamiliar with Scientology, a helpful bibliographical guide is provided online by Marco Frenschkowski, "L. Ron Hubbard and Scientology: An annotated bibliographical survey of primary and selected secondary literature," *Marburg Journal of Religion* 4, no. 1 (July 1999). It is accessed on the Internet at http://www.uni-marburg.de/ fb03/religionswissenschaft/journal/mjr/frenschkowski.html.

18.   Scientologists have focused upon the parallels between their thought world and that of various Eastern religions, parallels which exist and are shared by other Esoteric groups. See *Theology & Practice of a Contemporary Religion: Scientology* (Los Angeles, Calif.: Bridge Publications, 1998). However, many have missed the essential relationship of Scientology to the Esoteric tradition as Western Esotericism has only in the late twentieth century been defined as an academic topic worthy of concentrated study. On Western Esotericism, see Antoine Faivre's two volumes: *Access to Western Esotericism* (Albany, N.Y.: State University Press of New York, 1994) and *Theosophy, Imagination, Tradition: Studies in Western Esotericism* (Albany, N.Y.: State University Press of New York, 2000).

19.   An overall picture of The Bridge, including the OT Levels, can be put together from such readily available church publications as *Take Your Next Step to Total Freedom Now* (Los Angeles, Calif.: Church of Scientology International, 1999); *Get Trained/Go OT* (Los Angeles, Calif.: Church of Scientology International, 1998); and *Freewinds: A Complete Guide to the Freewinds-Only OT Hatting Cources* (Church of Scientology Flag Ship Service Organization, 1999). OT VIII and other courses offered only aboard the *Freewinds* are also discussed in the various issues of the periodical *Freewinds*. While published primarily as advertising items for the courses and supportive activities, they also reveal the basic outlines of the cosmology and the continuity of the OT Levels with the lower stages of The Bridge.

20.   L. Ron Hubbard, *Have You Lived Before This Life?* (East Grinstead, UK: Publications World Wide, 1968).

21.   As with all religions, Scientology has experienced individuals who have joined the church, participated in its activities, and later lost their faith in its teachings. While many former members continue to appreciate their participation in the movement, some former members rejected their former beliefs. The scope of opinion, both supportive and opposed to Scientology belief and practice and which may be expressed in highly emotive language, constitute theological assessments. As such they are outside the scope of this essay that takes no position on the truth or falsity of Scientology.

22.   Today the Advanced Organization offer OT I-V, and the Flag Land

Base offers Levels I-VII. OT VIII, released in 1988, is now available only aboard the ship *Freewinds.*

23.   Myth here is, of course, used in its technical meaning currently employed in the field of religious studies as a narrative that expresses the values that a community of people hold.

24.   The church has gone to great lengths to prevent the publication of the confidential documents, which it made the subject of a set of court cases in the mid-1990s. These cases were especially directed toward several former members who attempted to post the materials on the Internet. A small cadre of former members who had access to the documents prior to their leaving have dedicated a significant amount of time to various attempts to publish the materials in such a way that the church could not prevent access to them. The church has continually moved against such attempts (from dumping the documents into court records to entering them into various government proceedings).

25.   Those who wish to understand the cosmology of Scientology should begin with L. Ron Hubbard, *The Factors* (Los Angeles, Calif.: Bridge Publications, 1990); and the guide to the OT materials, *Ron's Legacy of OT* (Los Angeles, Calif.: Golden Era Productions, n.d.). Further definition of the cosmology is found in *Ron's Journal* 67 (Hubbard's annual report for 1967) and in several of his tape sets such as *The Dawn of Immortality, The Time Track of Theta, Secrets of the MEST Universe,* and *A Series of Lectures on the Whole Track.* These are available in most Scientology bookstores.

26.   In carrying out the Counter-Reformation, the church relied heavily on several of its ordered communities, especially the Dominicans and the newly founded Society of Jesus, popularly known as the Jesuits. Founded to evangelize the Holy Land, the Jesuits emerged just as the Reformation was expanding from its base in Saxony. The rise of Protestantism diverted the order from its original goal and gave it a new mission as the defender of the Catholic faith in Europe. Historians have given it credit for checking Protestantism's advance in many places and reclaiming some areas where Protestantism had become prominent, including Belgium, France, Poland, and Hungary.

27.   To date, the story of all that occurred in the Guardian's Office has yet to be assembled. Anti-Scientology literature has discussed many of the activities, though often in their attack upon the present Church of Scientology, they are discussed in such a way as to obscure the fact that they are talking about the GO in the 1970s. The church has naturally been less than eager to highlight what is an embarrassing part of its history. Above and beyond the attempt to gather the material from the IRS and FBI files that brought the Guardian's Office down, many of the more egregious activities are now well known. They include a spectrum of covert operations such as a plan (never implemented) to have journalist Paulette Cooper (who had written an anti-Scientology book) incarcerated in some manner; break-ins at the offices of people who opposed Scientology; and various "dirty tricks" designed to embarrass or call into question the credibility of Scientology's critics. It is hoped that a full account of the Guardian's Office can be produced in the near future, but is, unfortunately, beyond the scope of this essay.

28.   Cf. Clifford Longley, "Scientology Officers Expelled," *The Times* (London), 17 August 1983.

29. During his reign, Gregory moved to end the practice of simony (buying an ecclesiastical position) in the church and to take the selection of bishops and priests out of the hands of the king and nobles in whose lands they would work. He asserted the universality of the pope's jurisdiction and established the principal of papal elections by the College of Cardinals, a change cemented by the First Lateran Council in 1123. On Gregory, see William R. Cannon, *History of Christianity in the Middle Ages* (New York: Abingdon, 1960), 160-68. Interestingly enough, Gregory relied on his allies in the several ordered communities to accomplish his changes.

30. It should be noted that almost all of the questionable acts mentioned in anti-Scientology literature carried out by church officials and members were instigated by the Guardians Office during the 1970s.

31. The Celebrity Centres hearken back to previous efforts by different churches to provide space for members of the entertainment industry to develop their spiritual life apart from the glare of the media and the constant reactions by other church members to them as celebrities. Hollywood Presbyterian Church has had a program not unlike the Celebrity Centres for many years. One of its prominent members, Henrietta Mears, founded the Hollywood Christian Group to reach out to the entertainment industry. See J. Edwin Orr, *The Inside Story of the Hollywood Christian Group* (Grand Rapids, Mich.: Zondervan Publishing House, 1955). Most recently the Group has evolved into "Inter-Mission." See the Hollywood Presbyterian Church site at: http://www.fpch.org/. In the last generation, of course, various religious groups have attempted to interact with celebrities, possibly the most notable example being the Fellowship of Christian Athletes and the parallel attempts by Evangelical Christians to place "chaplains" with professional sports teams. Evangelical Christians have especially valued the testimonies of celebrities. See the FCA website at http://www.gospelcom.net/fca/index.php.

32. The issue of how many people belongs to the Church of Scientology and the basis of counting church members remains a matter of discussion between church officials, church critics, and other knowledgeable observers of the organization. The resolution of that issue is beyond the scope of this essay.

33. In the summer of 2001, the Church of Scientology moved to replace the famous "Billion Year Contract" with a new document, the Billion Year Commitment, the word commitment being a more descriptive term of what was actually occurring to those who signed it.

34. As part of the training it provides to new Sea Org members, the Estates Project Force is one of the organizations that oversee the maintenance and appearance of the buildings inhabited by the Sea Org and the associated grounds. In this capacity it operates with the guidance of the Base Crew Organization that has general oversight of the building and grounds.

35. Command Intention refers to policies set by an organization at it upper echelons. Those working in a particular organization at the lower echelons may compare what they are doing by reference to the overall policies and goals (broad targets) of the organization. The concept was more fully explained in Flag Order 3793-8 as issued on 21 September 1980.

36.   The Fourth Dynamic Engram refers to an event in the pre-historic past according to Scientology's understanding of the evolution of the human race. A disaster befell humans some 75 million years ago and its effect is universal. Removing the negative effects of this disaster is part of the ultimate work of the Sea Org.

37.   The appearance of the Sea Org facilities in Los Angeles, Copenhagen, and Clearwater are a testimony to the proficiency that members have developed over the years.

38.   A schedule of the daily schedule of the different orders is routinely printed in the introductory brochures and informational materials given to people inquiring about the order, particularly those who might consider joining it.

39.   Julia Lieblich, "The Cloistered Life," *New York Times Magazine*, 10 July 1983, 16. See also Patricia Curran, *Grace Before Meals: Food Ritual and Body Discipline in Convent Culture* (Urbana, Ill.: University of Illinois Press, 1989); and Suzanne Cita-Malard, *Religious Orders of Women* (New York: Hawthorn Books, 1964).

40.   It had been asserted in some anti-Scientology literature that the church had, at least for a time period, demanded that any female Sea Org members who became pregnant obtain an abortion. I have been unable to find any verification of that allegation. Hubbard spoke against abortion in his seminal book *Dianetics* (Los Angeles, Calif.: Bridge Publications, 1954, 1999), and officially the church has no position on the practice. Given the nature of the church, were this ever to have become a policy of the Sea Org, there would have undoubtedly been a paper trail of documents which, if they existed, have never been produced.

41.   In 1990 the age was raised from six to ten.

42.   This lack of SO organization partially accounts for the relative paucity of material on its life and work.

43.   A more concise discussion of Scientology ethics is offered in *What Is Scientology* (Los Angeles, Calif.: Bridge Publications, 1998), 285-91.

44.   L. Ron Hubbard, *Introduction to Scientology Ethics* (Los Angeles, Calif.: Bridge Publications, 1989), 12. The 446-page current edition of the *Ethics* book is considerably expanded over the earlier editions published in the 1980s (which were less than one hundred pages). A number of Hubbard's shorter writings on ethical topics have been incorporated into the text, thus making for a more thorough and systematic approach to the subject.

45.   One also sees in Hubbard's understanding of the Dynamics, at least at a cursory level, a correlation with Abraham Maslow's levels of human need beginning with bare survival and reaching at the higher levels the needs of self-actualization. Like Hubbard, Maslow also proposed understanding the self as basically good.

46.   Ibid., 15.

47.   One of the difficulties in discussing Scientology among non-Scientologists is the massive jargon introduced by Hubbard, both in his coining of new terms and his use of words in a very different manner than that commonly understood in public discourse. The discussion of ethics is additionally complicated by the use of a set of terms that in common discourse carry immense emotional baggage (enemy, treason, suppressive person, potential trouble source) in a technical

sense in Scientology literature. As much as possible, such jargon is avoided in this essay.

48.   This discussion of Hubbard's ethics has been extremely brief and points out the need for more specialized considerations of it both as a system and in its actual operation within the Sea Org, where it appears to have functioned with some degree of success for the last three decades.

49.   The operation of the Scientology justice relative to a person who has been expelled has been the source of problems for the church due to Hubbard's use of language, which has much different meanings within the church than in common parlance. Basically, Hubbard advocated excommunication as an act of abandoning the individual to the world. The excluded individual was henceforth cut off from all of the benefits available to a church member; however, the language of the ethical texts could, upon a cursory reading, imply that the church would continue to involve themselves in the lives of former members and that Hubbard was, by his statements, giving Scientologists permission to harm them in various ways. These seeming permissions became the justification for the actions of the Guardian's Office in the 1970s. Since that debacle, the church has taken pains to state clearly that such permission is neither implied nor intended.

50.   The preparation of this part of my essay consumed a considerable portion of my total research time. I reviewed the existing literature concerning the RPF, including the set of thirty documents on the RPF written by Hubbard as Flag Orders between 1974 and 1985, as well as visits to the Sea Org and RPF facilities in Los Angeles, Clearwater, and Copenhagen in the summer and fall of 2000, and St. Hill in April 2001. During these visits, structured interviews were conducted with more than fifteen present participants of the RPF program and ten former members of the RPF who are still members of the Sea Org. In addition, of course, I reviewed a number of critical accounts of their experience written by former Sea Org members. I also made reference to the highly critical paper by Stephen Kent, "Brainwashing in Scientology's Rehabilitation Project Force (RPF)," based upon his survey of the reports of the hostile former Sea Org members. A revised version of the Kent paper entitled "Scientology—Is It a Religion?" was published in the online *Marburg Journal of Religion* 4, no. 1 (July 1999). This essay, originally delivered at the Society for the Scientific Study of Religion in 1998, may be found on the Internet at http://www.uni-marburg.de/fb03/religionswissenschaft/journal/mjr/mjr_past.html. Kent's article was completed apart from any first hand inspection of the RPF and references only a limited collection of relevant church documents. He primarily relied on the reports of ex-Scientologists. In my research, I found that he had neglected important aspects of the program, mixed accounts from the RPF's formative years with more recent accounts, and confused incidents not a part of RPF with incidents that occurred within it. He also adopted the "concentration camp" image of the RPF that had been generated with the anti-Scientology literature for use against the church in court. I have found no evidence to substantiate the use of such an extreme image either from the ex-member literature or from my examination of the sites at which the RPF is and was housed. Kent has also found little response

from his fellow social scientists for his attempt to use the RPF to revive the discarded theories of "brainwashing" as applied to new religious groups. A more detailed critique of Kent's departures from standard sociological methodology can be found in Canadian sociologist Lorne L. Dawson's "Raising Lazarus: A Methodological Critique of Stephen Kent's Revival of the Brainwashing Model," in *Misunderstanding Cults*, ed. Benjamin Zablocki and Thomas Robbins (Toronto: University of Toronto Press, 2001).

51. "On the Excommunication for Faults," in *St. Benedict's Rules for Monasteries*, trans. by Leonard Doyle (Collegeville, Minn.: Liturgical Press, 1948), 43. On the operation of the system of rules in another setting, see Dom André Louf, *The Cistercian Alternative* (New York: Gill and Macmillan, 1985).

52. Ivor Shapiro, "Finding Words," *Saturday Night* (May 1989): 48.

53. Bernard van Acken, *A Handbook for Sisters* (St. Louis, Mo.: B. Herder Book Co., 1931); Adam C. Ellis, *Religious Men and Women in Church Law* (Milwaukee, Wis.: Bruce Publishing Company, 1958).

54. The *Vinaya-pitaka* is part of the Pali Canon and is used as the monastic rule for Theravada Monks. Mahayana monastic communities have their own sets of monastic rule derived from this earlier one. For example, Pai-Chang Huai-hai (749-814 C.E.) established a set of monastic rules for Ch'an (Zen) monks in China called the *Ch'ing-Kuei* or Pure Rules. A Korean revision appeared later as *Kyech'iosim hagin-mun* or Admonitions to Beginning Students. See Simon Young-suck Moon, *Korean and American Monastic Practices* (Lewiston, N.Y.: Edwin Mellen Press, 1996).

55. See Jane Bunnag, *Buddhist Monk, Buddhist Layman* (Cambridge, Mass.: Cambridge University Press, 1973), for a discussion of the operation of the Vinaya in a modern setting in Thailand. See also Sukumar Dutt, *Early Buddhist Monachism, 600 B.C.-100 B.C.* (London: Kegan Paul, Trench, Thübner & Co., 1924) for a more detailed discussion of the system of rules and punishments actually laid down in the *Vinaya*.

56. Moon, *Korean and American Monastic Practices*, 124-25.

57. "The Rehabilitation Project Force," Flag Order 3434RE-1, RPF Series 1 (10 June 1974): 1.

58. This part of the process includes a signing of documents to the effect that they understand what RPF is about and want to participate.

59. One theme that runs through anti-Scientology writings on the Sea Org and the RPF is the lack of informed assent by the participants. This appears to be an unsubstantiated charge. At the time of joining, members of the Sea Org go through an extensive orientation process as well as a screening process by the church to determine their fitness for the organization. That orientation program is conducted by the Estates Project Force, the same structure that oversees the RPF. In like measure, entrance into the RPF program includes an explanation of options open to individuals choosing participation and at several points during the entrance process they are called upon to make a conscious decision about continuing. As with the acceptance of any process of recovering one's status in a religious community whose rules one has broken, the participant can at any time choose to leave the community as an alternative to continued participation. Those who parti-

cipated in the program indicated that they chose to go through the program because they wished to remain a member of the Sea Org.

60.   Individuals may join the Sea Org from any point in their progress up the Bridge. Pre-Clears who join may serve in position that have little to do with auditing, and thus while they may receive personal auditing, they never learn how to be an auditor and counsel another person. Such a person in the RPF must learn how to audit before actually beginning the program.

61.   A dozen or more accounts of life in the RPF are posted on the Internet, a few being posted in multiple sites. A selection of these postings came be found in the references to Kent, "Brainwashing." In general, these accounts offer valuable research data concerning several individual's negative experience in the RPF, as far as they go. It is the case that some abuse of authority appears to have been experienced by individuals while serving in the Sea Org or participating in the RPF. The RPF includes numerous people who were in the program for "out Tech," and that activity does not automatically stop when one enters the RPF. The church's own literature and later revisions of rules for the Sea Org and RPF indicate reactions to problems. I have, however, found no evidence of any pattern of abuse as a common element of life in the RPF. As with accounts of present and former members who remain in Scientology, these accounts, while very useful, must be received with a critical eye. The accounts of members must be understood in light of their commitments and desires to be part of the Scientology program. Those of ex-members have a few similar problems. First, many were written as depositions for court cases and are thus quite selective in their discussion of RPF. Following a pattern also seen in accounts of former monks and nuns who have left a Roman Catholic order, they have imported later appraisals of their experience into their story. Some have incorporated the popular anti-Scientology analogy of the RPF as a prison camp, and thus, for example, they speak of their withdrawal from the program as "escaping" the RPF. As members have praise for Scientology and the auditing process, former members often include harsh opinions of Scientology belief and practice, especially the auditing process. Second, one must struggle with the significant omissions in the ex-member literature. They were not designed as complete stories of their experience in the church, but merely brief accounts of their bad experiences, usually for use in a court case. For example, almost none include any discussion of the role played by the person with whom they were paired during their stay in the RPF. That being said, if critically approached, the accounts of former members remain one valuable source of information on the operation of the Sea Org and RPF. It should also be noted that church authorities have questioned the veracity of several of the former members. People who were present and even mentioned in the accounts of Andre Tabayoyon and Dennis Erlich have suggested that they had both distorted accounts of incidents upon which they reported and on several occasions created incidents that had never occurred.

62.   The present RPF facility has been used since the mid-1980s. Prior to that time, it was in two different locations in the Fort Harrison Hotel. It was first located in what is now the bakery and later in what is now the primary ethics office. In each case, it was inside the hotel in space

adjacent to the parking lot. The parking lot is completely open with no doors to lock.

63. Locks on Sea Org facilities through which a departing RPF member might have to pass are such as to prevent someone from coming into the building but not prevent an egress from it. The fences around the present Sea Org residences in Clearwater were erected after an incident in which an outsider came into the complex and discharged a firearm. They were designed to keep possible troublemakers out, not prevent anyone from leaving.

64. This is confirmed in the accounts of former members such as Lynn Froyland, Hana Whitefield, and Ann Rosenblum, all of whom simply walked away from the Clearwater RPF. The only exception to this possibility concerns the RPF at the Gilman Hot Springs center. Gilman Hot Springs is a former resort that the Church of Scientology purchased and now uses as its international dissemination headquarters. Located there are a professional level recording studio, a large building for shooting dissemination and training films, and a large auditorium. It is frequently used by people from the nearby community of Hemet, California, for non-Scientology community events. It is located in the countryside, and intermittently in the 1980s and 1990s, there was a RPF unit there. That unit was housed at a location several miles away. While it would not be difficult to walk away from either Gilman or the housing site, it would be a long walk to the next town.

65. The first observation of the Zen Buddhist rule of monastic life, attributed to the honored Buddhist monk Pai-chang (720-814 CE) stated, "A day of no work is a day of no eating." Buddhist scholar D. T. Suzuki put is thusly, "Manual labor forms one of the most essential features of the Zen life . . . Life meant to the Chinese monks to be engaged in physical labour, to move their hands and feet, to handle tools, in order to accomplish some visible and tangible ends." D. T. Suzuki, *The Training of the Zen Buddhist Monk* (New York: University Books, 1959), 33.

66. See Koji Sato, *The Zen Life* (New York: Weatherhill/Tankosha, 1977), 148-49.

67. L. Ron Hubbard. "False Purpose Rundown," *Auditing Rundowns*, vol. 3 (Los Angeles, Calif.: Bridge Publications, 1991). Over the years of Hubbard's life, he periodically introduced upgraded forms of various auditing procedures, and such new upgrades have continued to be released. As these upgrades were published, they were, as appropriate, introduced into the RPF. The method of operating the "False Purpose Rundown" is spelled out in a series of Bulletins from the Hubbard Communication Office, the "False Purpose Rundown Series, 1-7" published as *HCO Bulletin*, 5-11 June 1984; rev. January 1990.

68. In spite of Steven Kent's study of Scientology over the last decade, he continually makes fundamental errors in reporting on Scientology's beliefs and practices. For example, his lack of knowledge of Scientology is manifest in his discussion of the False Purpose Rundown. It is one of a set of what in Scientology is called "security checks," or "sec checks." Kent asserts that "sec checks" are not covered by the same rules of confidentiality as auditing. In fact, security checks, of which the "False Purpose Rundown" is an example, are one form of auditing—the kind used to deal with overts and withholds, and is covered by all of the con-

fidentially rules governing auditing. See Kent, "Brainwashing." On the
other hand, interviews made during investigations by a Scientology
official or committee to determine the facts when a person has been
accused of a crime such as stealing money from the church or dishonesty on the job (sometimes called HCO security checks) are not considered auditing. In situations where someone might confuse the two,
an explicit denial that the session is to be considered auditing is made.
Also, all auditing sessions begin by noting the formal situation that the
individual has entered.

69.   "RPF Organization." Flag Order 3434RE-25, 7 January 1974; revised
      8 May 1997, 1-7.

70.   Quite obviously, not everyone adapts to the RPF regimen, and some
      people choose to leave which they are free to do at any point. Some
      who left the program are now quite critical of it. From the perspective
      of an ex-member, who no longer believes in Scientology, they have
      reinterpreted their life from their new perspective. These accounts bare
      a noticeable resemblance to similar accounts of others who have left the
      austerities of Roman Catholic orders. For example, Patricia Curran,
      who studied the rituals around food in several convents, noted that
      some of her informants had very different views of the behavior pat-
      terns expected of them: They described them [particular actions they
      were ordered to perform] as various outdated holdovers from Europe;
      daily reminders of belonging to the "club" of religious life; condition-
      ing to "perfect obedience" (the instantaneous execution of the superi-
      or's command). A great number argued that the effects the practices
      had on them provided the best indicator of purpose. They found them
      humiliating, particularly when kissing the feet of the sisters, asking
      prayers, or making the act of reparation. The penances were constant
      reminders of the self-concept that was held as an ideal: to consider one-
      self the least, lowest, and last in importance in the community. They
      regarded the penances also as a negation of all that was natural in favor
      of all that was spiritual, when these were considered to be in conflict.
      One named them the tools whereby each person's spirit was broken so
      that she could be remolded in the new corporate image. Once one no
      longer sees the purpose in their ordered life, its rules and regulations
      take on the appearance of a straightjacket. Life in the group no longer
      is seen as service to the cause and a means to nurture spiritual exis-
      tence, but an oppressive existence characterized by the following of a
      false religion and arbitrary rules. See Curran, *Grace Before Meals*.

Chapter 4

1.   See Lawrence Foster, *Religion and Sexuality* (New York: Oxford
     University Press, 1981), on the lives and philosophies of sexuality of
     Mother Ann Lee and John Humphrey Noyes.

2.   Rosabeth Moss Kanter, *Commitment and Community: Communes and
     Utopias in Sociological Perspective* (Cambridge, Mass: Harvard
     University Press, 1972).

3.   Prudence Allen, "Two Medieval Views of Woman's Identity," in *Studies
     in Religion* 16 (1985): 294.

4.   Susan J. Palmer, *Moon Sisters, Krishna Mothers, Rajneesh Lovers:
     Women's Roles in New Religions* (Syracuse, N.Y.: Syracuse University
     Press, 1994).

5. Eileen Barker, *The Making of a Moonie: Choice or Brainwashing?* (New York: Basil Blackwell, 1984). See also James Grace, *Sexuality and Marriage in the Unification Church* (Toronto: The Edwin Mellen Press, 1985).

6. Ruth Wangerin, "Women in the Children of God: 'Revolutionary Women' or 'Mountain Maids'?," in *Women in Search of Utopia: Mavericks and Mythmakers*, eds. Ruby Rohrlich and Elaine Hoffman (Baruch, N.Y.: Schocken Books, 1984), 130-39.

7. J. Z. Knight, *A State of Mind, My Story* (New York: Warner Books, 1987).

8. Lewis Carter, "The New Renunciates of Bhagwan Shree Rajneesh," *Journal for the Scientific Study of Religion* 26, no. 2 (1987): 148-72. See also Francis Fitzgerald, "A Reporter at Large: Rajneeshpuram I," *New Yorker*, 22 September 1986.

9. Palmer, *Moon Sisters, Krishna Mothers, Rajneesh Lovers: Women's Roles in New Religions*.

Chapter 5

1. See Malcolm Spector and John I. Kituse, *Constructing Social Problems* (New York: Aldine de Gruyter, 1987), Joseph Schneider, "Social Problems Theory," *Annual Review of Sociology* 11 (1985): 209-29. See Joel Best, ed., *Images of Issues: Typifying Contemporary Social Problems* (New York: Aldine de Gruyter, 1989), for more detailed explications of social constructionism, and Peter Conrad and Joseph Schneider, *Deviance and Medicalization* (St. Louis, Mo.: Mosby, 1980), for some examples of specific problems that have been constructed in Western societies.

2. The term moral entrepreneur was added to the sociological lexicon by Howard Becker in his famous study of marijuana smoking. See Howard Becker, *Outsiders: Studies in the Sociology of Deviance* (New York: Free Press, 1963).

3. See Spector and Kituse, *Constructing Social Problems*, for delineation of the term claims making.

4. Cohen defines a moral panic as a situation, "in which a minor social problem expresses and preempts a deeper related one." See Stanley Cohen, *Folk Devils and Moral Panics* (London: Granada, 1972). For a more contemporary use of the term, see Philip Jenkins, *Intimate Enemies: Moral Panic in Britain* (Hawthorn, N.Y.: Aldine de Gruyter, 1993); and Philip Jenkins, *Moral Panic: Changing Concepts of the Child Molester in Modern America* (New Haven, Conn.: Yale University Press, 1998).

5. See James Richardson, Joel Best, and David Bromley, *The Satanism Scare* (New York: Aldine de Gruyter, 1991) for a collection of research studies from various disciplinary perspectives, as well as Jeffrey Victor, *Satanic Panic: The Creation of a Contemporary Legend* (Chicago, Ill.: Open Court, 1993); also see Jenkins, *Intimate Enemies*. See an informative book by a law enforcement person, Robert Hicks, *In Pursuit of Satan: The Police and the Occult* (Buffalo, N.Y.: Prometheus Books, 1991).

6. William Bainbridge, *Satan's Power: A Deviant Psychotherapy Cult* (Berkeley, Calif.: University of California Press, 1978). Also see William Bainbridge, "Social Construction from Within: Satan's

Process," in Richardson, Best, and Bromley, *The Satanism Scare*, 297-310.

7.   Bill Ellis, "Legend Trips and Satanism: Adolescents Ostensive Traditions as 'Cult' Activity," in Richardson, Best, and Bromley, *The Satanism Scare*, 279-96.

8.   Note that other youthful activities sometimes get labeled as Satanic. See David Martin and Gary Fine, "Satanic Cults, Satanic Play: Is 'Dungeons & Dragons' a Breeding Ground for the Devil?" in Richardson, Best, and Bromley, *The Satanism Scare*, 107-25. Also see James Richardson, "Satanism in the Courts: From Murder to Heavy Metal," in Richardson, Best, and Bromley, *The Satanism Scare*, 205-20, which discusses Satanist accusations associated with heavy metal music.

9.   See David Bromley and Anson Shupe, *The New Christian Politics* (Macon, Ga.: Mercer University Press, 1984), and Erling Jorstad, *Holding Fast/Pressing on: Religion in American in the 1980s* (New York: Praeger, 1990) for some descriptions of the rise of Christian fundamentalism in America.

10.   The best source for the development of the child saver movement is Joel Best, *Threatened Children* (Chicago, Ill.: University of Chicago Press, 1990); also see his "Endangered Children and Antisatanist Rhetoric," in Richardson, Best, and Bromley, *The Satanism Scare*, 95-106.

11.   See Jenkins, *Intimate Enemies*.

12.   See Debbie Nathan, "Satanism and Child Molestation: Constructing the Ritual Abuse Scare," in Richardson, Best, and Bromley, *The Satanism Scare*, 75-94.

13.   See Philip Jenkins and Daniel Maier-Katlin, "Occult Survivors: The Making of a Myth," in Richardson, Best, and Bromley, *The Satanism Scare*, 127-44, and Sherrill Mulhern, "Satanism and Psychotherapy: A Rumor in Search of an Inquisition," in Richardson, Best, and Bromley, *The Satanism Scare*, 145-74.

14.   See Anson Shupe and David Bromley, *The New Vigilantes* (Beverly Hills, Calif.: Sage, 1980); Anson Shupe and David Bromley, eds., *Anti-Cult Movements in Cross Cultural Perspectives* (New York: Garland, 1994); and Marat S. Shterin and James T. Richardson, "Effects of the Western Anti-Cult Movement on Development of Laws Concerning Religion in Post-Communist Russia," *Journal of Church and State* 42 (Spring 2000): 247-71.

15.   See Michael Langone and Linda Blood, *Satanism and Occult-related Violence* (Weston, Mass.: American Family Foundation, 1990).

16.   See Jenkins, *Intimate Enemies*.

17.   Ibid., 174-76.

18.   I have attended such seminars in the U.S. and Australia, and reviewed materials from those in other countries such as New Zealand and the U.K. Jenkins's *Intimate Enemies* talks about them in Britain among social workers, and law enforcement involvement is described in Ben Crouch and Kelly Damphouse, "Law Enforcement and the Satanic Crime Connection: A Survey of 'Cult Cops'," in Richardson, Best and Bromley, *The Satanism Scare*, 191-204. Also, see Mulhern, "Satanism and Psychotherapy," for the role played by such seminars in "converting" therapists to accept the reality of repressed memories of ritual abuse.

19. See chapters by Phillips Stevens, Jeffrey Burton Russell, and David Bromley in Richardson, Best, and Bromley, *The Satanism Scare*, that analyze the historical and cultural import of Satan and Satanism in Western societies.

20. See especially Laurel Rowe and Grey Cavender, "Cauldrons Bubble, Satan's Trouble: But Witches are Okay: Media Constructions of Satanism and Witchcraft," in Richardson, Best, and Bromley, *The Satanism Scare*, 263-78. Also see other chapters in the Richardson, Best, and Bromley book (n. 5), many of which discuss the role played by media coverage in spreading concern about Satanism.

21. See James Richardson, "The Satanism Scare: Social Construction of an International Social Problem, *Australian Journal of Social Issues* 32 (1997): 61-85. Also see Jenkins, *Intimate Enemies*, and Jean La Fontaine, "The Extent and Nature of Organized Ritual Abuse: A Report to the Department of Health," (London: HMSO, 1994), on the situation in Britain; and Jenny Barnett and Michael Hill, "When the Devil Came to Christchurch," *Australian Religious Studies Review* 6 (1994): 25-30, which discusses ritual abuse claims in New Zealand, and the work of U.S. "missionaries" in spreading the concern about Satanism there.

22. See Rowe and Cavender, "Cauldron Bubbles," for a fascinating discussion of this difference in treatment by some, but not all mass media.

23. This claim is disputed by some, but whether Gardner developed his ideas out of whole clothe or received them as he claimed, his influence has been felt in modern witchcraft on both sides of the Atlantic and beyond. See Margot Adler, *Drawing Down the Moon* (Boston, Mass.: Beacon Press, 1986); and Helen Berger, *A Community of Witches: Contemporary Neo-Paganism and Witchcraft in the United States* (Columbia, S.C.: University of South Carolina Press, 1999) for discussions of these early beginnings of Wicca in the U.S.

24. See Starhawk, *The Spiral Dance: A Rebirth of the Ancient Religion of the Great Goddess* (New York: Harper & Row, 1979) for the most influential statement of ancient origins. But also see Charlotte Allen, "The Scholars and the Goddess," *Atlantic Monthly*, January 2001, disputing these old ties.

25. See Berger, *A Community of Witches*, 9, who analyzes the methodology of estimates that have been made and suggests that a more accurate figure might be 150,000 to 200,000.

26. Adler, *Drawing Down on the Moon*; and Berger, *A Community of Witches*, 23.

27. Lynne Hume, "Exporting Nature Religions: Problems in Praxis Down Under," *Nova Religio* 2 (1999): 287-98.

28. This activity on military bases by Wiccan groups, which is growing, has been controversial, in part because they are so different from normal religions, but also because part of the belief system of Wiccan groups involves pacifism. Thus, some have claimed that Wiccans cannot make good soldiers who will follow orders, including orders to "shoot to kill."

29. There are those who take a more cynical view of the witch craze and talk about the use of this definition by the Church to accrue the property of those accused of witchcraft, and to gain political advantage using accusations and the threat of accusations as a social weapon of great power.

30.   Recall the study by Rowe and Cavender, "Cauldrons Bubble," that shows some important differences between media coverage of Wicca and Satanism.

Chapter 6

1.   There is an interesting footnote here. I made a case for this charge in an editorial that appeared both in the *Houston Chronicle* and the *Beaumont Enterprise* (see Stuart A. Wright, "What the Waco Jury never Heard," *Houston Chronicle*, 23 July 2000; Stuart A. Wright, "Jurors didn't hear the whole story of Branch Davidian incident," *Beaumont Enterprise*, 23 July 2000). Mr. Bradford, whose U.S. Attorney's office is headquartered in Beaumont, responded to the editorial with a missive of his own in the *Beaumont Enterprise* (see J. Michael Bradford, "Waco critic purely biased," *Beaumont Enterprise*, 30 July 2000). Mr. Bradford attacked my scholarship and opined that my institution should not allow me to unduly influence students in the classroom with ideas critical of the government. I found the U.S. Attorney's apparent effort to abridge free speech both ironic and revealing, particularly since his responsibility as a civil servant is to uphold the Constitution, not to advocate its violation. The spirited exchange led to a public debate on the Waco trial, organized by the Southeast Texas Press Club on 15 September 2000. The event drew a standing room only crowd at the Press Club luncheon and made headlines in the local newspaper on the local TV news the next day. We sought to have the debate televised over the Web through a local company that expressed interest. However, Mr. Bradford threatened to pull out of the debate if it were televised.

2.   Many questions had multiple parts so that the questionnaire actually consisted of over a hundred items.

3.   While these questions were relevant to issues in the case, some were entirely too invasive. As such, jurors should have been informed that they could refuse to answer. But to the contrary, the judge's instructions in the questionnaire state: "This is not a voluntary endeavor, as you are required to answer the questions." Jury questionnaire is reproduced in Jack DeVault, *The Waco Whitewash* (San Antonio, Tex.: Rescue Press, 1994), 264-82.

4.   *U.S. v. Brad Branch et al.,* U.S. District Court, Western District of Texas, W-93-CR-046, 2.

5.   See Stuart A. Wright, ed., *Armageddon in Waco: Critical Perspectives on the Branch Davidian Conflict* (Chicago, Ill.: University of Chicago, 1995).

6.   See Alan W. Bock, *Ambush at Ruby Ridge* (Irvine, Calif.: Dickens Press, 1995); Jess Walter, *Every Knee Shall Bow* (New York: Harper/Regan Books, 1995).

7.   On appeal, the U.S. 9th Circuit Court *en banc* agreed to hear the arguments for this motion.

8.   Susan Gamboa, "Immunity Helped Turn Waco Trial," Associated Press, 15 July 2000.

9.   Christopher Simpson, *Science of Coercion: Communication Research and Psychological Warfare 1945-1960* (New York: Oxford University, 1994), 12.

10. Stuart A. Wright, "Anatomy of a Government Massacre: Abuses of Hostage-Barricade Protocols during the Waco Standoff," *Journal of Terrorism and Political Violence* 11 (1999): 39-68.

11. Michael J. McMains and Wayman C. Mullins, *Crisis Negotiations: Managing Critical Incidents and Hostage Situations in Law Enforcement and Corrections* (Cincinnati, Ohio: Anderson, 1996), 125.

12. Ibid., 129.

13. Ibid.

14. *Report to the Deputy Attorney General on the Events at Waco, Texas, February 28 to April 19, 1993* (Washington, D.C.: U.S. Department of Justice, 1993), 138.

15. Alan A. Stone, *Report and Recommendations Concerning the Handling of Incidents Such as the Branch Davidian Standoff in Waco, Texas*. Report to the Deputy Attorney General, 8 November 1994, 28.

16. Robert Cancro, letter to Deputy Attorney General Philip B. Heymann, *Recommendations of Experts for Improvement in Federal Law Enforcement After Waco* (Washington, D.C.: U.S. Department of Justice, 1993), 4.

17. Stone, *Report and Recommendations*, 10.

18. *Investigation into the Activities of Federal Law Enforcement Agencies*, 3 (emphasis added).

19. Lee Hancock, "Davidians' attorney vents anger at judge," *Dallas Morning News*, 13 September 2000.

20. Quoted in David B. Kopel and Paul H. Blackman, *No More Wacos: What's Wrong with Federal Law Enforcement and How to Fix It* (Amherst, N.Y.: Prometheus, 1997), 238.

21. Michelene E. Pesantubbee, "From Vision to Violence: The Wounded Knee Massacre," in *Millenialism, Persecution, and Violence: Historical Cases*, ed. Catherine Wessinger (Syracuse, N.Y.: Syracuse University Press, 2000), 62-81.

Chapter 7

1. Jess Walter, *Every Knee Shall Bow: The Truth and Tragedy of Ruby Ridge and the Randy Weaver Family* (New York: HarperPaperbacks, 1995).

2. James Tabor and Eugene V. Gallagher, *Why Waco? Cults and the Battle for Religious Freedom in America* (Berkeley, Calif.: University of California Press, 1995); Stuart A. Wright, ed., *Armageddon in Waco: Critical Perspectives on the Branch Davidian Conflict* (Chicago, Ill.: University of Chicago Press, 1995); Carol Moore, *The Davidian Massacre: Disturbing Questions about Waco Which Must Be Answered* (Franklin, Tenn., and Springfield, Va.: Legacy Communications and Gun Owners Foundation, 1995); Catherine Wessinger, *How the Millennium Comes Violently: From Jonestown to Heaven's Gate* (New York: Seven Bridges Press, 2000), 56-119.

3. Wessinger, *How the Millennium Comes Violently*; John R. Hall, "Public Narratives and the Apocalyptic Sect: From Jonestown to Mt. Carmel," in Wright, ed., *Armageddon in Waco*, 205-35; James T. Richardson, "Minority Religions and the Context of Violence: A Conflict/Interactionist Perspective," in *Terrorism and Political Violence* 3 (Spring 2001): 103-33.

4.   Wessinger, *How the Millennium Comes Violently*, 47, 121, 143, 274-75, 280-81.

5.   Wessinger, *How the Millennium Comes Violently*, 30-55, 120-57; John R. Hall, *Gone from the Promised Land: Jonestown in American Cultural History* (New Brunswick, N.J.: Transaction Books, 1987); Mary McCormick Maaga, *Hearing the Voices of Jonestown: Putting a Human Face on an American Tragedy* (Syracuse, N.Y.: Syracuse University Press, 1998); Rebecca Moore, "'American as Cherry Pie': Peoples Temple and Violence in America," in *Millennialism, Persecution, and Violence: Historical Cases,* ed. Catherine Wessinger (Syracuse, N.Y.: Syracuse University Press, 2000), 121-37; Ian Reader, *A Poisonous Cocktail? Aum Shinrikyo's Path to Violence* (Copenhagen: Nordic Institute of Asian Studies Books, 1996); Ian Reader, *Religious Violence in Contemporary Japan: The Case of Aum Shinrikyo* (Richmond, Surrey, UK: Curzon Press, 2000); Robert J. Kisala and Mark R. Mullins, eds., *Religion and Social Crisis in Japan: Understanding Japanese Society through the Aum Affair* (New York: Palgrave, 2001).

6.   David G. Bromley and James T. Richardson, eds., *The Brainwashing/ Deprogramming Controversy: Sociological, Psychological, Legal and Historical Perspectives* (New York: Edwin Mellen Press, 1983).

7.   Thomas Robbins and Dick Anthony, "Sects and Violence: Factors Enhancing the Volatility of Marginal Religious Movements," in Wright, ed., *Armageddon in Waco*, 236-59.

8.   Robert D. Baird, *Category Formation and the History of Religions* (The Hague: Mouton, 1971).

9.   Wessinger, *How the Millennium Comes Violently,* 5-6. My definition of millennialism builds and expands on the definition provided by Norman Cohn, *The Pursuit of the Millennium* (London: Secker & Warburg, 1957).

10.   Catherine Wessinger, "Millennialism With and Without the Mayhem: Catastrophic and Progressive Expectations," in *Millennialism, Messiahs, and Mayhem: Contemporary Apocalyptic Movements,* eds. Thomas Robbins and Susan J. Palmer (New York: Routledge, 1997), 47-59; Wessinger, *How the Millennium Comes Violently;* Catherine Wessinger, "The Interacting Dynamics of Millennial Beliefs, Persecution, and Violence," in Wessinger, *Millennialism, Persecution, and Violence*, 3-39.

11.   Wessinger, *How the Millennium Comes Violently*, 158-217; Wessinger, "The Interacting Dynamics," 35-38.

12.   Scott Lowe, "Western Millennial Ideology Goes East: The Taiping Revolution and Mao's Great Leap Forward," in Wessinger, *Millennialism, Persecution, and Violence*, 220-40; Robert Ellwood, "Nazism as a Millennialist Movement," in Wessinger, *Millennialism, Persecution, and Violence,* 241-60; Richard C. Salter, "Time, Authority, and Ethics in the Khmer Rouge: Elements of the Millennial Vision in Year Zero," in Wessinger, *Millennialism, Persecution, and Violence,* 281-98. "Speed progress up to an apocalyptic rate" is Robert Ellwood's phrase.

13.   Adam Szubin, Carl J. Jensen, Rod Gregg, "Interacting with 'Cults': A Policing Model," *FBI Law Enforcement Bulletin* (September 2000): 16-24, <http://www.fbi.gov/library/leb/2000/sep00leb.pdf>.

14. Szubin, Jensen, Gregg, "Interacting with 'Cults'"; Lonnie Kliever, "Meeting God in Garland: A Model of Religious Tolerance," *Nova Religio: The Journal of Alternative and Emergent Religions* 3, no. 1 (October 1999): 45- 53.
15. Wessinger, *How the Millennium Comes Violently.*
16. Grant Underwood, "Millennialism, Persecution, and Violence: The Mormons," in Wessinger, *Millennialism, Persecution, and Violence*, 43-61.
17. Linda E. Olds, *Fully Human: How Everyone Can Integrate the Benefits of Masculine and Feminine Sex Roles* (Englewood Cliffs, N.J.: Prentice-Hall, 1981).
18. Phillip Lucas, "How Future Wacos Might Be Avoided: Two Proposals," in *From the Ashes: Making Sense of Waco,* ed. James R. Lewis (Lanham, Md.: Rowman & Littlefield, 1994), 209-13; Jayne Seminare Docherty, "When the Parties Bring Their Gods to the Table: Learning Lessons from Waco," Ph.D. diss., George Mason University, 1998, published as *Learning Lessons from Waco: When the Parties Bring Their Gods to the Negotiation Table* (Syracuse, N.Y.: Syracuse Univesrsity Press, 2001).
19. Tabor and Gallagher, *Why Waco?*; James D. Tabor, "The Waco Tragedy: An Autobiographical Account of One Attempt to Prevent Disaster," in Lewis, *From the Ashes*, 13-21.
20. Wessinger, *How the Millennium Comes Violently*, 73-74, citing negotiation audiotape no. 129.
21. Wessinger, *How the Millennium Comes Violently*, 75-76; James D. Tabor, "The Events at Waco: An Interpretive Log" (1995), <http://home.maine.rr.com/waco/ww.html>.
22. Wessinger, *How the Millennium Comes Violently*, 22, 93-94; on the Davidians cheering at the prospect of coming out, see House of Representatives, Investigation into the Activities of Federal Law Enforcement Agencies toward the Branch Davidians: Thirteenth Report by the Committee on Government Reform and Oversight Prepared in Conjunction with the Committee on the Judiciary together with Additional and Dissenting Views, Report 104-749 (Washington, D.C.: U.S. Government Printing Office, 1996), 65; "Last Recorded Words of David Koresh, April 16-18, 1993" audiotape introduced by James Tabor, transcribed and published in Wessinger, *How the Millennium Comes Violently*, 105-12.
23. Wessinger, "The Interacting Dynamics"; Wessinger, *How the Millennium Comes Violently.*
24. Underwood, "Millennialism, Persecution, and Violence: The Mormons"; Michelene E. Pesantubbee, "From Vision to Violence: The Wounded Knee Massacre," in Wessinger, *Millennialism, Persecution, and Violence,* 62-81; Christine Steyn, "Millenarian Tragedies in South Africa: The Xhosa Cattle-Killing Movement and the Bulhoek Massacre," in Wessinger, *Millennialism, Persecution, and Violence,* 185-202.
25. Maaga, *Hearing the Voices of Jonestown*; Moore, "'American as Cherry Pie,'"; Hall, *Gone from the Promised Land;* Wessinger, *How the Millennium Comes Violently*, 30-55.
26. Wessinger, *How the Millennium Comes Violently,* 120-57; Reader, *A Poisonous Cocktail?*

27. Szubin, Jensen, and Gregg, "Interacting with 'Cults.'"
28. Wessinger, *How the Millennium Comes Violently,* 271.
29. Ibid., 60-65.
30. The following is a refinement of my discussion of characteristics that cause concern and reassuring characteristics in Wessinger, *How the Millennium Comes Violently,* 275-82.
31. Benjamin Zablocki, "The Blacklisting of a Concept: The Strange History of the Brainwashing Conjecture in the Sociology of Religion," *Nova Religio: The Journal of Alternative and Emergent Religions* 1 (October 1997): 96-121.
32. Wessinger, *How the Millennium Comes Violently,* 158-217; Jean E. Rosenfeld, "The Justus Freemen Standoff: The Importance of the Analysis of Religion in Avoiding Violent Outcomes," in Wessinger, *Millennialism, Persecution, and Violence,* 323-44.
33. Wessinger, *How the Millennium Comes Violently,* 229-52.
34. Lorne L. Dawson, "When Prophecy Fails and Faith Persists: A Theoretical Overview," *Nova Religio: The Journal of Alternative and Emergent Religions* 3, no. 1 (October 1999): 60-82.

Chapter 8

1. Gary North, "Gary North's Y2K Links and Forums," accessed from Internet, 12 December 2000.
2. Ibid.
3. Referring to the Communist scheme for utopia, North writes, "the year 2000 . . . has been the target date for over 200 years." Gary North, "The Final Phase: East Side," *Remnant Review* 17 (19 January 1990): 1.
4. Gary North, *Millennialism and Social Theory* (Tyler, Tex.: ICE, 1990); Gary North, *Rapture Fever: Why Dispensationalism is Paralyzed* (Tyler, Tex.: ICE, 1993).
5. Amazon search for "Y2K" on the Internet site, accessed 8 January 2001.
6. Gary North, quoted in Rob Boston, "2000: Apocalypse Now?," *Church and State* (March 1999): 8.
7. Gary North, *Political Polytheism: The Myth of Pluralism* (Tyler, Tex.: ICE, 1989), 590, emphasis his.
8. North, *Millennialism,* 273.
9. "Gary North is a Big Fat Idiot," accessed 22 May 2000, www.garynorth.shadowscape.net.
10. See Boston, "2000," 8-12.
11. Catherine Wessinger, *How the Millennium Comes Violently: From Jonestown to Heaven's Gate* (New York: Seven Bridges Press, 2000), 16-17.
12. Greg Bahnsen, "Postmillennialism and the Reformed Faith," accessed from the Internet 2 March 2001, forerunner.com/beast; Ray Sutton, "Covenantal Postmillennialism," *Covenant Renewal* 3 (February 1989): 1; Kenneth Gentry, "Whose Victory in History?" in *Theonomy: An Informed Response,* ed. Gary North (Tyler, Tex.: ICE, 1991), 213; North, *Millennialism,* 238.
13. Gary North, Preface, *Christian Reconstruction: What It Is, What It Isn't,* eds. Gary North and Gary DeMar (Tyler, Tex.: Institute for Christian Economics, 1991), xi.

14. The organization is named "Chalcedon" in reference to the A.D. 451 council, and the Chalcedonian creed is the keystone of Rushdoony's interpretation of orthodox Christianity.

15. Sandlin explains, "As a result of a series of fax exchanges between North and me, North agreed in a signed fax of April 28, 1995 to abandon any acrimonious criticism of Rushdoony and Chalcedon. In fact, he stated that, for the most part, he does not intend to criticize Rushdoony at all; when he does, he pledges that the criticism will occur in a context of reasoned academic discourse. He willingly called his statement a 'truce.' I had already stated in my April 27 fax to North: '[W]e want no trouble; we simply wish to be left alone. We did not start this fracas, we did not attack you, and we have never meant you harm. Aside from responding to specific views you address with which we disagree, we do not intend to mention you in the future. We expect you to act in kind.'" Andrew Sandlin, "Deconstructing Reconstruction: Review of Gary North's *Baptized Patriarchalism: The Cult of the Family*" [online article], accessed from the Internet 2 March 2001, chalcedon.edu/articles.

16. Anson Shupe, "The Reconstructionist Movement on the New Christian Right," *The Christian Century*, 4 October 1989, 880-82; Rodney Clapp, "Democracy as Heresy," *Christianity Today*, 20 February 1987, 17-23; Mark Karlberg, Review of *Covenant and Common Grace*, *Westminster Theological Journal* 50 (1988): 323-37. Richard John Neuhaus, "Why Wait for the Kingdom? The Theonomist Temptation," *First Things* 3 (May 1990): 14.

17. Michael Gabbert, "An Historical Overview of Christian Reconstructionism," *Criswell Theological Review* 6, no. 2 (1993): 281.

18. For instance, Rob Boston begins his 1988 article by stating, "The Reconstructionists' ideal is a country where a fierce God reigns supreme and government is based on the Law of Moses . . . [and] homosexuals, atheists, sabbath-breakers and 'infidels' face execution." Boston's presentation is biased from the start against the Reconstructionists. His article has not aided the public's understanding of the movement as much as it and other articles like it have instilled a fear of CR. Rob Boston, "Thy Kingdom Come," *Church & State* (September 1988): 6. Of course, not all publications are as brutal. Mark Karlberg's review of *Covenant and Common Grace* in the *Westminster Theological Journal* (1988): 323-37, is an exemplary work of respectability and scholarship.

19. While many are beginning to prefer the term "Reformed" to "Calvinist," the latter is used here because it is the term Sandlin chooses in his "Creed of Christian Reconstruction" dated 1999-2000. Andrew Sandlin, "The Creed of Christian Reconstruction," accessed from the Internet 31 May 2000,

20. See Gary DeMar, *The Debate over Christian Reconstruction* (Fort Worth, Tex.: Dominion Press, 1988), 63-65.

21. Total depravity; Unconditional election; Limited atonement; Irresistible grace; Perseverance of the saints.

22. Sandlin, "Creed."

23. For instance, see Gary North, *Puritan Economic Experiments* (Tyler, Tex.: ICE, 1988).

24. Gary DeMar, "What is Christian Reconstruction?," in *Christian Reconstruction,* 81.

25. Andrew Sandlin, "Glossary of Frequently Used Terms," accessed from the Internet on 31 May 2000, www.chalcedon.edu.html.
26. Greg Bahnsen, *By This Standard* (Tyler, Tex.: ICE, 1985), 3.
27. Ibid.; italics his.
28. In fact, the analogy of the Constitution comes the closest to depicting the CR position. Reconstructionists believe that one day, the Bible will in fact replace the Constitution and that the legislative and judicial branches of the government will study the Bible, not the Constitution, for rulings.
29. Capital punishment is required for murder, striking or cursing a parent, kidnaping, adultery, incest, bestiality, sodomy or homosexuality, unchastity, rape of a betrothed virgin, witchcraft, offering human sacrifice, incorrigible delinquency, blasphemy, Sabbath desecration, propagation of false doctrines, sacrificing to false gods, refusing to abide by a court decision, and failing to restore the pledge or bail. In this penal system, prisons will not exist. A criminal will either repay his victim's loss, be exiled, or be executed.
30. Regarding slavery, David Chilton, in his *Productive Christians in an Age of Guilt Manipulators* (written in response to Ronald Sider's *Rich Christians in an Age of Hunger*), argues that resisting slavery is futile. Slavery has always existed and continues to exist everywhere, even in America, just not always in the forms historically associated with it. Furthermore, "If slavery were a sin, *God* would not have provided for it. Indeed, since God is the Standard of right and wrong, the fact that He gives rules for the proper management of slavery shows that to *disregard* the laws of slavery is a sin." David Chilton, *Productive Christians in an Age of Guilt Manipulators* (Tyler, Tex.: ICE, 1981), 60, italics his. Chilton argues that Christians should not attempt to abolish slavery wherever it may be found, but instead we should "follow God's laws for slavery." Ibid., 61. These laws, drawn directly from Exodus, Deuteronomy, and Leviticus, stipulate conditions for obtaining, caring for, and freeing slaves. The problem with American slavery in the South was that there was no process for gradually freeing the slaves. From a biblical perspective, people can be indentured for six-year stints, but had to be freed or hired as servants in the seventh year. Rushdoony agrees with Chilton's proposals and insists that because slavery was not outlawed, but indeed provided for under God's law, white Americans should not feel guilty for their ancestors' role in slavery in the states. He believes that historical distortion has "systematically indoctrinated [the white man] into believing that he is guilty of enslaving and abusing the Negro." R. J. Rushdoony, *Politics of Guilt and Pity* (Fairfax, Va.: Thoburn Press, 1970), 3-4, 19, 25. At any rate, no debt could be imposed for more than six years. This is because alongside the hard-line approach to capital punishment and slavery is a hard-line approach to jubilee. Thus, long term mortgages would be a thing of the past in a reconstructed society.
31. Gary North, *Backward Christian Soldiers? An Action Manual for Christian Reconstruction* (Tyler, Tex.: ICE, 1984), 66.
32. In an effort to reduce state power, CR opposes almost all forms of tax. National tax should be a flat tax of no more than 10 percent or, even better, the church, which in turn would support the governmental agencies, should levy a tithe tax.

33. R. J. Rushdoony, *The Institutes of Biblical Law* (Phillipsburg, N.J.: Presbyterian and Reformed, 1973), 747.

34. DeMar, *Christian Reconstruction*, 82.

35. In an extensive discussion on "The Idea of Progress and Inheritance," North says, "History is progressive because corporate sanctification is progressive. It is not simply that history is linear; it is also progressive." Gary North, "The Covenantal Ideal of Economic Growth," *Biblical Economics Today* 21 (April/May, 1999): 3-4.

36. Sandlin, "Creed."

37. North, *Political Polytheism*, 87.

38. Gary North, "The Intellectual Schizophrenia of the New Christian Right," *Christianity and Civilization* 1 (Spring 1982): 25.

39. North offers a full exposition on humanism, its evolution, and influence on American democracy in *Conspiracy: A Biblical View* (Tyler, Tex.: Dominion Press, 1996).

40. See R. J. Rushdoony, "Publisher's Foreword: Can We Legislate Morality?," [online article] accessed on the Internet 2 March 2001, www.chalcedon.edu/report/2000jan.

41. Gary North, *Liberating Planet Earth: An Introduction to Biblical Blueprints* (Tyler, Tex.: Dominion, 1987), 150-51. North infers that all parts are therefore equally normative. The preacher must not limit himself to "a chapter or two in Exodus, the Book of Amos, Acts 2 and 4, and 2 Corinthians 8. No, he must preach the whole law," 151.

42. Ray Sutton, "Covenantal Postmillennialism" *Covenant Renewal* 3 (February 1989): 2-4.

43. North, *Political Polytheism*, 67.

44. Ibid., 590.

45. Gary North, *Treasure and Dominion: An Economic Commentary on Luke* (Tyler, Tex.: ICE, 2000); and his *Cooperation and Dominion: An Economic Commentary on Romans* (Tyler, Tex.: ICE, 2000).

46. Gary North to author (personal email), 30 May 2000.

Chapter 9

1.   *The Baptist Standard,* vol. 113, no. 6 (5 February 2001): 1.

2.   Clinton Rossiter, ed., *The Federalist Papers* (New York: Penguin Books, 1961), 422-23.

3.   See Pew Forum Updates, 9 April 2003, available at http://pewforum.org/faith-based-initiatives/.

4.   *Church and State,* vol. 54, no. 6 (June 2001): 5.

5.   Executive Order: Establishment of White House Office of Faith-Based and Community Initiatives. 29 January 2001. Available at: http://www.tgci.com/faithbased/articles/eo012901.htm

6.   *Church and State* vol. 54, no. 4 (April 2001): 5.

7.   *The Report from the Capitol*, Baptist Joint Committee, vol. 56, no. 12 (13 June 2001): 1.

8.   *Church and State*, vol. 54, no. 4 (April 2001):5.

9.   Quoted in *Church and State*, vol. 54, no. 6 (June 2001): 10.

10. SMART Press Release, 28 February 2001. Available at: http://www.sikhmediawatch.org/news_events/pr20010228.htm

11. Letter to George W. Bush, Dick Cheney, and Honored Government Officials, available at http://www.aren.org/lettersig.html.

12. Ibid.
13. Laura Meckler, "Plan for Religious Groups Debated." *AP Online*, 6 May 2001.
14. Ibid.
15. Janet Weiland, "Scientology Responds to Faith-Based Accusations." Available at: http://www.beliefnet.com/story/74/story_7439_1.html
16. *Church and State,* vol. 54. no. 4 (April 2001): 5.
17. Rossiter, "Federalist 51," *James Madison*, 324.
18. Ibid., 6.
19. Christy Karras, "Mormons Reject Bush Charity Plan," *AP Online*, 25 April 2001.
20. *Church and State,* vol. 54. no. 4 (April 2001): 6.

Chapter 10

1. Indeed, Wiccans point out that "Satan" is a Christian construct, and not known to the pagans who were forcibly conquered by Christianity in the early Middle Ages. Neither Satan, nor Satan-like demons or devils, are part of the normative Wiccan pantheon of gods and goddesses.
2. J. G. Melton, *The Encyclopedic Handbook Of Cults In America* (New York, Garland Publishing, 1986), 211, 213. It is important to emphasize that the spiritual belief system related in Melton's *Handbook* is normative for the Wiccan movement as a whole. Indeed, the Wiccan Rede is, "And you harm none, do what you will." Deviant exceptions to the norm, of course, may be found in every religious group, and thus Christian anti-Wiccan groups who search for such deviance will probably find it. But no religious denomination as a whole can be branded for the outrageous or evil acts of those few deviants. Jimmy Swaggart's behavior was not considered normative for his Protestant denomination, nor was Protestantism as a whole blamed or condemned for Jim Jones's activities. Nor is the occurrence of incidents of child molestation among Catholic priests typical or at all representative of Catholic beliefs and practices. One might also anticipate that anti-Wiccan groups will come up with a scandalous story or two from "former Wiccans" who have since experienced a conversion. Such a printing of sensational, "insider" exposés is a well-worn tactic used by zealots against feared and hated religious groups. Indeed, this tradition goes back at least as far as the anti-Catholic, nativist movements before the Civil War; the most notorious propaganda tool of this period was a book purportedly written by a woman named Maria Monk in 1836, titled *Awful Disclosures of the Hotel Dieu Nunnery of Montreal.* Maria Monk purportedly wrote of her first-hand experiences as a young woman living in a nunnery, and included such horror stories as priests having unbridled sex with nuns in the confessional, nuns essentially kept as concubines, newborns of these nuns being baptized and then immediately strangled, and so forth. Noted historian of American religion, Sidney Ahlstrom, however, stated that this book was "published (and in large part written) by a group of New York anti-Catholics, lay and clerical." S.E. Ahlstrom, *A Religious History Of The American People* (New Haven, Conn.: Yale University Press, 1972), 561. Three hundred thousand copies of this book had been sold by 1860, and a new edition appeared after the Civil War. Edwin Gausted explained

the Maria Monk phenomenon as follows: "Most Americans, never having been inside a nunnery, often wondered—or worried—about what went on in there."Maria Monk" was only too glad to tell, not in explicit salacious detail (that would become the fashion of the next century), but in suggestion and intimation. The facts were hair-raising, the only problem being that they weren't facts at all, only nativist fancy." E.S. Gausted, ed., *A Documentary History of Religion In America: To The Civil War* (Grand Rapids, Mich.: Wm. B. Eerdmans Publishing Co., 1982), 462. Similar combinations of ignorance, fear, curiosity and revulsion exist today about Wicca/Neo-Paganism.

3.   Melton, *The Encyclopedic Handbook,* 213-14.

4.   (All materials described below and in subsequent footnotes were supplied to the author by Wiccans.) Kathy Keys Snowden, LCSW, "Satanic Symbols" (privately reproduced hand-out, n.d., Richmond, Va.). This one-page illustration bore the following attribution: "Condensed from material of: Michael True, Assistant to Pres., Evangelical School of Theology, Meyerstown, Penn. 17067."
    In the sheet titled, "Key Dates in Orthodox Satanism," Satanic holidays are listed as follows: New Year's Day, St. Winebold Day, January 17 Satanic Revels, Candle Mass, St. Walpurgis Day, Spring Equinox, Mocking Good Friday, Walpurgis Night, Beltane/May Day, Summer Solstice, Midsummer's Eve, July 1 Demon Revels, St. James Day, Lammas Day, August 3 Satanic Revels, St. Bartholomew's Day, Marriage To Beast of Satan, September 20 Midnight Host, Fall Equinox, All Hallows Eve, Halloween, Winter Solstice/St. Thomas Day, December 24 Demon Revels, as well as phases of the moon, particularly full moons. Kathy Keys Snowden, LCSW, "Key Dates in Orthodox Satanism" (privately reproduced handout, n.d., Richmond, Va.).
    As is obvious by a comparison with the previously-mentioned Wiccan holy days, there is some similarity (although by no means a complete overlap) in the names and time periods of celebration. But Satanic holidays were/are not meant to be celebrations of pre-Christian European pagan holy days but, rather, an attack on and perverse mockery of *Christian* holy days. The Satanists were not striving to be pre-Christian European pagans, but, rather, were striving to be the opposite of Christianity. Satanism first arose in the Middle Ages in opposition to and thus as a reverse of Christianity (Christianity "inside-out"). Christianity at that time had assimilated and Christianized the old pagan celebrations into its liturgical calendar, hence the similarities. As already noted, Wiccans do *not* worship demons or devils of any type.

5.   Catherine Gould, "Signs and Symptoms of Ritualistic Abuse in Children," (Checklist, privately printed, 1988).

6.   Catherine Gould, "Symptoms Characterizing Satanic Ritual Abuse and Sexual Abuse" (two-page list, privately printed, n.d.).

7.   Kathy K. Snowden, LCSW, "Satanic Cult Ritual Abuse" 9 (privately reproduced hand-out, rev. Richmond, Va.: February 1990).
    One Wiccan interviewed had attended a talk by a state college professor to a local group, and he reported that the professor stated that Smurfs were Satanic because they believe in magic, showed common Wiccan symbols (including a hexagram Star of David in a circle), and stated "these are satanic symbols and if you see people wearing these

symbols you can be sure that they are involved in Satanism," and then continued by connecting Satanism with murder, child-eating, and drugs. Personal interview, M.L., 16 July 1992.

8.   Personal interviews, M.L., R.C., 16 July 1992; telephone interview, S.B., April 1992. File letters, OH; MN; MD. Personal narratives included in this paper were obtained in three ways: in-person or telephone interviews, correspondences sent to me directly, and several hundred correspondences on file with Circle/Lady Liberty League, a Wiccan center/clearinghouse for Wiccan religious freedom issues located in Wisconsin. For purposes of privacy, confidentiality, and personal safety, all Wiccans who authored letters or who were personally interviewed will not be identified (including the few who did give permission for their names to be used).

9.   File letter.

10.   File letter, 1991.

11.   See, for example, *Dept. Of The Army, Religious Requirements And Practices Of Certain Selected Groups: A Handbook For Chaplains.* 28 April 1978 (Pamphlet 165-13). Wicca is addressed in Chapter VII, "Other Groups." Also included in this section is the Native American Church, Baha'i Faith, Foundation Faith of the Millennium, the Church of Satan (carefully distinguished from "classical Satanism" which practiced human sacrifice), and Churches of Scientology. The introduction section on "Magick" is informative, even-handed, and respectful. Ibid., VII-2, VII-3.

12.   Scott James, "By the Power Vested In Me: Witches Wage War on City Hall, Win Sweeping Reform," *Liberty* 2-3 (July/August 1985) (photocopy forwarded by personal letter, NY, 12 June 1992). The reporter observed: "The story of witch Judith Harrow and Covenant of the Goddess is not a conspiracy. It does show what happens when a few government officials let personal beliefs interfere with their official duty." Ibid., 3.

13.   Personal interview with S.F., 6 June 1992.

14.   Personal interview with G.O., 6 June 1992.

15.   Telephone interview, S.B., April 1992.

16.   Personal interview with M.L., 16 July 1992.

17.   Reports of such progress have been received from Indiana, Ohio, and South Carolina. Personal interview with M.L., 16 July 1992. Telephone interview with S.B., April 1992. Personal letter, SC, n.d..

18.   Wiccan narratives uniformly refer to their harassers as "fundamentalists" although it is by no means clear that this term is used by Wiccans in the same way as it is used by academics. Interestingly, while religious intolerance stemming from a scientific/rational worldview is probable (witness the battle over scientific creationism), no Wiccan narratives this author has heard or reviewed ever referred to this type of worldview as a basis for intolerance or harassment.

19.   E.J. Lawless, *God's Peculiar People: Women's Voices & Folk Tradition in a Pentecostal Church* (Lexington, Ky.: The University Press of Kentucky, 1988), 14-15, 24.

20.   Ibid., 14.

21.   Ibid., 15 (emphasis in the original).

22.   Personal interview with M.L., conducted on 16 July 1992.

23.   Telephone interview with Anne Penway, American Library

Association, 27 September 1992. These groups include: Dr. James Dobson's group in Colorado, Focus on the Family; the Reverend Donald Wildman's group, American Family Association; and a group called Citizens For Excellence in Education, which is part of Robert Simon's group, The National Association of Christian Educators.

24. Paul deParrie and Mary Pride, *Ancient Empires of The New Age* (Westchester, Ill.; Crossway Books, 1989).

25. Ibid., 103 (emphasis added).

26. Exodus 23:18 (RSV). The King James Version uses the term "witch."

27. Ibid., 42.

28. Exodus 34:11-17, quoted in deParrie and Pride, *Ancient Empires,* 79-80.

29. deParrie and Pride, *Ancient Empires,* 80, 83-84.

30. Luke 11:23, quoted in deParrie and Pride, *Ancient Empires,* 175.

31. deParrie and Pride, *Ancient Empires,* 193-94.

32. Ibid., 195.

33. See, for example, newspaper articles cited throughout this article.

34. File letters: Ohio; Maryland. Personal letters: Pennsylvania, 5 December 1992; Ohio, 1 August 1992. Telephone interview, S.B., April 1992. Personal interviews: S.F. 6 June 1992; M.L. and R.C., 16 July 1992.

35. File letter, "Lorcalann" of Circle Caer Myrddin, about 1985.

36. File letter dated 12 May 1991. Other Wiccans personally interviewed also reported hearing of the existence of such a fundamentalist underground.

37. The minister of a local Lutheran church, for example, was quoted as follows in a local newspaper report concerning the zoning matter:"There is a definite interest [in the zoning application] in that this is what we don't want in our community," [said the minister, who] . . . charges they are devil worshippers despite their denials.""I've [the minister] seen their publication, it is full of symbols which represent devil worship and the occult.We intend to use whatever legal means, such as the zoning laws, to get them out of here."Dan Wilson, "Zoning Issue Becomes Witch Hunt," *Mount Horeb Mail,* 24 July 1986, 1, 4.

38. Of course, few, if any, Christian churches would seek out or need large acreages of farmland for religious purposes, but even if they did so (for a retreat house, for example), now they, too, are banned from that county, unless, of course, they could get a majority of the county board to agree to change the zoning.

39. Personal interview with S.F., 6 June 1992 (and newspaper articles on the matter).

40. File letter.

41. File letter. Statement made in particular reference to a judge's calling her taking her child to Wiccan ceremonies and celebrating pagan holidays, "child abuse."

42. File letter from New Mexico, 1985.

43. "Holiday invitation to witch withdrawn," *The Home News,* 24 October 1991 (New Brunswick, New Jersey) (photocopy supplied by Wiccan correspondent).

44. "Misunderstood, say protesting witches," *The Philadelphia Inquirer,* 27 October 1991, 1-B, 4-B (photocopy supplied by Wiccan correspondent).

45.   *Miami Herald*, 10 July 1986 (photocopy supplied by Wiccan correspondent).

46.   *San Francisco Examiner*, 13 July 1986 (photocopy supplied by Wiccan correspondent).

47.   *Abingdon School District v. Schempp*, 374 U.S. 203 (1963) at 300 (Brennan, J., concurring).

48.   *Epperson v. Arkansas*, 393 U.S. 97 (1968) at 107 (quoting opinion of Clark, J. in the case of *Joseph Burstyn, Inc. v. Wilson*, 343 U.S. 495 (1952) at 505.

49.   H.R. 3389, 99th Cong., 1st Sess., 131 *Congressional Record* 24288 (1985). This bill, which was referred to the House Ways and Means Committee, did not make it out of Committee.

50.   H.R. 3036, Amend. 705, 99th Cong., 1st Sess., 131 *Congressional Record* 25074 (1985) (Appropriations Bill for 1986).

51.   Interestingly, it was this very same 20/20 segment that was shown at the church meeting organized to oppose the zoning variance requested by the Wisconsin Wiccan group discussed earlier.

52.   131 Congressional Record 25077 (1985).

53.   131 Congressional Record 25080 (1985).

54.   Ibid., (emphasis added). Ironically, Senator Helms made the following statement in Congress just three months prior to his efforts to deny religious freedoms and legitimacy to Wiccans: "Mr. President, as long as I am a U.S. Senator, I will fight to preserve the freedoms of the religious organizations of this country. These institutions have supported and nourished the moral resolve of our citizens, upon which the strength and stability of this republic is based. Without this strong moral base, the freedoms we hold dear will slip away and be forever lost. And with the loss of these freedoms follows the jeopardizing of our democracy." 131 *Congressional Record* 14158 (1985) (remarks of Sen. Helms).

55.   131 *Congressional Record* 25085 (1985).

56.   Personal interviews with S.F., 6 June 1992 and 17 November 1992.

57.   Dr. C. Everett Koop, quoted in *Nova: The Controversial Dr. Koop* (PBS television air-date: 10 October 1989) (Transcript by Journal Graphics, Inc., 3-14).

58.   File letters: NC; IL; IN. Personal interview, M. L., R. C., 16 July 1992. Personal letters: NH, 12 June 1992;

59.   The Wiccan's job as Victim's Assistance Coordinator was funded by federal state and local government funds. The court held: "Based on the facts in the present case, the effect of the government substantially, if not exclusively, funding a position such as Victim's Assistance Coordinator and then allowing the Salvation Army to choose the person to fill or maintain the position based on religious preference clearly has the effect of advancing religion and is unconstitutional." See *Dodge v. Salvation Army*, 48 Empl. Prac. Dec. (CCH) par. 38,619 (1989) (S.D. Miss., civil action no. S88 0353 (R)).

60.   File letter from Lindenhurst, Illinois.

61.   File letter from North Carolina.

62.   File letters: Michigan; Maryland; Iowa. Personal letters: Florida, postmarked 4 January 1993; Indiana, letters 2 June 1992, 20 July 1992; letter from California indicated that Texas and Nevada prisons refuse Wiccan literature to inmates, postmarked 17 November 1992.

63. File letter, Maryland.
64. Personal letter, Oregon, 17 November 1992. The Wiccan notes: "There are many items in this policy which are made available to inmates of the Islamic, Judaic, Christian, or Native American Indians that can be comparable to Wiccan items. Robes are obvious! Prayer rugs/alter [sic] cloth. Islamic inmates are allowed essence oils, Buddhist inmates are allowed incense, Native American Indians have an outside area for worship."
65. File letter, Wisconsin.
66. File letter, California.
67. Personal letter, California, postmarked 12 November 1992.
68. File letter from Tryon, North Carolina.
69. File letter of 27 October 1985, from Greenwood, South Carolina.
70. One must keep in mind the atmosphere of threats in which Wiccans practice (this was Salem immediately after a vigorous anti-Wiccan rally) in order to fully understand how this woman interpreted what was happening to her. Also recall the common currency of stories of an alleged "fundamentalist undergrounds" that "rescues" children from Wiccan parents, for example.
71. Telephone interview with Capt. Paul Murphy, 28 September 1992.
72. Coincidentally, the same time that Rep. Walker introduced his anti-witchcraft bill in the House of Representatives.
73. Letter from Lady Galadriel, and accompanying photocopies of legal documents and newspaper articles, including: "Atlanta Witches Fight Suspicion, Resent Association with Satanism," *The Atlanta Constitution*, 16 October 1985, 10-B; "Metro in Brief: Trespass Case on Witches' Land Dropped," *The Atlanta Constitution* and *Atlanta Journal WEEKEND*, 14 December 1985; "Witches vow to cease ceremonies in Lithonia," *The Atlanta Journal*, 19 September 1985, 1C, 6C.
74. Telephone interview, S. B., April 1992; personal interview, S. F., 6 June 1992; personal interview, M.L., 16 July 16 1992; File letters: Oregon; Tennessee.
75. File letters: Ohio; South Carolina; California; Texas; Illinois (successful appeal within the company after Christian group demanded she be fired from her job in a print shop); Chicago, Illinois; Indiana; California; Maryland. Personal letters: 18-year-old lost her job when a fellow student reported to her manager that she was "a satanic witch" 4 December 1992; mental health assistant taken off full time status, lost all benefits, placed on "call as needed" status (his card in the call-in box is persistently missing), after a relative told one of his patients he was a Wiccan and the patient told a visiting student minister from Bob Jones University 22 February 1992, South Carolina, forwarded by Wiccan Pagan Press Alliance, Pennsylvania, 7 April 1992.
76. Personal interview, M. L., 16 July 1992; telephone interview, S. B., April 1992; file letters: Vermont; Wisconsin; Texas; Illinois; Florida; Ohio; Indiana; Indiana; Tennessee; Georgia. Personal letters: one Wiccan reported being "kicked out" of a park for worshipping and praying at a "ritual place" on Samhain. Letter, 4 December 1992.
77. File letter, Oregon.
78. File letters: Illinois (personally assaulted by two men "who were not two fanatics. They were merely two young men who had been so per-

suaded by what they read and had been taught that they believed what I taught and worshipped was 'evil' and should be 'dealt' with"); California ("was injured when some kids from a local bible college saw my pentacle and slammed me to the ground"); California (harassed at work when she wears her pentagram).

79.   File letters: Coven Lothlorien, New Port Ritchey, Florida. Personal letter, Georgia.

80.   That the fear of religious violence is widespread among the Wiccan community is evidenced by the reaction from this community to a proposed television series by ABC titled, "The Craft." The central motif of the series was the kidnapping of a baby by a coven of witches. The weekly focus was to be centered on the terrible harm which threatened to befall the innocent child and the mother's frantic efforts to find and rescue her child. The response against the proposed series was strong enough to convince ABC to cancel the project, although, to recoup its monetary losses on the pilot, ABC sold it to a cable channel which occasionally airs it as a movie. The overwhelming majority of the over two hundred and seventy-five letters addressed to ABC and copied to Circle (a Wiccan religious group and central clearinghouse) expressed not so much an anger at the negative image per se of witches that was being presented, but rather a resounding and terrible fear that the weekly show would promote a wave of violence against them: physical violence, not "mere" defamation, was the clear concern.

81.   John Rawls, *A Theory of Justice* (Cambridge, Mass.: Harvard University Press, 1971), 388 (emphasis added) (stated in the context of a discussion as to when civil disobedience is justified).

Chapter 11

1.   Victor Rotnem, "Criminal Enforcement of Federal Civil Rights," *Lawyers Guild Review* (May 1942): 18-23; Francis H. Heller, "A Turning Point For Religious Liberty," *Virginia Law Review* 29 (1943): 440-59; Edward F. Waite, "The Debt of Constitutional Law to Jehovah's Witnesses," *Minnesota Law Review* 28 (1944): 209-46; Hollis W. Barber, "Religious Liberty v. Police Power—Jehovah's Witnesses," *American Political Science Review* 41 (1947): 226-47; William Shephard McAninch, "A Catalyst for the Evolution of Constitutional Law: Jehovah's Witnesses in the Supreme Court," *Cincinnati Law Review* 55 (1987): 997-1077; and David P. Currie, "The Constitution in the Supreme Court: Civil Rights and Liberties, 1930-1941," *Duke Law Review* (1987): 800-30; "Jehovah's Witnesses: Definers of Freedom," in *Congressional Quarterly's Guide to the U.S. Supreme Court*, 3rd ed., vol. 1, ed. Joan Biskupic & Elder Witt (Washington, D.C. CQ Press, 1997), 453; Lee Epstine and Thomas G. Walker, *Constitutional Law for A Changing America, Rights, Liberties and Justice*, 3rd ed. (Washington, D.C.: CQ Press, 1998), 101; and Shawn Francis Peters, *Judging Jehovah's Witnesses: Religious Persecution and the Dawn of the Rights Revolution* (Lawrence, Kans.: University Press of Kansas, 2000).

2.   John E. Molder and Marvin Comisky, "Jehovah's Witnesses Mold Constitutional Law," *Bill of Rights Review* 2 (1942): 262-68.

3.   Harlan Fiske Stone to Charles Evans Hughes, 24 March 1941, quoted by Peters, *Judging Jehovah's Witnesses*, 186.

4.   M. James Penton, *Apocalypse Delayed: The Story of Jehovah's Witnesses* (Toronto: University of Toronto Press, 1985), 88.

5.   David R. Manwaring, *Render Unto Caesar: The Flag Salute Controversy* (Chicago, Ill.: The University of Chicago Press, 1962), 27.

6.   Barbara Grizzuti Harrison, *Visions of Glory: A History and a Memory of Jehovah's Witnesses* (New York: Simon & Schuster, 1978), 185-86.

7.   Barber,"Religious Liberty v. Police Power," 227.

8.   Manwaring, *Render Unto Caesar,* 26; and Harrison, *Visions of Glory*, 185.

9.   See *Commonwealth v. Palms,* 14 A.2d 484 (Penn. 1940).

10.   William J. Whalen, *Armageddon Around the Corner: A Report on Jehovah's Witnesses* (New York: John Day Company, 1962), 57-58.

11.   Huey B. Howerton, "Jehovah's Witnesses and the Federal Constitution," *Mississippi Law Journal* 17 (1946): 347-71, 352; Charles G. Hanson, "Note: Constitutional Law–Jehovah's Witnesses," *Notre Dame Lawyer* 22 (1946): 82-94; and Jerry Bergman, "The Modern Religious Objection to Mandatory Flag Salute in America: A History and Evaluation," *Journal of Church and State* 39 (Winter 1997): 215-36.

12.   Morton Grodzins, *The Loyal and the Disloyal: Social Boundaries of Patriotism and Treason* (Chicago, Ill.: University of Chicago Press, 1956), 18.

13.   For a summary of these attacks, see Manwaring, *Render Unto Caesar,* 163-67.

14.   *Minersville School District v. Gobitis,* 310 U.S. 586 (1940).

15.   James A. Beckford, *The Trumpet of Prophecy: A Sociological Study of Jehovah's Witnesses* (New York: John Wiley & Sons, 1975), 35.

16.   See also, Joseph T. Tinnelly, "A Current Problem in Freedom of Speech and of Religion," *St. John's Law Review* 16 (1941): 108-17, 112-13, n. 44: "The Witnesses have been charged with sedition, disrespect to the flag, riot, breach of the peace, disorderly conduct, conspiracy against the government, trespassing, offending and annoying people, vagrancy, soliciting and canvassing with out a license, inciting riot, assault and battery, distribution of obscene literature, blasphemy, violating the Sabbath laws, and distributing circulars without a permit." An example of such legal action in West Virginia is in the case of a woman and young girl, who were attacked repeatedly while distributing Jehovah's Witnesses literature in Grantsville. They were permanently enjoined from distributing religious literature in the county. See *Matthews v. West Virginia ex rel. Hamilton*, Chancery Orders of Calhoun County Circuit Court, 16 November 1942 (vol. 11, 319).

17.   Victor W. Rotnem and F. G. Folsom, Jr., "Recent Restrictions Upon Religious Liberty," *American Political Science Review* 36 (1942): 1053-67, see esp. 1061.

18.   Robert J. O'Brien, "Persecution and Resistance: Jehovah's Witnesses and the Defense of Religious Liberty in West Virginia." an unpublished manuscript in my possession. This article examines the expulsion of Jehovah's Witnesses children from school in Barbour, Hancock, Harrison, Kanawha, Nicholas, Upshur, and Wood Counties. It also discusses or enumerates attacks on Jehovah's Witnesses with the complicity of government officials in the West Virginia towns of Bluefield, Clarksburg, Follansbee, Holliday's Cove, Huttonsville, Keyser,

Martinsburg, Morgantown, New Martinsville, Phillippi, Richwood, St. Marys, Wellsburg, and Williamson. Dr. O'Brien, a professor at West Virginia Wesleyan College, is writing a comprehensive book on the persecution of Jehovah's Witnesses.

19. Minutes of the Hancock County Board of Education, 22 May 1941.

20. "Jehovah's Witnesses Indicted," *The* (New Cumberland, W.Va.) *Independent*, 16 April 1942, 1.

21. *Minersville School District v. Gobitis,* 310 U.S. 586.

22. Quoted in *West Virginia State Board of Education v. Barnette*, 319 U.S. 624 (1943) at 621.

23. *State v. Frank Clementino, Sr., State v. George Maupin, State v. Joe Mercante, State v. Pete Mercante*, and *State v. Arthur Ginier;* files of the Hancock County Circuit Clerk. The grand jury returned all these indictments on 14 April 1942. Based on the number of children they had in school, all the men except Ginier were named in two indictments.

24. This Order is in the *Maupin* file.

25. 1941 W. Va. Acts 32., codified at W. VA. Code § 1851(1) (1943).

26. "Judge J.H. Brennan Gives Opinion In Flag Salute Cases," *The* (New Cumberland, W.Va.) *Independent* 4 June 1942, 1.

27. "Memorandum of Opinion," *State v. Mercante,* 4 June 1942, 12; located in the Joe Mercante file.

28. Donald E. Wilkes, Jr., "The New Federalism in Criminal Procedure: State Court Evasion of the Burger Court," *Kentucky Law Journal* 62 (1974): 421-51; Robert D. Bursack, "Of Laboratories and Liberties: State Protections of Political and Civil Rights," *Georgia Law Review* 10 (1976): 533-64; William J. Brennan, Jr., "State Constitutions and the Protection of Individual Rights," *Harvard Law Review* 90 (1977): 489-504; and Ronald K. Collins, Peter J. Galie, and John Kincaid, "State High Courts, State Constitutions and Individual Rights Litigation Since 1980," *Publius* 16 (1986): 141-61.

29. Constitution of West Virginia, Article III, § 15.

30. "Memorandum of Opinion," *State v. Mercante,* 1 June 1942, 12.

31. The other decisions were *Brown v. Skustad,* Minnesota, St. Louis County District Court, 1942 (unreported), cited in Marwaring, *Render Unto Caesar,* 193; *State v. Smith,* 127 P.2d 518 (Kan. 1942) and *Bolling v. Superior Court,* 133 P.2d 803 (Wash. 1943).

32. Interview with Harding Legg, Mount Lookout, W. Va., 26 September 1996 [tape recorded]; and "Stipulation of Facts," 1, *United States v. Catlette* Docket no. 9390 (S.D.W.Va. 1942) unreported decision. National Archives and Record Administration–Mid Atlantic Region, Philadelphia, Pa. Record Group 21, [hereinafter NARA-RG 21, *Catlette*].The petition protested the Ohio State Fair Association's cancellation of a contract for use of the Ohio State Fair Grounds for a national convention of Jehovah's Witnesses.

33. "Court's Charge," 11, NARA-RG 21, *Catlette.*

34. Legg interview; and Leonard A. Stevens, *Salute! The Case of the Bible vs. the Flag* (New York: Coward, McCann & Geoghegan, Inc., 1973), 13.

35. Rotnem & Folsom, "Recent Restrictions," 1061, n. 23.

36. The earliest scholarly reference to the event is a two sentence description in a footnote by Rotnem and Folsom, Ibid. A brief summary of the case's importance is provided by Frank Coleman, "Freedom From

Fear On the Home Front," *Iowa Law Review* 29 (1944): 415-29, see esp. 421-22; and by John T. Elliff, *The United States Department of Justice and Individual Rights, 1937-1962* (New York: Garland, 1987, reprint of Elliff's Harvard thesis, 1967), 93-94. A more extensive examination is found in a study of the first years of the U.S. Department of Justice Civil Rights Section; see Robert K. Carr, *Federal Protection of Civil Rights: Quest For A Sword* (New York: Cornell University Press, 1947), 134-35, 143-44, and 155-59. Brief references to the Richwood incident are included in Manwaring, *Render Unto Caesar,* 166 and 179. A detailed, but poorly documented, description of the attack is found in Stevens, *Salute!,* 11-17. The Richwood case is also discussed in Peters, *Judging Jehovah's Witnesses,* 89-92, 113-14, and 120-23.

37. "Stipulation of Facts," 2, NARA-RG 21, *Catlette.*
38. Ibid., 2.
39. See Manwaring, *Render Unto Caesar,* 6, 63, 64, 77, 165, 166, and 175-76; Heller, *A Turning Point for Religious Liberty,* 446; William Pencak, *For God & Country: The American Legion, 1919-1941* (Boston, Mass.: Northeastern University Press, 1989), 303 and 318; and Peters, *Judging Jehovah's Witnesses,* 107-13.
40. "Affidavit of C. A. Cecil," 8 July 1940, American Civil Liberties Union Archives 2249:180, Seeley G. Mudd Manuscript Library, Princeton University, [hereinafter, ACLU Archives]. All material from the ACLU Archives is used by permission of the Princeton University Library.
41. This information comes from an account in the 29 June 1940, issue of a mimeographed newspaper, the Richwood Daily News Letter. Jim Comstock, a high school English teacher, launched the paper as a student summer project. I have a photocopy of this issue and the 1 July 1940 issue, made from the files of *The Richwood* (W. Va.) *Nicholas Republican.* Comstock. He later became well known as publisher of the weekly newspaper, the *West Virginia Hillbilly.* This account has been reprinted in several newspapers; see Jim Comstock, "Mandatory flag-saluting has ugly history," *Charleston* (W. Va.) *Gazette,* 16 October 1988, 5.
42. "More About Jehovah's Witnesses," *Richwood Daily News Letter,* 1 July 1940, 3-4.
43. Vi Finlinson, "Jehovah's Witnesses Pro's and Con's," *The Richwood* (W. Va.) *Nicholas Republican,* 11 July 1940, 3.
44. "Stipulation of Facts,"2, NARA-RG 21, *Catlette.*
45. Ibid., 2-3.
46. Ibid.
47. Legg interview.
48. "Stipulation of Facts," 3, NARA-RG 21, *Catlette.*
49. Comstock, "Mandatory flag-saluting.
50. "2 Held Guilty in Civil Rights Case of Jehovah's Witnesses," *Charleston* (W. Va.) *Gazette,* 4 June 1942.
51. A columnist in the Richwood newspaper presented a digest of the views of the town's residents; see Finlinson, "Jehovah's Witnesses Pro's and Con's." Two letters to the editor criticized the attack: A Citizen, "In The Mail," *The Richwood* (W. Va.) *Nicholas Republican,* 11 July 1940, 1; and M. B. McClung, "Readers' Forum," *The Charleston* (W. Va.) *Gazette,* 11 July 1940, 8. A brief Associated Press story provided a sketchy, somewhat inaccurate account of the attack: "9 Refuse to

Salute Flag, Are Fed Castor Oil by Richwood Mob," *The Charleston* (W. Va.) *Gazette,* 1 July 1940, 7.

52. Carr, *Federal Protection of Civil Rights,* 156.
53. Manwaring, *Render Unto Caesar,* 177-79.
54. Ibid., 133-34.
55. Harry P. Stumpf, *American Judicial Politics* (New York: Harcourt, Brace, Jovanovich Publishers, 1988), 107.
56. Lemuel R. Via to Wendell Berge, 18 December 1941, National Archives and Records Administration, Record Group 60.U.S. Department of Justice Central Files, Case 171891-1. At the time this article was researched, some of the Department of Justice correspondence files were missing from the National Archives. I determined the content of some of the correspondence cited here from records slips of the correspondence that were compiled by Department of Justice clerks and which served as an index of the correspondence files. The record slips identified the sender, recipient, date, subject and Department of Justice file number of each letter [hereinafter NARA-RG 60].
57. Ibid.
58. Raoul Berger, Memorandum of 21 April 1942, quoted in Carr, *Federal Protection of Civil Rights,* 134-35.
59. Wendell Berge to Lemuel R. Via, 17 April 1942, NARA-RG 60 *Catlette.*
60. See *Mackin v. United States,* 117 U.S. 348 (1886); *United States v. Moreland,* 258 U.S. 433 (1922); and *Duke v. United States,* 301 U.S. 492 (1937).
61. Although the strategy of indictment by information proved successful in this instance, its usefulness is limited by several considerations. As Carr, *Federal Protection of Civil Rights,* 135-36, argues, it limits prosecutions of those who are officers of the law. Others who deprive persons of their civil rights must be tried under 18 U.S.C. § 51 (1925), conspiracy to deprive persons of their civil rights, which, because it is a felony, requires indictment by a grand jury. This meant that because it was difficult to convince the local people, who made up grand juries to indict those who attacked Jehovah's Witnesses, it was possible to prosecute only law officers acting under color of law.
62. The statute had its origins in the Civil Rights Act of 1866, see 14 Stat. 27, c. 31 § 2.It was retained in the *Revised Statutes* of 1873 as section 5510 and carried over and given its present wording in the *Criminal Code of 1909* as section 5440, see 35 Stat. 1092, c. 321 § 20. In 1942, this provision was found in the *United States Code* of 1925, 18 U.S.C. § 52 (1925).
63. *United States v. Buntin,* 10 Fed. 730, 732 (C.C.S.D. Ohio 1882); and *United States v. Stone,* 188 Fed. 836, 841 (D.C. Md. 1911).
64. The U.S. Supreme Court upheld this application of the statute in *United States v. Classic,* 313 U.S. 299 (1941).
65. "Court's Charge," 6 and 11, NARA-RG 21, *Catlette.* The only victim of the attack who did not testify at the trial was C. A. Cecil.
66. Ibid., 12.
67. Ibid., 15-16.
68. "Order on trial, guilty verdict," 1, NARA-RG 21, *Catlette;* and *2 Held Guilty In Civil Rights Case,* 1 and 12.

69. "Order Overriding Motion to Set Aside Verdict and Imposing Judgment," 1, NARA-RG 21, *Catlette*.

70. "Appellant's Brief," 5, *Catlette v. United* States No. 4992, National Archives and Record Administration–Mid Atlantic Region, Philadelphia, Pa. Record Group 276, [hereinafter NARA-RG 276, *Catlette*].

71. Wendell Berge to Claude M. Dean, 16 November 1942, NARA-RG 276 *Catlette*.

72. *Catlette v. United States*, 132 F2d 902 (4th Cir. 1943), at 906.

73. Ibid.

74. Ibid.

75. Ibid.

76. For an extensive discussion of the legal significance of this case see Chuck Smith, "Jehovah's Witnesses and the Castor Oil Patriots: A West Virginia Contribution To Religious Liberty," *West Virginia History* 57 (1998): 95-110.

77. *Screws v. United States*, 325 U.S. 91 (1945). For a note mentioning that *Catlette* contributed to this development, see G. L. Clark, "Annotation: Validity and construction of statutes making conspiracy to deprive or deprivation of constitutional right a federal offense," 162 A.L.R. 1373, 1396 (1946).

78. George C. Schmidt to J. E. Mayeur, 4 June 1942. West Virginia and Regional History Collection, West Virginia University Libraries, A&M 2423–Window Glass Cutters League of America, Series 2, Legal Matters 1924-73, Box 2, Folder 13, Jehovah's Witness Case 1941-43 [hereinafter WVRHC, Jehovah's Witnesses file]. All materials from this collection are used with permission of the West Virginia University Libraries.

79. Franklin D. Roosevelt, "Address to Congress Requesting War Declaration," 8 December 1941, in *The Public Papers and Addresses of Franklin D. Roosevelt,* vol. 10 (New York: Russell & Russell, 1950, reissued 1969), 514.

80. Ibid.

81. "Affidavit of Fred Kroll, Brief of Pittsburgh Plate Glass Company," 20, The National Archives and Records Administration: Record Group 228, Committee on Fair Employment Practice, Headquarters Records/Legal division–hearings, Entry 19 530-53-41-07, Box 336, [hereinafter NARA RG 228, Hearing Records].

82. "Verbatim transcript of proceedings," 66, NARA-RG 228, Hearing Records.

83. Ibid., 48.

84. "Affidavit of Howard L. Halbach, Brief of Pittsburgh Plate Glass Company," 18, NARA-RG 228, Hearing Records.

85. "Verbatim Transcript of Proceedings," 124; and "Affidavit of Clarence James, Brief of Pittsburgh Plate Glass Company," 39; both in NARA-RG 228, Hearing Records.

86. "Witnesses Examined," *Time*, 29 July 1941, 40.

87. "Minutes of the Harrison County School Board of Education," 5 August 1941, Minute Book 4, 100.

88. "Non-Saluters Open School in Northview," *The Clarksburg* (W.Va.) *Exponent*, 25 September 1941, 9.

89. "Minutes, Norwood Local," 16 December 1941, West Virginia and

Regional History Collection, West Virginia University Libraries, A&M 2423–Window Glass Cutters League of America, General Correspondence, Records 1924-73, Series 3, General Correspondence, Box 26, Folders w/Norwood Local Correspondence [hereinafter WVRHC, Window Glass Cutters, Gen. Cor.].

90. Ibid.

91. "Schoolroom Flags," *The Clarksburg* (W.Va.) *Exponent*, 19 December 1942, 6.

92. "Intermediate Findings and Directions," 21 December 1942, 1; West Virginia and Regional History Collection, West Virginia University Libraries, A&M 2423–, Glass, Ceramic, and Sand Silica Workers, Local 2, Records, 1934-1974, Series 1 Correspondence, Box 5, Folder 31, General Correspondence, 1939-44 [hereinafter WVRHC, G.C.&S.S.W].

93. "Verbatim transcript of proceedings," NARA-RG 228, Hearing Records.

94. Stanley Meredith to Harry D. Nixon, 19 December 1940, WVRHC, Window Glass Cutters, Gen. Cor.

95. "Verbatim transcript of proceedings," 41, NARA-RG 228, Hearing Records. The seven fired workers were Clyde Seders, Paul G. Schmidt, Bernard L. Schmidt, Woodrow Parson, Charles W. Faris, Brown H. Russell, and Charles R. Ferris.

96. Ibid. Stanley Meredith to Harry D. Nixon, 27 December 1940, WVRHC, Jehovah's Witnesses file.

97. Francis Schmidt, interview by author, Clarksburg, W. Virginia, 12 September 1998 [hereinafter, Schmidt interview]. Francis Schmidt is the son of Paul Schmidt. During the interview, he gave me a 1905 photograph of the West Fork Local of the Window Glass Cutters League. Paul Schmidt is among the workers in the picture. He is also pictured among glass workers at the Lafayette glass plant in a 1912 photograph published in Ron Borum, ed., *Harrison County 76* (Clarksburg-Harrison Bicentennial Commission, 1976), 36.

98. "Verbatim transcript of proceedings," 142, NARA-RG 228, Hearing Records.

99. For a more complete description of the efforts Paul Schmidt made to regain his job, see Chuck Smith, "Paul Schmidt: A Workingman's Tenacious Pursuit of Religious Liberty," *Journal of Law and Religion* 14 (2000): 101-19.

100. Executive Order 8802, 25 June 1941, The National Archives and Records Administration, Record Group 11, General Records of the United States [hereinafter NARA-RG 11].

101. James W. Rush, "The Fair Employment Practice Committee and the Shipyard Hearings of 1943-1944," *Prolog: Quarterly of the National Archives and Records Administration* 29 (1992): 279-89, 281.

102. Charles Zaid, *Preliminary Inventories: No. 147, Records of the Committee on Fair Employment Practice* (National Archives and Records Administration 1962), at 4.

103. Executive Order 8802, 25 June 1941; Executive Order 8823, 18 July 1941; Executive Order 9111, 25 May 1942; and Executive Order 9346, 27 May 1943, NARA RG 11.

104. Paul G. Schmidt to Clifford Forster, 7 March 1942, ACLU Archives 2428:128.

105. Ibid.
106. "Exhibit #11, Memorandum, Daniel R. Donovan to Lawrence W. Cramer," no date, NARA-RG 228, Hearing Records.
107. Accounts of this investigation are in William Saas to Philip Murray, 27 April 1942, WVRHC, Window Glass Cutters, Gen. Cor.; "Exhibit #11, Memorandum, Daniel R. Donovan to Lawrence W. Cramer," no date, NARA-RG 228, Hearing Records; and Paul G. Schmidt to Clifford Forster, 13 August 1942, ACLU Archives 2428: 139.
108. "Exhibit #11, Memorandum, Daniel R. Donovan to Lawrence W. Cramer," no date, 1, NARA-RG 228, Hearing Records.
109. Ibid., 2.
110. Frank Fenton to J. E. Mayeur, 20 May 1942, WVRHC, Jehovah's Witnesses.
111. Paul G. Schmidt to Clifford Forster, 13 August 1942, ACLU Archives 2428: 130.
112. Ibid.
113. Schmidt interview.
114. Lawrence W. Cramer to J. E. Mayeur, 19 August 1942, WVRHC, Jehovah's Witnesses file.
115. "Government Exhibit 6 — Lawrence W. Cramer to Irwin De Shetler," 19 August 1942, NARA-RG 228, Hearing Records.
116. Lawrence W. Cramer to Howard L. Halbach, 19 August 1942, The National Archives and Records Administration: Record Group 228, Committee on Fair Employment Practice, General Correspondence Entry 5, 530-53-41-02 Box53, [hereinafter NARA-RG 228, CFEP, cor.].
117. Lawrence W. Cramer to William Green, 19 August 1942, WVRHC, Jehovah's Witnesses file.
118. Stanley R. Meredith to Harry E. Nixon, 1 September 1942,WVRHC, Jehovah's Witnesses file.
119. Frank Fenton to J. E. Mayeur, 9 September 1942, WVRHC, Jehovah's Witnesses file.
120. J. E. Mayeur to Frank Fenton, 9 September 1942, WVRHC, Jehovah's Witnesses file.
121. Lawrence W. Cramer to J.E. Mayeur, 16 October 1942, WVRHC, Jehovah's Witnesses file.
122. Lawrence W. Cramer to Howard L. Halbach, 19 October 1942, NARA-RG 228, CFEP, cor.
123. "Agendum," 9 November 1942, National Archives and Records Administration: Record Group 228, Committee on Fair Employment Practice, Headquarters Records/office of the committee, Entry 3, 530-53-40-01. [hereinafter referred to as NARA-RG 228, office].
124. "Summary of actions taken at November 23 meeting of the committee," 24 November 1942, NARA-RG 228, office.
125. Malcolm S. MacLean to W.G. Koupal, 23 November 1942, NARA-RG 228, office.
126. Office of War Information, War Manpower Commission, "Advance release: For Sunday Morning Papers, Nov. 29, 1942," National Archives and Records Administration: Record Group 228, Committee on Fair Employment Practice, Headquarters Records/Information and Public Relations Division, Press releases, 1941-1945, R - Z, Entry 64, 530-53-50-05 - box 510.

127. Ibid.
128. "7 Of Jehovah Sect Ordered Rehired, *New York Times*, 29 November 1942, 32; "Bias Charged in Firings," *Business Week*, 26 December 1942, 62.
129. "Agendum, meeting of Dec. 7, 1942," NARA-RG 228, office.
130. "Verbatim transcript of proceedings," 95-96, NARA-RG 228, Hearing Records.
131. Lawrence W. Cramer to William M. Saas, 5 December 1942, WVRHC, G.C.&S.S.W. and Stanley R. Meredith to J. E. Mayeur, 11 December 1942, WVRHC, Jehovah's Witnesses file, n. 78.
132. Meredith, ibid.
133. Minutes, "meeting of Dec. 7, 1942," NARA-RG 228, office.
134. George M. Johnson to Committee Members, "Summary of actions taken at December 7 meeting of the committee," 9 December 1942, NARA-RG 228, office.
135. J. E. Mayeur to Lawrence W. Cramer, 16 December 1943, WVRHC, Jehovah's Witnesses file.
136. Ibid.
137. Rush, "Fair Employment Practice Committee."
138. The committee met from 11:30 a.m. to 1:00 p.m. and 2:30 to 6:00 p.m. Six member of the committee were present, as were nine workers who opposed the rehiring and their lawyer, two officials and two attorneys of the company; Paul Schmidt was the only one of the fired workers present. "Verbatim transcript of proceedings," 1, NARA-RG 228, Hearing Records.
139. "Brief of Pittsburgh Plate Glass Company, 220-44," NARA-RG 228, Hearing Records.
140. "Verbatim transcript of proceedings," 17 and 23, NARA-RG 228, Hearing Records.
141. "Brief of Pittsburgh Plate Glass Company," 3-10, NARA-RG 228, Hearing Records.
142. Ibid., 11-13.
143. Verbatim transcript of proceedings, 23-142, NARA-RG 228, Hearing Records
144. Paul G. Schmidt to Clifford Forster, 12 December 1942, ACLU Archives 2428:147.
145. "Verbatim transcript of proceedings," 143-44, NARA-RG 228, Hearing Records.
146. Paul G. Schmidt to Clifford Forster, 12 December 1942, ACLU Archives 2428:147.
147. Ibid., 147-48.
148. Ibid., 160-62.
149. Fred W. Perkins, "FEPC Expected To Risk Walkout In Jehovah Case," *World Telegram* (New York), 22 December 1942, clipping, ACLU Archives 2428:157;"Sees Walkout If Witnesses Are Employed," *The Clarksburg* (W.Va.) *Exponent,* 22 December 1942, 1-2.
150. Roger N. Baldwin to Lawrence W. Cramer, 22 December 1942, ACLU Archives 2428:155.
151. "Summary of Action Taken at March 1, 1943, Meeting of the Committee," NARA-RG 228, office.
152. Lawrence W. Cramer to Leland Hazard, 5 March 1943; Lawrence W. Cramer to Leland Hazard, 15 March 1943; both in NARA-RG 228, CFEP, cor.

153. Lawrence W. Cramer to Leland Hazard, 5 March 1943, NARA-RG 228, CFEP, cor.
154. William Saas to William Lewis, 20 March 1943, WVRHC, G.C.&S.S.W.
155. "Minutes," 15 March 1943, NARA-RG 228, office.
156. William Saas to William Lewis, 20 March 1943, WVRHC, G.C.&S.S.W.
157. W. G. Koupal, "Notice of Special Meeting All Union Employees of Works No. 12 Masonic Auditorium 8 p.m., March 26, 1943," WVRHC, G.C.&S.S.W.
158. "Jobs Offered To Witnesses," *The Clarksburg* (W. Va.) *Exponent*, 27 March 1942, 1.
159. Lawrence W. Cramer to Leland Hazard, 10 April 1943, NARA-RG 228, CFEP, cor.
160. W. G. Koupal, "Notice Concerning Jehovah's Witnesses," 27 March 1942, WVRHC, G.C.&S.S.W.
161. Paul G. Schmidt to Clifford Forster, 15 April 1943, WVRHC, G.C.&S.S.W.
162. Ernest G. Trimble to W.G. Koupal, 1 April 1943, NARA-RG 228, CFEP, cor.
163. Paul G. Schmidt to Clifford Forster, 15 April 1943, ACLU Archives 2428:168.
164. Schmidt interview.
165. For a detailed description and analysis of the significant of the resolution of this case see, Chuck Smith, "War Fever and Religious Fervor: The Firing of Jehovah's Witnesses Glassworkers in West Virginia and Administrative Protection of Religious Liberty," *American Journal of Legal History* 43 (1999): 133-51.
166. "Advance release," 29 November 1942, NARA-RG 228, press.
167. *The Civil Rights Cases*, 109 U.S. 3 (1883).
168. Rush, "The Fair Employment Practices Committee," 281.
169. Ibid., 288.
170. Charles E. Lindblom, *Politics and Markets: The World's Political Economic Systems* (New York: Basic Books, Inc., 1977), 12-13.
171. *Minersville School District v. Gobitis*, 310 U.S. 586 (1940).
172. "Verbatim transcript of proceedings," 83, NARA-RG 228, Hearing Records.
173. *Barnette*, 47 F. Supp. 251 (S.D.W.Va. 1942)
174. Manwaring, *Render Unto Caesar*, 11.
175. Ibid., 12-15.
176. Ibid., 30.
177. Ibid., 30-31.
178. At that time the Pledge of Allegiance was recited by placing one's right hand over the heart. When the words "I pledge allegiance to the flag" were recited, at the word "flag" the right arm was extended toward the flag with the palm up.
179. Manwaring, *Render Unto Caesar*, 31.
180. Exodus 20: 3-5. For a detailed explanation of this rationale see Bergman, "The Modern Religious Objections to the Flag Salute."
181. Manwaring, *Render Unto Caesar*, 56.
182. Ibid.
183. *Nicholls v. Lynn*, 7 N.E.2d 577 (Mass. 1937); *Leoles v Landers*, 192 S.E. 218 (Ga. 1937); *Hering v. Board of Education*, 194 Atl. 177 (N.J.

1937); *Gabrielli v. Knickerbocker*, 82 P.2d 391 (Cal. 1938); *People ex rel. Fish v. Sandstrom*, 18 N.E.2d 840 (N.Y. 1939); and *State ex rel. Bleich v. Board of Public Instruction*, 190 So. 815 (Fla. 1939).

184. *Leoles v. Landers*, 302 U.S. 656 (1937); *Hering v. Board of Education*, 303 U.S. 624 (1938); and *Gabrielli v. Knickerbocker,* 306 U.S. 621 (1939).

185. *Johnson v. Deerfield*, 306 U.S. 621 (1939).

186. My narration of the *Gobitis* case, unless otherwise noted, is drawn from Manwaring, *Render Unto Caesar,* 81-147; see also Peter Irons, *The Courage of Their Convictions* (New York: The Free Press, 1988), 13-35.

187. *1935-36 Pennsylvania Opinions of the Attorney General,* 100, 26 October 1935.

188. *Gobitis v. Minersville School District,* 24 F.Supp. 271 (E.D. Pa. 1938).

189. *Minersville School District v. Gobitis*, 108 F.2d 685 (3d Cir. 1939).

190. *Minersville School District v. Gobitis*, 309 U.S. 645 (1940).

191. Manwaring, *Render Unto Caesar*, 121.

192. Ibid., 123-31.

193. *Minersville* at 594-95.

194. *Johnson v. Deerfield*, 306 U.S. 621.

195. John Haynes Holmes, "The Case of the Jehovah's Witnesses," *Christian Century* 57 (17 July 1940): 896-98; see esp. 898.

196. Beulah Amidon, "Can We Afford Martyrs?" *Survey Graphic,* September 1940, 457-60; see esp. 457.

197. Ibid.

198. Manwaring, *Render Unto Caesar*, 187.

199. Ibid., 149. For a through discussion of scholarly and popular media response to the *Gobitis* decision, see Heller, *A Turning Point in Religious Liberty*, 450-53.

200. *Brown v. Skustad,* Minnesota, St. Louis County District Court, 1942 (unreported), cited in Manwaring, *Render Unto Caesar*, 193.

201. *State v. Smith,* 127 P.2d 518 (Kan. 1942); and *Bolling v. Superior Court*, 133 P.2d 803 (Wash. 1943).

202. "Complaint," 19 August 1942, *Barnette v. West Virginia State Board of Education,* National Archives and Records Administration—Mid-Atlantic Region, Philadelphia, Pa. Record Group 21, U.S. District Court for Southern West Virginia, Civil Cases, Case 242, hereinafter NARA-RG 21, *Barnette.*

203. "Order," 27 August 1942; ibid.

204. "Flag Salute Case Argued in Court," *The Charleston* (W. Va.) *Gazette*, 15 September 1942, 13.

205. "Board Reaffirms Flag Salute Rule," *The Charleston* (W. Va.) *Gazette*, 16 September 1942, 1; and "Salute Ruling Unchanged," *The Charleston* (W. Va.) *Daily Mail*, 16 September 1942, 7.

206. Ibid.

207. Ibid.

208. Manwaring, *Render Unto Caesar,* 212.

209. "Final Decree," 6 October 1942, NARA-RG 21, *Barnette.*

210. *Jones v. Opelika,* 316 U.S. 584 (1942).

211. Ibid., 623-24.

212. *Barnette v. West Virginia State Board of Education,* 47 F. Supp. 251 at 253 (S.D.W.Va. 1942).

213. *Murdock v. Pennsylvania*, 319 U.S. 105 (1943).

214. *Jones v. Opelika,* 316 U.S. 584 (1942).
215. Manwaring, *Render Unto Caesar,* 215-17.
216. Ibid., 217-20.
217. Ibid., 220-24.
218. *West Virginia State Board of Education v. Barnette*, 319 U.S. 624 (1943).
219. Stone, Black, Murphy, Douglas, Jackson, and Rutledge voted to over-rule *Gobitis*; Roberts, Frankfurter, and Reed voted to maintain it.
220. Ibid., 642.

About the Contributors

Susan E. Darnell is the branch manager of a major bank in Portage, Indiana, has extensive financial management experience, and has authored or co-authored a wide variety of publications, including newspaper articles and columns, professional journal articles dealing with the sociology of religion and criminology, and various national professional conference papers. She most recently co-edited (with Anson Shupe and William A. Stacey) *Bad Pastors: Clergy Misconduct in Modern America* (New York: University Press, 2001).

Derek H. Davis is director of the J.M. Dawson Institute of Church-State Studies, Baylor University, and editor of the award-winning *Journal of Church and State*. He is the author of *Original Intent: Chief Justice Rehnquist & the Course of American Church-State Relations* (1991), *Religion and the Continental Congress, 1774-1789: Contributions to Original Intent* (2000), and editor or coeditor of twelve additional books, including the *Legal Deskbook for Administrators of Independent Colleges and Universities* and *The Role of Religion in the Making of Public Policy*. The author is indebted to Kevin Holton, a graduate student in Church-State Studies at Baylor University, for assistance in the preparation of this chapter.

Catherine Cookson (J.D., Rutgers-Newark School of Law; M.A., University of Virginia; Ph.D., Indiana University at Bloomington) has served since 1998 as the Director of the Center for the Study of Religious Freedom at Virginia

Wesleyan College. Special interests include law and religion in American history and religion and social issues. The author acknowledges and thanks the many Wiccans who responded to her ads requesting information concerning their experiences (both positive and negative) of religious freedom. Special gratitude is extended to CIRCLE Coven staff and especially Selena Fox; without their time, many courtesies, and the access they gave to information, this article could not have been written.

Adam C. English is a Ph.D. candidate at Baylor University. He has forthcoming articles due to appear in *Perspectives in Religious Studies* and *Baptist History and Heritage*. Special interests include the relationship between faith and philosophy in the nineteenth and twentieth century as well as the postmodern situation in theology and philosophy. He is grateful to W. D. English and Bill Pitts for their assistance with earlier drafts of this essay.

Barry Hankins (B.A., M.A., Baylor University; Ph.D., Kansas State University) is associate professor of history and church-state studies in the J. M. Dawson Institute of Church-State Studies at Baylor University. He is author of *God's Rascal: J. Frank Norris and the Beginnings of Southern Fundamentalism* (1996); and *Uneasy in Babylon: Southern Baptist Conservatives and American Culture* (2002). He also co-edited with Derek Davis, *Welfare Reform and Faith-Based Organizations*. His articles have appeared in *Church History, Religion and American Culture, Fides et Historia, Journal of Church and State*, and other journals and magazines.

J. Gordon Melton is director of the Institute for the Study of American Religion, a research facility in Santa Barbara, California. He is also a research specialist with the Department of Religious Studies at the University of California-Santa Barbara. He is the author of the *Encyclopedia of American Religions* (6th ed., 1999), the standard reference work on American religious bodies, and more than thirty other books in American religious history, including most recently *American Religion: An Illustrated History* (ABC-Clio, 2000). He has specialized in the study of America's minority religious traditions and produced two widely used textbooks, *The Cult Experience* and *The Encyclopedia Handbook of Cults in America*.

Timothy Miller is professor of religious studies at the University of Kansas. With research specialization in American religious history, new religious movements, and communal groups, Dr. Miller has authored or edited a number of books, including *The 60s Communes: Hippies and Beyond* (1999), *The Quest for Utopia in Twentieth-Century America* (vol. one, 1900-1960) (1998), and *American's Alternative Religions* (editor, 1995).

Kendrick Moxon received his B.A. in Anthropology from American University in 1972 and his Doctor of Jurisprudence from George Mason University in 1981. He has worked extensively in the areas of civil liberties and freedom of information/government litigation. He is currently a practicing attorney in Los Angeles, California.

Susan J. Palmer teaches religious studies at Dawson College in Montreal and is an adjunct professor at Concordia University, Montreal. She is the author of *Moon Sister, Krishna Mothers, Rajneesh Lovers* (Syracuse, 1994), *Aids as an Apocalyptic Metaphor,* and co-author of *The Rajneesh Papers and Children in New Religions* (with Charlotte Hardman) as well as many articles. She is associate producer on *The Endtime,* a documentary film on The Family.

James T. Richardson is a professor of sociology at the University of Nevada-Reno. He is the author of a number of journal and book articles on topics associated with new religious movements and the law. He also co-edited *The Satanism Scare* (1991, with Joel Best and David Bromley) and edited *Money and Power in the New Religions* (1988).

Anson Shupe is professor of sociology at the joint campus of Indiana University-Purdue University, Fort Wayne, and is a member of the graduate faculties of both universities. He has also held positions at Alfred University and the University of Texas at Arlington. Author of over two dozen books and over seventy journal/book articles (and numerous popular writings for such outlets as *The Wall Street Journal* and *The Philadelphia Inquirer*), most of his research has focused on religious movements, from the cult-sect type to televangelism, and their political implications. While he has continued to monitor these areas over the past twenty-eight years, his most recent research emphasis is clergy malfeasance. In studying this subject, he is attempting to marry the sub-disciplines of the sociology of religion and criminology in analyzing clergy misconduct. His most recent publications on the subject are *In the Name of All That's Holy: A Theory of Clergy Malfeasance* (1995, Praeger), *Wolves within the Fold: Religious Leadership and Abuses of Power* (Edited, 1998, Rutgers University Press), and *Bad Pastors: Clergy Misconduct in Modern America* (co-edited with William A. Stacey and Susan E. Darnell, 2000, New York University Press).

Chuck Smith (B.A., West Virginia State College; M.A., University of New Mexico; Ph.D., University of Kentucky) is professor of political science at West Virginia State College. He is author of *The New Mexico State Constitution: A Reference Guide.* His articles have appeared in *West Virginia History, West Virginia Public Affairs Reporter, University of Arkansas at Little Rock Law Journal, State Constitutional Commentaries and Notes, Journal of Law and Religion,* and *American Journal of Legal History.* Special interests include judicial policymaking, dynamics of judicial-legislative relationships, and developments in civil liberties, especially religious liberty. Research for this article was partially funded by the West Virginia Humanities Council, a state program of the National Endowment for the Humanities, and by a Faculty Research Grant from West Virginia State College. The knowledge gained from his research into the contribution of Jehovah's Witnesses to the expansion of legal protections for religious liberty has led to an examination of how religious groups sometimes function as interest groups in both the judicial and legislative arenas.

Catherine Wessinger is professor of history of religions and women's studies, and chair of the religious studies department at Loyola University, New Orleans. She is a former chair of the New Religious Movements Group at the American Academy of Religion, and a member of the Executive Advisory Committee of *Nova Religio: The Journal of Alternative and Emergent Religions.* She was an adviser to the FBI during the Freemen standoff in 1996. She is the author of *Annie Besant and Progressive Messianism* (1988) and *How the Millenium Comes Violently: From Jonestown to Heaven's Gate* (2000). She is editor of *Women's Leadership in Marginal Religions: Explorations Outside the Mainstream* (1993) and of *Religious Institutions and Women's Leadership: New Roles Inside the Mainstream* (1996).

Stuart A. Wright is associate director of graduate studies and research and professor of sociology at Lamar University in Beaumont, Texas. Editor of *Armageddon in Waco,* he testified at the 1995 U.S. House of Representatives hearings on Waco and worked with the Senate Judiciary Committee on its Waco hearings later the same year. Portions of this essay appeared in Stuart A. Wright, "Justice Denied: The Waco Civil Trial," *Nova Religio* (Fall 2000), and are reprinted with permission.

Index